AN
INDEPENDENT
WOMAN

AN INDEPENDENT WOMAN

The Life of Lou Henry Hoover

Anne Beiser Allen

Contributions in American History, Number 188
Jon L. Wakelyn, Series Editor

Greenwood Press
Westport, Connecticut • London

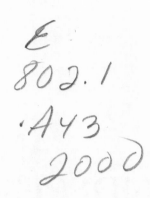

Library of Congress Cataloging-in-Publication Data

Allen, Anne Beiser, 1941–
    An independent woman : the life of Lou Henry Hoover / Anne Beiser Allen.
       p. cm.—(Contributions in American history, ISSN 0084–9219 ; no. 188)
    Includes bibliographical references (p.) and index.
    ISBN 0–313–31466–7 (alk. paper)
      1. Hoover, Lou Henry, 1874–1944.   2. Hoover, Herbert, 1874–1964.
    3. Presidents' spouses—United States—Biography.   I. Title. II. Series.
    E802.1.A45   2000
    973.91'6'092—dc21   99–462298
    [B]

British Library Cataloguing in Publication Data is available.

Library of Congress Catalog Card Number: 99–462298
ISBN: 0–313–31466–7
ISSN: 0084–9219

First published in 2000

Greenwood Press, 88 Post Road West, Westport, CT 06881
An imprint of Greenwood Publishing Group, Inc.
www.greenwood.com

Printed in the United States of America

The paper used in this book complies with the
Permanent Paper Standard issued by the National
Information Standards Organization (Z39.48–1984).

10 9 8 7 6 5 4 3 2 1

Copyright Acknowledgments

The author and publisher gratefully acknowledge permission to use the following material:

Letter written by Dorothy Bowen to Marjorie Gal.

Letters, diaries, and oral histories from the Hoover Library.

Except where noted, the photographs in this book are taken from the collection of the Herbert Hoover Presidential Library in West Branch, Iowa.

Every reasonable effort has been made to trace the owners of copyright materials in this book, but in some instances this has proven impossible. The author and publisher will be glad to receive information leading to more complete acknowledgments in subsequent printings of the book and in the meantime extend their apologies for any omissions.

I would like to extend my thanks to the staff of the Herbert Hoover Presidential Library for their cooperation and assistance with the research for this book. Their patience and support were invaluable.

Contents

Photo essay follows page 102.

Prologue

Who Was
Lou Henry Hoover?

Her friends and colleagues called her "the Lady"—as they called her husband "the Chief." Among those who had worked closely with the Hoovers during the hectic days of World War I, when they organized relief projects for noncombatants in Europe and later coordinated food production in the United States to support the war effort, these two inspired an admiration that amounted almost to awe. It seemed that there was no problem that this couple—together or singly—could not handle, from a calm, logical appraisal to a simple, rational solution.

This was particularly true of Lou Henry Hoover, a woman whose tact and generosity were legendary among those who worked with her. While her husband could at times be prickly, his impatience with those who disagreed with his appraisal of the situation inspiring accusations of arrogance, Lou was unfailingly courteous, thoughtful, and kind. She always knew exactly which of her many friends to call on for assistance with the project of the moment, and exactly what to say to persuade them to do as she wished. Whether it was collecting a boatload of California produce for starving Belgians, enlisting top quality volunteers for her beloved Girl Scout program, or securing financial support for the Women's Division of the National Amateur Athletic Federation, Lou Henry Hoover almost always succeeded—quickly, effectively and with a minimum of fuss.

It is difficult, even now, for a biographer to get at the deeper aspects of Lou Henry Hoover's nature. She was, in the words of her close friend Charlotte Kellogg, "an unusual combination of spontaneity and reserve."[1] She rarely shared her private thoughts, routinely burned personal letters, and maintained always an invisible barrier between her public image and her private self. Among the thousands of her letters on file at the Herbert Hoover Presidential Library in West Branch, Iowa, there are very few that touch on the most intimate concerns of her life. She asked her son Allan to burn her letters when he finished reading them. Fortunately for historians, Allan was less particular in this regard than his mother. Lou's chatty letters to her "Darling Boy" radiate with the intense love she had for her husband and sons.

This reticence carried over into her personal behavior also. One of her secretaries remarked on her "remarkable restraint." Mrs. Hoover never lost her temper, seldom even expressed her displeasure with someone openly.[2] What were her private griefs, her disappointments, her frustrations, her greatest joys? We find only glancing references to such things among her papers and in the observations of those closest to her, yet what is there paints a picture of a most remarkable woman, for her own time or for any other.

Modern feminist historians often dismiss Lou Hoover as a wealthy clubwoman. Certainly she belonged to a number of women's clubs, although she tended to use them for her own purposes rather than to find her purpose in them. It is important, also, to realize that the thousands of upper-middle-class women who founded the women's clubs in the period from 1890 to 1910 were not mere dilettantes, but pioneers in the realm of social activism. They were a new breed of woman, nurtured in the nineteenth-century concept that woman's chief role was as wife and mother, but redefining that role in a way that drew them out of the home and into the community. To be a good wife and mother, they felt, a woman must be well educated, take a lively interest in the world around her, and work diligently to improve the society in which her family lived. For women like Lou Hoover, the women's clubs provided a training ground for the organizational and leadership skills that they could apply in other venues. Clubwomen funded libraries, cultural organizations, and civic beautification projects. They founded settlement houses, hospitals, and homes for the elderly and infirm. They set up scholarships for young women, and encouraged the establishment of night schools and extension courses for the convenience of working people. They held national conferences on subjects ranging from scientific home management and women's sports to juvenile delinquency and prostitution. Their financial position made them ideal fund raisers, and they had the time to serve without pay on governing boards. Though few of them identified with the more radical feminists of the period, they helped to create a social climate in which women could emerge from the shelter of the home without censure by society at large.[3]

Lou Hoover did not campaign actively for women's rights. She believed that more could be accomplished by persuasion and perseverance than by confrontation, and once said that she "never thought women were downtrodden by the men before they had the vote." All that women needed to do "was to sit down and talk it over with our fathers and our husbands and our brothers and . . . when we convinced them we were serious about it they would give it to us, as they had given us everything else sensible we ever wanted."[4]

The experiences of her own life—the close, unbiased relationship she enjoyed with her husband and her father, and the privileged economic circles in which she lived—sometimes blinded her to the difficulties faced by less fortunate women. She believed that if a woman wanted to do something, she should simply do it, and that if she worked at it hard enough, she would succeed as well as any man. Lou Hoover also never completely understood the barriers that prevented non-white Americans from participating fully in American society. These things did not prevent her from being an effective advocate of independent womanhood.

As head of the Girl Scouts and chairman of the Women's Division of the National Amateur Athletic Federation, she championed a woman's right to excel. She often reiterated her belief, stated in 1932 to an audience in Toledo, Ohio, that a "modern mother may build a home and at the same time, have a career."[5] In fact, she told her Girl Scouts, a woman who does nothing more than keep house in the modern world "is lazy."[6]

To a woman who had written a biographic sketch of Lou and her husband in 1942, she wrote, "I can but smile at [your characterization of me as having] 'no taste for a career'—for, depending exactly upon what one's definition of 'career' may be, I have not said that! All kinds of projects I should like to have put through. A number of professions or callings I should like to have followed, and was prepared to begin. But always duties, interests, activities of the moment, pushed further back the moment for taking up any long-to-be-continued cause or profession. . . . Mary Austin's famous sentence, 'She said her only ambition was to be a background for Bertie' is too absurd to need a denial. . . . And then I love to settle back with a feeling of being 'gentle, coupled with a passive nature'!"[7]

Although it is difficult to identify specific instances where Lou may have influenced her husband in his political work, the unusually close relationship that they shared means that her role cannot be totally discounted. She actively supported many of his projects, making speeches on behalf of Belgian relief work and food conservation during World War I and later urging local organizations such as the Girl Scouts to combat the Depression through individual effort and grass-roots initiative, in accordance with her husband's economic policy. In two of Hoover's high-profile undertakings during his presidency—the establishment of a national Quaker Meeting House and of the President's School for underprivileged children in the Virginia mountains near the presidential retreat at Rapidan—it was Lou and her aides who did most of the actual work. And one of her most controversial actions—inviting the wife of black Congressman Oscar DePriest to tea at the White House—was taken only after careful consultation with Hoover and his staff.

Her personal record as a philanthropist is impressive. By the time her husband was elected president, Lou Hoover had coordinated relief efforts for stranded American women in Europe in 1914, raised funds for the relief of Belgian war victims, and given years of service to programs for America's youth. The number of individuals whom she assisted on a one-to-one basis throughout her lifetime will probably never be known, because of her deliberate efforts to keep such acts out of the public eye. However, from the documentary evidence in the files at the Hoover Presidential Library in West Branch, Iowa, it is clear that she rarely refused a deserving petitioner. In 1917, while her husband was head of the U.S. Food Administration, she used her own funds—which she described as a "loan"—to establish three boarding houses and a cafeteria in Washington, D.C., for young single women who worked in her husband's department. She paid for the education of several of her own and her husband's relatives with "loans" that she refused to let them repay, asking them instead to pass the money on to someone else who needed it.

During the desperate years of 1929–1932, Lou utilized her wide network of personal friends—some wealthy, others with wide contacts in their communities—as an unofficial welfare service. She hired a secretary whose only job was to screen all pleas for assistance and deal with those that seemed genuine. If a government agency existed that could help the petitioner, she (most of these pleas were from women, who felt more comfortable addressing the president's wife than his government) was directed to that agency. If not, Lou notified one of her friends in the petitioner's neighborhood, and frequently sent money herself to be given anonymously through a "friend of a friend."

Canny at all times in matters relating to finance, she never publicized her private charities, although she was willing to lend her name—as well as her time and energy—to a cause if she deemed it worthy. The Girl Scouts, the Red Cross, the Salvation Army, Stanford University, and many others all benefited from her assistance over the years. When she died, her family found a large number of uncashed checks in her desk—attempted repayments of "loans" which she had refused to accept.

The new century into which Lou Hoover stepped in 1899 as the bride of a young mining engineer called for a new type of woman, intelligent, self-confident, able to make her own decisions, unshadowed by the men around her. *Fin-de-siècle* society had redefined the concept of a lady. The term no longer meant merely a well dressed, politely spoken ornament for a successful husband to display. To be a lady now meant being able to combine domestic life with public action, for the benefit of society as a whole.[8] As wife of a man who regarded her as his equal, mother of two intelligent, well adjusted sons, and organizer or chair of a mind-boggling assortment of cultural, charitable and educational organizations and committees, Lou Henry Hoover embraced those ideals as few in her generation were able to do. She was more than just a lady. She was a truly independent woman.

Chapter 1

From Iowa to California

Waterloo, Iowa, was barely twenty years old when Lou Henry let out her first squall in an upstairs bedroom at 426 West Fourth Street on Sunday, March 29, 1874. A plump, healthy baby, weighing in at just over seven pounds, with bright blue eyes and light brown hair, Lou was the first child of Charles Henry and Florence Weed. Her parents had come to Iowa, separately, only a few years before from the town of Wooster, Ohio, where they had grown up and moved in the same social circles.

Charles' grandfather, William Henry, came to America from Ireland at the age of three. He grew up in Pennsylvania, studied law, married, and in 1807 moved to Ohio, where he helped to found the town of Wooster in Wayne County. He served from 1814 to 1816 in the Ohio legislature, and then was elected associate judge of Stark County. His son and namesake, William Henry, was born in 1818 in Wooster. In 1844 the younger William married Mary Ann Dwire, a tall, slender, self-assured seventeen-year-old schoolteacher with dark hair and eyes, who had boarded with Judge Henry's family. William and Mary Ann had three sons: Charles Delano Henry, born in 1845, William Dwire Henry in 1847, and Addison Morgan Henry in 1848.

Mary Ann's strength of character would be tested all too soon. Her husband had owned a hardware shop in Wooster, but in the 1850s he became superintendent of Ohio Bitumen Coal in Massillon. Because Massillon, located on the Ohio Canal, was subject to epidemics of malaria, William Henry left his family in Wooster and commuted weekly to work by train. Returning home one afternoon in 1856, he fell between two cars and was crushed to death. He was thirty-eight years old.

Mary Ann Henry was left to raise her three young sons alone, though because of the family's relative prominence in the town, she was not destitute. Lou would remember her grandmother Henry as a strong, stately woman, always dressed in black or purple "widow's weeds." Mary Ann was a practical person, with little time for frivolous activities like the "Christmas gew-gaws" her daughter-in-law Florence enjoyed creating.

When the Civil War broke out, Lou's father, Charles Henry, was sixteen. Because his mother was a widow with three minor children, he would have been exempt from the draft imposed two years later. There is no record of his having seen military service, although many of his classmates did.

He met Florence Weed in 1867 at a masquerade party at the American House Hotel in Wooster, which was owned by her paternal step-grandfather, Horace Howard. Florence's maternal grandfather, Dr. John Scobey, had left his native New Hampshire in 1825, making his way through a series of frontier settlements to Jackson, Ohio, where his daughter Philomelia Sophia met a young man from Stark County—Phineas K. Weed. Phineas and Philomel were married in 1848 and made their home in Wooster. Their daughter Florence Ida was born the next year. She was followed by Jennie Alice in 1852, Wallace Phineas in 1858, and Jessie Scobey in 1866.

In 1856 Philomel's father, Dr. John Scobey, moved to Iowa, settling on a farm in the Shell Rock area. Several of his children, including Philomel and her husband, followed. The Weeds lived briefly in Waverly, where in 1870 Florence worked as a clerk in a dry goods store. By 1872 the Weeds had purchased a farm in Shell Rock, on which they would spend the rest of their lives.

Around 1872 Mary Ann Henry and her two older sons also moved to Iowa. Charles and Will found jobs as bookkeepers in the First National Bank. Charles renewed his acquaintance with Florence Weed, and the two were married on June 13, 1873, at the Weed home in Shell Rock. The young couple settled in a two-year-old house in Waterloo, where their daughter Lou was born the following March.

When Lou was two years old, her father decided to leave the bank and try his hand at operating a woolen mill in Shell Rock. According to Mary Ann Henry, his health had been suffering from stress caused by internal bickering among the personnel at the bank. For the next year the young Henrys lived a frugal existence in an unpainted three-room house "on ham, potatoes, bread and butter very much like farmers," as Mary Ann wrote to her son Will, then abroad in Paris.[1]

Charles' youngest brother, Addison, who had graduated from West Point in 1873 and was serving as an army lieutenant on the frontier, visited his brother in Shell Rock. He reported to his mother that although Charlie was confident of success, he himself doubted that the mill would survive.[2] Addison was right. The depression caused by the financial panic of 1873 forced Charles to sell the mill in 1877 and return to his old job at the Waterloo bank.

At that time, Waterloo was a community of some 5,500 people. Sitting firmly astride the Cedar River, it boasted twelve churches, three newspapers, three banks, six restaurants and eight hotels. Although the streets were still unpaved and live-stock often foraged along the roadsides, the town had already acquired a solid in-dustrial base built on flour, woolen, and lumber mills. The Illinois Central Railroad had established its main shops there. As county seat for Blackhawk County, it was also a political center. In 1877, not long after the Henrys' return, the first opera house opened at Commercial and Main Streets, and street lights were installed along the city's major thoroughfares.

The young Henrys lived comfortably, if frugally. Charles walked to work each day, crossing the river on the iron bridge at the foot of Fourth Street. The town was small enough that they didn't need to own a horse and carriage. When they wanted to visit Florence's family, they could take the train, which passed through Shell Rock on its way to Minneapolis. There were plenty of friends with whom Florence could gossip as her clever fingers kept busy with their sewing. Her younger sisters, Jennie (now Mrs. Judson Powers) and Jessie, visited frequently.

Lou was a bright and lively child, her father's delight. He enjoyed taking her on walks along the river, teaching her to fish and to set snares for rabbits. On holidays at Grandfather Weed's farm, she learned to ride horseback and rambled with her father through the orchards, gardens, berry patches, meadows, and maple woods. Sometimes they would pitch a tent and spend the night sleeping under the stars.

Biographers have said that Charles Henry raised his older daughter as "the son he never had," but this fails to capture the true nature of their relationship. Charles and Florence were united in their determination to give their daughters every op-portunity to develop their individual talents and pursue their interests without consulting conventional roles. In Lou, Charles seems to have found a child who shared many of his own interests and outlooks. The two remained quite close until Charles' death in 1928.

Still not content with his situation at the bank, Charles decided in 1879 to move his family to Corsicana, Texas. It was April when the family took the three-day train trip south to this county seat of Navarro County, set in the middle of cot-ton and grain country some fifty-five miles southeast of Dallas. The journey made a deep impression on five-year-old Lou.

"Although it was scarcely ten years after the close of the [Civil] war, we were re-ceived as hospitably as though we were old friends," she would write ten years later. She retained a vivid memory of the houses with their wide verandas and uncar-peted floors. It intrigued her to discover that "just back of nearly every house is a small cabin, usually made of logs, in which live the darkie help. Over one third of the population of Corsicana was colored."[3] This impressed her particularly, as Wa-terloo at that time had barely half a dozen black inhabitants.

But Charles Henry once again failed to find the business success he was seeking, and the family returned to Waterloo in early 1880. Six-year-old Lou was enrolled in school. "Kindergartens were very new at that time, and I remember my mother and her friends feeling a bit smug over their progressive ideas in keeping their chil-dren out of school at such a late age and permitting them to play with toys instead of sitting stolidly down and learning lessons!"[4] On June 30, 1882, her mother gave birth to a second daughter, Jean.

Lou was growing into a slim, energetic child endowed with a strong vitality and an eager curiosity about the world about her. Her mother, a frail, feminine figure, instructed her in the domestic arts of sewing, knitting, and household management. But Lou preferred to be outdoors playing baseball in the street, or going for hikes in the country with her father. Charles Henry not only shared with his elder daughter his love of the outdoors, but as she grew older he discussed business matters with her as well. "Grandpa believed that a girl should know all about business," Lou told her sons many years later, and gave her "a really thorough training, practically, in the subject."[5] She went fishing and boating on the Cedar River, swimming in Black Hawk Creek, and sledding on the snow-covered hills in winter. During frequent visits to Florence's family in Shell Rock, she listened to her great-grandparents' tales of life on the frontier in the earlier part of the century. Aunt Jessie, who was only eight years older than Lou, still lived on the family farm. Wallace married Lillian Stewart in 1882 and went into farming with his father. Jennie's husband died, and she moved to Waterloo, where in 1886 she worked as a clerk in a store.

By the mid-1880s, the frontier had moved beyond Iowa onto the high plains. In 1883 Lou's grandmother Mary Ann Henry accompanied her son Will to the Dakota Territory. The fifty-five-year-old widow spent a winter living alone in a shanty in Day County to "prove up" a homestead. She was sustained by occasional visits from distant neighbors and letters from her family. After the claim was proved, she moved to Wahpeton, North Dakota, where Will had become cashier of the Wahpeton bank. The letters from this strong, independent-minded woman, relating her adventures on the prairie, made a deep impression on her young granddaughter.

In May 1883 Florence Henry and her friend Esther Sweet gave a children's masquerade party for their daughters at the Sweets' Commercial House hotel. Some 150 guests attended the party, which was the social event of the season. Lou went dressed as the Waterloo *Tribune* newspaper, and Anna Sweet as its rival, the Waterloo *Courier*.

When the national fad of roller skating reached Waterloo in the early 1880s, Lou took up the sport with enthusiasm. One day, a contest was held at a rink owned by a local dairy farmer, who also operated a creamery in town. A series of small tables were placed down the center of the rink's floor. On them, the proprietor placed nineteen candles. The contestants were challenged to blow out all nineteen candles, while skating past the tables without stopping. Competing against men and women twice her age, little Lou zipped around the course at lightning speed, her short brown hair whipping around her face, ankle-length skirts swishing around her legs. When she reached the end of the course, all nineteen candles had been extinguished. Ten-year-old Lou was awarded the grand prize, a pink silk umbrella, by the proprietor's wife, to the accompaniment of cheering from the audience.

Charles Henry had now worked for ten years at the First National Bank, but he was still not happy with his position there. He wanted to be his own boss. Florence's health was another concern. The Iowa climate had caused her to develop chronic bronchitis. Fearing that she might have contracted tuberculosis, which in those days was common and frequently fatal, Charles began to consider moving to a milder climate.

The Henrys spent several months in Clearwater, Kansas, in 1887, where Charles helped a friend set up a bank. But another friend had suggested he come to California, where a group of Quakers was founding a town not far from Los Angeles. Feeling that the climate in California would be better for his wife's health, Charles decided to move his family there.

Twelve-year-old Lou, who was developing a talent for sketching, spent much of her time in Clearwater drawing pictures of the wildflowers that grew abundantly on the prairie around the town. "I remember Clearwater with such pleasant memories," she wrote years later, "even though we stayed there for such a few months."[6] The interlude caused a temporary disruption in her schooling: "I was not put in school before the summer vacation and then when the autumn term began we were about to leave for California so I was not entered at that time."[7]

The family returned to Waterloo briefly in the fall to clear up a few last details and prepare for their journey. In late September, they said goodbye to their friends and relatives and embarked on the long train ride west to where the fledgling town of Whittier was rising amid fields of wild mustard.

Situated at the foot of the Puente Hills, Whittier was only about twenty miles from the Pacific Ocean. The scenery, so different from the wide prairies of Iowa, made a strong impression on Lou. "On clear days we can easily count the vessels in San Pedro Harbor, twenty miles away," she wrote in December 1887 to *St. Nicholas* magazine, which she took regularly. "And the Santa Catalina Island, thirty-five miles from shore, is in sight nearly all the time . . . here we have only to turn around to see ocean, mountains and valley, perpetual snow and perpetual summer."[8]

This enthusiasm for her new home would remain with her lifelong. She relished the sense of living in a new land, where the future was what you made it. Though she later traveled around the globe, mingling with the power brokers of her time, she would always manage to return regularly to California. Even when her husband's work required them to live elsewhere, Lou maintained a pied-à-terre in her beloved state. Most of her closest friends had some connection with California. She had a strong affinity for the Western psyche, which she considered most completely democratic and unfettered by tradition or social stratification.

Whittier was still under construction when the Henrys arrived. As they approached the town, all they could see were dirt streets, with here and there a pile of lumber or a half-constructed building standing among the yellow barley and mustard. Lou was fascinated by the orderly arrangement of the proposed community. She enjoyed walking with her father around the site, while he explained to her what was going on.

Believing that it was important to get his banking business into operation as soon as possible, Charles Henry had a tiny two-room frame building constructed. This temporary bank had a counter in the front room and a desk, a small safe, and a few chairs in the back—the minimum necessary to transact business. After a few months, a regular brick bank building was completed, and the bank moved to more imposing quarters. Lou spent many happy hours in both buildings, watching her father at work and learning the mechanics of banking from him. "Everything he did was of very great interest to me."[9] He taught her to roll coins, and introduced her to the intricacies of double-entry bookkeeping.

During their first year in Whittier, the Henrys rented a house on a large block on Painter Avenue. With its spacious garden and orchard, it felt more like a country bungalow than a house in town. Charles Henry had bought ten acres of land on the hills above Painter Avenue, intending to build a home there, but by 1888 the economy in Whittier had begun to falter, and Charles decided to wait awhile before putting money into a house. When their lease on the Painter Avenue house ended in December 1888, the Henrys moved into an apartment over the bank.

Evergreen School, originally built to serve the area's farm children, had to be enlarged to serve the increasing population from the new town. Lou attended sixth grade there. In the fall of 1888 the Bailey School opened in the town of Whittier itself. Lou Henry was one of some two hundred students in this four-room, eight-grade structure, and a member of its first graduating class. Among the students at the Bailey School were the three children of a black man, Mark Anthony, who was the town's barber. One of the boys, Jo, did odd jobs for the Henrys for a time. Lou was quite interested in the old barber's tales of his early life as a slave. He "gave the town its vision of pre–Civil War conditions."[10]

The Puente Hills, 1,500 feet above sea level, provided "splendid" opportunities for the picnics and hiking Lou enjoyed so much. There were dances and visits with friends. Lou was popular among her classmates, who recognized her leadership skills. When a fan drill team was formed at Bailey School, Lou was elected its captain. And when in June 1890 she and a group of friends formed the Dickens Club in honor of the popular novelist, Lou became its first president.

In 1889 the state of California decided to build a reform school in Whittier. The cornerstone was laid in February 1890 with much ceremony. Lou and her friends helped serve refreshments. When Lou poured coffee for the governor, "he asked me if I liked pickles after I had passed them to him for the third time."[11]

While the Henrys' primary affiliation was with the Episcopal Church, they were not rigid in their doctrine. Charles' grandmother had been a Quaker, and Florence's New England–born grandparents came from a Congregationalist background. There was no Episcopal church in Whittier, so the Henrys attended services at either the Methodist Episcopal church or the local Quaker meeting house. Whittier had been founded by Quakers, and many of Lou's friends were of that faith. This early exposure to Quaker practices would stand Lou in good stead years later, when she married the son of a Quaker preacher.

Baseball was still one of Lou's favorite pastimes. There was no ball diamond in Whittier, so the young people decided to make one in a vacant lot filled with mustard weed. Lou suggested that the two teams compete to see who could clear away the weeds from their side of the lot first. The losers would then treat the winners to a "feed." Although Lou's team won, she provided the refreshments to the group anyway.[12]

The building boom in California collapsed in 1890. Whittier was one of the communities seriously affected: "My father's bank did not crash . . . he pulled things through and nobody lost a cent; he was always proud of that. But prosperity was finished in that section."[13] Charles Henry sold his bank to a firm represented by an old Iowa colleague, Charles Mason, on May 1. Moving his family to Los Angeles, Charles found temporary work auditing the books of the *Tribune* company.

Now that Lou had graduated from the Bailey School, she faced the question of what to do about her future. Across the country, thousands of young middle-class women were refusing to stay at home until marriage, as their mothers had done. Large numbers of these women became teachers, secretaries, nurses, and bookkeepers. Salaries in these professions remained low (men preferred not to work in them any longer, since they did not pay enough to support a family). Nevertheless, as new career options they were a step up for women from the previous generation, which had been limited largely to working at dress and hat-making, low-paying factory work, or acting as a servant or paid companion in someone else's home.

As standards in these new fields rose, training schools were established. Lou's mother, before her marriage, had worked as a store clerk and a teacher in a small country school—positions for which she had received minimal training. Now, however, women were attending colleges and business schools in order to improve their qualifications for the jobs they confidently planned to hold—at least until they married, when they were expected to give up their careers to become homemakers and mothers. Although it would be another generation before teacher training advanced from the secondary to the college level, giving teachers the same professional standing as doctors, lawyers, or ministers of religion, many states had established specialized schools called normal schools for the specific purpose of training teachers. Lou's parents were among the growing number of parents willing to give their daughters as much education as they wanted, and to offer them full support in whatever careers they proposed to follow.

In the fall of 1890, Lou, now sixteen, enrolled at the Los Angeles Normal School in a three-year course leading to certification as a teacher. Although she spent only two years at Los Angeles Normal, she enjoyed her time there. Behind the main building was a large two-story gymnasium, where she spent many happy hours. On Halloween in 1891 she and her friends "decorated" the gym with odds and ends of clothing as a prank. She was delighted to note, a few years later, that no one ever found out who the culprits were! Her favorite classes were physical education, physical geography and botany; she was less fond of vocal music, for which she had little talent. She particularly liked the botany field trips, when she and her

classmates hiked around the countryside collecting and sketching plant specimens. She proved to have considerable talent at drawing. She also did well in English and literature; her written prose is excellent. Years later, she would leave her
mark on her husband's works, often editing his erratic grammar and spelling before publication.

Although the days of the forty-niners were long past, gold-mining was still big
business in California, and prospectors still roamed the hills looking for strikes.
During the summer of 1891, the Henry family camped out in the mountains near
Acton, where Charles Henry had bought a prospect in a small mine. Charles had
been commuting to the mine since February, traveling by train and horseback. Lou
thrived on this outdoor life, riding bareback on a pony called Molly, or driving the
wagon behind old Bill the horse to visit their few neighbors at nearby farms or
mines. She even learned to run the mine's water pump.

In August Lou reluctantly left the mountains to return to school. In September
1891 she and ten of her closest friends formed a club, which they called the Agassiz
Association after the noted scientist Louis Agassiz. Lou Henry was its first president. The club's stated purpose was to study botany, zoology, microscopy, and taxi-
dermy, and to make additions to the school's natural history collection. The girls
met weekly in a room off the school museum, and went out on field trips as often as
they could to collect "specimens"—horned toads, grasshoppers, bees, butterflies.
Lou described one of these outings in her diary: "We climbed big hills, explored
deserted castles and most wonderful canons [*sic*], saw snakes, fell down hillsides,
stepped on cactus and did many other delightful things."[14]

In November her father received a letter from a friend in Monterey telling him
of an opening for a qualified man as cashier at the Bank of Monterey. Closing
down the mine for the winter, Charles hurried north and returned December 9
with the news that he had been hired. At the end of January, Charles, Florence and
Jean left Los Angeles for Monterey.

Lou stayed behind to finish out her second year at Los Angeles Normal. She
boarded for a time with the family of a classmate, but the arrangement was unsatisfactory, and in May she moved to a rooming house, where she could have a room to
herself. In June, when classes ended, she boarded the coastal steamer *Eureka* for the
two-day voyage north along the coast to Monterey.

Over the summer Lou helped her father at the bank, counting and rolling coins
and collecting money. She also took lessons in manual training at a local planing
mill, which she enjoyed. In Lou's absence, Jean had begun accompanying their father on his fishing expeditions. During the summer Lou joined them on frequent
junkets into the mountains or along the coast. Sometimes Florence came along,
too, if the outing was not too strenuous. She would sit by the roadside in the shade
of a tree while the others climbed up and down hills or frolicked on the beach.

In Monterey Charles Henry at last found the economic security for his family
that he had been seeking. The move to California had improved Florence's health;
the long, painful coughing spells had vanished with the cold Iowa winters. The

Henry home on Pacific Street was a comfortable two-story structure with a large bay window overlooking the street. The family kept Bill the horse, and acquired a dog named Shivers. A Mexican-American woman came daily to help Florence with the housework and the cooking. Jean, now ten years old, was taking piano lessons and displaying considerable musical talent.

Because of the distance involved, the family decided that Lou should not return to Los Angeles in the fall, but transfer instead to San Jose Normal School, just over fifty miles from Monterey, for her final year. She boarded with a professor's family, attended football and baseball games, and taught classes in the town of Utopia under the supervision of a Miss Cozzens. The light-hearted gaiety of her years at Los Angeles Normal is missing from this period of her life. Her diary no longer contains lively tales of high-jinks with fellow students. She seems to have made few close friends, concentrating instead on completing her schoolwork and acquiring her teacher's certification. She compensated by making frequent visits home.

In March Florence's youngest sister Jessie came to visit. On her return to Iowa she told Grandma Weed that Lou "could go right into teaching, having unsolicited offers at different places, Whittier among them; also a place was ready for her in the bank with her father," which struck Grandma Weed as best of all.[15]

Despite Aunt Jessie's confident assessment of her future, Lou graduated on June 23, 1893, with no definite plans for the fall. On May 24 she had written to her mother asking her whether there were any teaching positions available in the Monterey area. She would consider a position with the bank, she said, provided she could be guaranteed an income of $275 a month. Whether or not the bank agreed to this condition is unknown, but she did work there as an assistant cashier until March of 1894, when the Monterey School Board hired her as a substitute teacher for the remainder of the school year.

From most people's point of view, Lou Henry was now well set on a way of life that would keep her productively busy until she could marry. But Lou was not satisfied. Teaching, although it was what she had trained for, did not hold her interest. Banking was more interesting, but her prospects there were limited; women did not become bank officers in the last decade of the nineteenth century. Where would she find a career that would challenge her varied capabilities?

In late spring of 1894 she attended a public lecture that would change her life forever.

Chapter 2

Stanford University and Herbert Hoover

The lecture, given by Dr. John Casper Branner, professor of geology at Stanford University, was entitled "The Bones of the Earth." Branner was an enthusiastic and inspiring speaker, and Lou, whose interest in earth sciences dated back to her hikes through the mountains with her father and that exciting summer when she helped him operate the mine in Acton, was hooked. She decided to enroll at Stanford to study geology under Dr. Branner.

Leland Stanford Junior University was only three years old. It had been founded in 1891 by California Senator and rail baron Leland Stanford in memory of his son, Leland Jr., who had died of typhoid seven years before at the age of fifteen. Located on the 8,800–acre Stanford ranch, the university was thirty miles from San Francisco and seventy-five from Monterey. Its buff sandstone buildings had been designed by architect Frederick Olmsted, who also designed New York's Central Park. They were arranged in an open quadrangle, joined by long sandstone arcades with red tile roofs. Grain fields surrounded the campus, punctuated here and there by an occasional live oak or eucalyptus tree. Several horse farms were nearby; Stanford himself raised racehorses. On the northeast corner of the ranch stood a single sequoia—the tall tree (or *palo alto*) that gave the community growing up around the campus its name. Tuition at Stanford was free, and from the first the school was fully coeducational.

When Lou started classes at Stanford in the fall of 1894, many buildings were still under construction, and new departments were being added each year. Ellen Coit Elliott, wife of the school's registrar, complained that the campus looked "exactly like a factory."[1] Roble Hall, the women's dormitory, had been built rather quickly of reinforced concrete in 1891; it accommodated perhaps half of the female student body. Those women unable to find rooms in Roble Hall boarded in the nearby towns of Mayfield or Menlo Park, or with faculty members. Similar conditions prevailed for the male students, whose dormitory was called Encina. A few enterprising souls had built boardinghouses for students on or near the campus in Palo Alto.

The rough condition of the campus, however, inspired an intense partisanship in the ranks of the student body. To have been a member of one of the early "pioneer" classes at Stanford would be something to brag about in later years. Forced by their somewhat isolated circumstances to rely on their own ingenuity for entertainment, the students and younger faculty became very close. Many of the friendships formed under these circumstances lasted for a lifetime.

Lou was the only woman student in the geology department. At first the young men were skeptical of her ability to do the work required, but this changed after the first field trip, when she vaulted a fence without assistance, as limber as any of the men. Her personality helped, too; she was warm and open with everyone, confident and capable, the kind of woman men referred to as a "good sport." She was quickly accepted by her fellow students as one of the boys. Hoover's biographer Will Irwin, who knew her then, has described her as a slim woman, supple as a reed, whose face "had a beautiful bony structure, regular and delicate yet firm." She wore her long brown hair coiled up on her head. She was also a fine horsewoman, who "rode like a centaur."[2]

According to legend, Lou was in Professor Branner's laboratory one day, discussing the origin of a certain rock with him, when the door opened and a young man entered.

The professor introduced them, then said, "Miss Henry thinks that this rock belongs to the precarboniferous age. What do you think, Hoover?"

Herbert Hoover, the story goes, examined the specimen and gave his considered judgment, but his mind was not on rocks.[3] He was entranced by this tall, energetic, unconventional young woman. He recalls in his *Memoirs* that he was captivated by her "whimsical mind, her blue eyes and a broad grinnish smile that came from an Irish ancestor."[4]

Lou saw a tall, slender, diffident young man whose broad shoulders tended to stoop slightly. His mouse-colored hair was straight and his hazel eyes tended to avoid making contact with those to whom he spoke. He wore an uninspired double-breasted blue serge suit, with one hand often thrust deep into his pants pocket, jiggling the coins or keys he carried there. Though not a scholar, he was Dr. Branner's prize pupil because of the intensity he brought to bear on those things that—like geology—interested him. Although Hoover was a senior, he and Lou were the same age (she was in fact nearly six months older) and both were natives of Iowa.

An earnest, unpretentious young man with a quirky sense of humor, Bert had survived a difficult childhood. By the time he was ten, both his parents had died, his father in 1880 and his mother in 1884. Bert, his older brother Theodore, and their younger sister Mary were parceled off among various aunts and uncles. His family were all sober, devout Quakers; he would later claim that he was twelve years old before he realized that it wasn't a sin to enjoy life. In the fall of 1884 he was sent by emigrant train to Oregon to live with his uncle, Dr. Henry John Minthorn. The Minthorns were fond of Bert and treated him well, though Dr. Minthorn's personality was on the cold side. For four years, Bert attended a small Quaker school that Dr. Minthorn had founded in Newberg; then he worked for his uncle's land office in Salem, studying math and accounting on his own in the evenings. Dr. Minthorn wanted to send him to a church-affiliated college, but Bert, then seventeen, had other ideas. He had heard about a new university opening in California, and he announced that he intended to go to Stanford to study science. Irritated by his nephew's obstinacy, Dr. Minthorn told Bert that if he insisted on attending Stanford, he'd have to pay for it himself. Bert promptly agreed.

Bert's share of his father's modest estate by this time was only $822.67, and although Stanford charged no tuition, the costs of room, board, books, and other living expenses would deplete it rapidly. His preparatory education barely qualified him for entrance. Undeterred by these obstacles, he enrolled in Stanford's first university class in the fall of 1891. When Professor Branner joined the faculty the following year, Bert became a geology major.

"It never occurred to him," Lou would later write to a friend, "to wait on tables or do professors' gardening or do typewriting," as other needy students did. Instead, he organized a laundry service, lectures, football games, and "every student body interest that he could lay his hands on."[5] He became known as a leader among the "barbarians," or nonfraternity men on campus and was elected class treasurer his junior year—but only on the understanding that he would receive no salary for the job. With an efficiency that foreshadowed much of his future work as a public servant, he eliminated the class debt of $2,000, set up a voucher system to guard against fraud and helped to write a student constitution.[6]

Lou Henry soon discovered that behind his shy, unimposing exterior, Bert Hoover was an intelligent young man whose dry sense of humor matched her own. Her sister Jean would later complain that the two of them often laughed together over things that she could see no humor in at all.[7] Bert rarely laughed out loud, generally contenting himself with a chuckle.[8] As a student, his work was solid but not brilliant; he flunked German, and barely passed the university's English writing requirement in time for graduation. None of this diverted him. He seldom wasted time worrying about the future, preferring to deal with the present in the most efficient way he could manage.

Although he didn't much care for dancing, Bert escorted Lou to her first Stanford dance. Through the remainder of the year their romance flourished modestly—she didn't introduce him to her parents until much later—but it acquired the solid grounding of close friendship. By the time he graduated in 1895, Bert

Hoover had determined to marry Lou Henry as soon as his financial situation permitted it.

It took the penniless orphan less time to achieve financial security than might have been expected. Through a combination of luck and sheer audacity, he was able in less than a year to work his way up from day laborer in a series of California mines to personal assistant to Louis Janin, a prominent San Francisco mining engineer. Bert and Lou exchanged numerous letters—none of which she kept for posterity—and he managed to see her frequently while on business trips to Stanford.

Meanwhile, Lou was thoroughly enjoying her four years at the university. In addition to her classes, there were dances, concerts, debates, ball games, and plays; there were good friends with whom she would remain close throughout her life. She bought a bicycle and learned to ride it, despite her Grandma Henry's contention that bicycles were not appropriate for young ladies. She didn't talk much about Bert to her friends, though, preferring to keep her feelings for him private. One of her classmates, Sue Dyer, observed some years later that "we knew there was someone, but Lou—well, she was friendly with everybody."[9]

Lou corresponded regularly with her parents in Monterey, keeping her father informed about her finances and her mother about the status of her wardrobe. Periodically, packages of food would arrive on the north-bound train, including the excellent tamales made by the Henrys' housemaid Amalia, which Lou shared with her friends. In 1895, her sister Jean spent several months with her while studying violin with one of the university professors.

The first year, Lou lived in Roble Hall, the women's dormitory on campus. When Jean came, she moved to a rooming house. Later she shared rooms in another boardinghouse with her sisters of the Kappa Kappa Gamma sorority.

Sororities were a fairly recent phenomenon in colleges, a by-product of the increasing numbers of young women flocking to higher education. Most of them were founded on the highest principles of scholarship, character, and morals. These were idealistic young women, breaking away from the old notion that women were lesser beings. They were determined to prove that they could achieve on an equal level with the male students around them. For encouragement, they banded together with other young women with whom they shared ideals and outlooks. Sororities provided them with a secure community in which they could exchange ideas and experiences and form friendships that in many cases would be lifelong.

Lou was introduced to Kappa Kappa Gamma (KKG) by Lucy Evelyn Wight, an older student who would become one of her closest friends. A native of Brooklyn, New York, Evelyn had been initiated into the sorority's St. Lawrence University chapter and later served as its first national president. In that capacity, she had presided over the first national Panhellenic convention in Boston in 1891. She transferred to Stanford the following year, and organized the Stanford chapter of KKG in 1892. Lou was initiated in 1894. In 1896 the girls rented the second floor of a house on Forest Avenue, owned by a Mrs. Mitchell, whose son and daughter were students at Stanford. By the following year they were able to rent a whole house. It cost them twenty-five dollars a month, complete with maid and cook. Only nine girls lived in the house that year, but they hoped to have more the following year. The father of one of the members offered to help them find any necessary furnishings.[10]

Lou enjoyed the fellowship that the sorority provided. After she graduated, the Kappas built a house of their own on campus. Adeline Fuller, who lived there as house manager a few years later, claimed in her oral history that Lou had paid for it, and that the sorority paid rent to her in those early years.[11] As time went on, however, and sororities grew both more exclusive and more dedicated to social than intellectual pursuits, Lou became disillusioned with the entire concept. The Stanford chapter's refusal to rush the daughters of her good friends the Herbert Starks in 1915 angered her. She came to believe that sororities were no longer a beneficial influence on young women. In 1937, she wrote to another friend whose daughter was entering college, "I think not having [sororities] makes for a much pleasanter, healthier (not physically) student body."[12]

As an undergraduate, Lou tackled her courses—chemistry, physics, bionomics, botany, economics, English literature, and of course, geology—with enthusiasm. Although a fourth of Stanford's female students were science majors, Lou was the first to major in geology, and the first woman in the country to receive a college degree in that field. Most women graduates expected to teach following graduation, but it was not Lou's intention to use her degree in such a passive manner. She wanted to do geodetic survey work, a field generally closed to women because it involved much work outdoors in rough country.

She received little encouragement. Even Dr. Branner had doubts about the wisdom of Lou's plans. A male friend wrote to her in July 1898, after her graduation, that Dr. Branner had told him Lou would be wiser to go back to school and specialize in "a kind of chemistry of geology," involving the study of geologic specimens through the microscope, rather than attempting field work, which "the conventionalities of life" would prevent her from doing.[13] However, Branner did make an effort on Lou's behalf, writing to various colleagues to ask whether they would be willing to take on a female scientist.[14]

The results were not promising. Shortly after her graduation, Lou wrote to Evelyn Wight, then teaching in New York City: "Well, dearest, here it is more than two whole weeks since '98 was thrown out on an already overstocked market, and you have not yet had a letter from this A.B. (which unfortunately does not stand . . . for 'A Boy'—ah, what wouldn't I give just about now to be one!)"[15]

While she waited for an acceptable job to appear, she helped her mother with Red Cross work in Monterey, where the government was gathering soldiers to send to the Philippines. The Spanish-American War had just begun, and war interest was high on the west coast; Stanford had fielded half a company of recruits for the Manila campaign. Lou agreed to serve as treasurer of the local Red Cross chapter. But other events were occurring that would soon affect her future.

In 1897, when the West Australian gold boom hit, the British firm of Bewick Moreing & Co. contacted Louis Janin in San Francisco, asking him to recommend an American engineer as a consultant to work in their Australian mines. Because America was the only country at that time that gave its engineers scientific training as well as practical experience, American engineers were in great demand.

Janin recommended Herbert Hoover. Since Bert was barely twenty-three years old, Janin suggested that he grow a moustache on his way to London for the interview, and blandly added twelve years to Bert's age in his letter of recommendation. The moustache was not a great success. The Moreing official who interviewed him observed in a bemused fashion, "How remarkable you Americans are. You have not yet learned to grow old. . . . Now you, for example, do not look a day over twenty-five."[16] Nevertheless, he offered Bert the job, with its impressive salary of $600 a month.

Bert was elated. The money would free his brother Theodore from the necessity of supporting their sister Mary and make it possible for Theodore to go back to college. Bert had felt he could not consider marrying until he had achieved this goal.[17] He desperately wanted to marry Lou. He confided to his cousin, Harriette Miles, that he was afraid of losing her if he waited too long. To another friend he wrote, "I'm growing impatient about waiting to marry a certain beautiful geology student but the London office is offering me a big opportunity in Australia where I'll be on my own in developing a mine."[18]

On the eve of his departure for Australia, Bert had dinner with the Henrys. It was the first time that they had met Lou's "young man." By this time an arrangement, if not quite a formal engagement, had been more or less agreed upon between them. "We carried on a correspondence," Bert wrote laconically in describing his courtship.[19]

It was characteristic of Bert Hoover to seize whatever opportunity he was offered, and improve upon it to the best of his considerable ability. By November 1897 he had been made a junior partner in Bewick Moreing, and shortly afterwards he became superintendent of the Sons of Gwalia mine, one of the most productive gold mines in the area—thanks to Herbert Hoover. He was now earning close to $10,000 a year—a good third of which he "loaned" to friends and relatives, often anonymously, to help them with educational expenses. His Quaker training, and his own struggle to find the means to achieve an education, had left him with the firm belief that wealth was meant to be shared. It was a concept with which Lou Henry agreed wholeheartedly.

In mid-1898, soon after Lou graduated, Bert was presented with an even bigger opportunity. Bewick Moreing had made a deal to provide the Chinese government with a consulting engineer to help develop its coal-mining and cement manufacturing industries. The position, which the Chinese offered to Bert, carried the princely salary of $20,000 a year.

A few days later, a new postmistress in Monterey received what she took to be a business message between two men. She posted the cable on the bulletin board. It was addressed to Lou Henry, and read, "Going to China via San Francisco. Will you go with me?" and was signed "Bert."[20] If Lou was embarrassed by the public exhibition of this rather cryptic marriage proposal, which greatly amused her friends, there is no record of it. She wired back her acceptance in an equally brief cable, and immediately set about making preparations for her wedding.

They would have preferred a Quaker ceremony, Hoover observed in his *Memoirs*, but there was no meeting in that part of the state. Lou had asked her father's good friend the Reverend Dr. Thoburn to officiate, but he died six weeks before Bert's arrival. So they turned to a Catholic priest whom Lou had met during her teaching days in Monterey. Father Ramon Mestres, pastor of San Carlos Church in Monterey and Carmel Mission, was an energetic young man who encouraged clubs for children and built playgrounds and athletic fields for them. He had held marriage services for many Protestants, and foresaw no difficulty about the arrangement.

Bert reached California on January 28 and planned to set sail with Lou for China on February 11. The wedding therefore had a rather hasty feeling. It was held in the front room of the Henrys' home. Promptly at noon on February 10 Charles Henry led his daughter down the little hall into the sitting room, where Bert was waiting by the bay window.

"I particularly noticed that I wasn't asked to obey the young gentleman!" Lou recalled. "Otherwise, it was an adaptation of the Catholic service, in most ways similar to the Episcopal one."[21]

Both bride and groom appeared in matching brown suits—a coincidence that much amused Lou's mother. "We had made up our minds not to like him very well," she wrote to a friend after the ceremony, "but after he had been here a few days"—thirteen days in all—"we all liked him about as much as Lou did."[22]

Bert's brother and sister were present, as well as the Henry family. After a quick wedding luncheon, the young couple boarded the two o'clock train for San Francisco. Lou had written Sue Dyer that they would be passing through Palo Alto around 3:30, and a bevy of Lou's sorority sisters gathered at the Palo Alto station to see them off. Theodore later claimed that he managed to distract the girls' attention long enough for Lou and Bert to elude their notice.[23] Sue, who claimed that there were only two or three girls present, said that Lou came out on the platform to speak to them, but Bert stayed inside, perhaps too shy to face them.[24] As the train pulled away, the girls waved energetically.

That afternoon the newlyweds boarded a steamship in San Francisco harbor. They would have a short honeymoon in Honolulu, staying in the original Royal Hawaiian Hotel and getting stuck in the mud while sightseeing on Mount Palikea.

And then—on to China.

Chapter 3

A Chinese Adventure

The Hoovers reached Shanghai on March 8, having taken nearly a month to travel from San Francisco by way of Honolulu and Japan. Impressed by "picturesque" Kyoto, Lou reported the Chinese to be "more ostentatious and bizarre, but less picturesque than Japan—and *much* dirtier."[1] After four days in Shanghai's Astor Hotel, Bert and Lou sailed north to Tianjin (then known as Tientsin), where they would make their headquarters.

China in 1899 was in a state of flux. The Manchurian dynasty that had ruled the country since the seventeenth century was in decline. Military ineffectiveness, bureaucratic corruption, and widespread poverty in a steadily growing population all contributed to increasing political unrest. This governmental weakness had been exploited during the nineteenth century by European nations seeking cheap natural resources and new markets for their own burgeoning industrial economies. Using aggressive diplomacy backed by superior military power, the Europeans secured privileged status for their representatives. By the end of the century, agents of rival European powers were diligently vying for influence in a state torn between the forces of modernization, surrounding the weak but well-meaning Emperor Kuang Hsu, and of conservatism, gathered around his grandmother, the old Dowager Empress. Playing one faction against the other, both the Manchurian nobility and the European and Japanese diplomats contributed to the further weakening of the central government and a correlative increase in the inefficiency and corruption in the bureaucratic machine that administered the state.

Tianjin was the foreigners' capital in China at the turn of the century. A series of forced treaties had established a concession area two miles below the Chinese city on the bank of the Pei Ho. In this extraterritorial strip, one-and-a-half miles long by a mile wide, each foreign treaty nation—England, France, and Germany—maintained its own laws and property. The houses there were built according to European tastes, primarily of brick. A paved embankment, the Bund, had been built along the river where wealthy foreigners could promenade as they did in their native lands. Chinese servants, under the direction of a Number One Boy, ran the households of the foreigners, much as they did those of the wealthy Chinese in the Old City to the north. Streets were filled with vendors, beggars, and servants all noisily going about their business.

"Its 300 foreign families each lives in the centre of a large garden," Lou wrote of her new home, "with a high mud brick wall around it . . . so the streets are like the bottoms of high-banked canals, through which lines of coolies are usually carrying great boxes and bales of something."[2] Because of the heavy amount of foreign trade carried on through the Concession area, and because Tianjin was a provincial capital, the space between the city proper and the Concession area had filled in over the past thirty-some years with "a sea of one-storied Chinese houses and a maze of narrow alleys, until now the Foreign Settlement can be said to form one end of Tientsin City, and the old Walled City the other."[3] The two were joined by a highway, the Taku Road. The railway station was across the river from the foreign settlement. Around the entire area, Chinese city and foreign settlement alike, was a mud wall fifteen feet high.

Lou spent her first week in Tianjin at the Astor Hotel, recuperating from the ill effects of vaccinations and what she referred to as "getting acclimated." Bert was kept busy traveling back and forth to Beijing, talking with Chinese officials and trying to get an idea of the scope of his new job. He then took off for a two-month tour of Mongolia. Mrs. Ursula Johnson Stanley, a stout, elderly missionary who had spent nearly forty years in Tianjin, offered to rent Lou a room in her house until Bert returned. As the hotel was far from comfortable, Lou accepted the invitation gratefully.

In the next weeks, Lou began to take lessons in Chinese, which she thoroughly enjoyed. With plenty of time on her hands during Bert's lengthy absences, she applied her intellectual curiosity eagerly to this challenge. Her tutor, a Chinese Christian scholar named Chu'an Yueh-tung, remembered her years later as a good pupil with a kind manner and a humble attitude, who learned to read 60,000 characters—more than he could read himself.[4] She wrote to her parents that Bert's name in Chinese was *Hoo Yah*, while hers was *Hoo Lu*. *Hoo*, she went on to explain, meant wild or reckless, and *Lu* meant deer. Bert commented in his *Memoirs* that Lou had a "natural gift for languages," which he himself lacked entirely. After a while, the Chinese would speak to Lou in Chinese, and to him in English. In later years, Lou never let Bert forget any of the hundred or so words of Chinese he did manage to learn, using them to speak to him on what he called "*sotto voce* occasions."[5]

While she stayed with the Stanleys, Lou became acquainted with some of the other members of the European community. Formal afternoon calls and invitations to tea were as much a common practice in the foreign community of Tianjin as they were in Europe or America. As the wife of an important figure in China's department of mines, Lou was in some demand in the community's social hierarchy.

Gustav Detring, a shrewd German expatriate with curly black hair, neatly trimmed van Dyke beard and pince-nez, was personal adviser to Chang Yen-Mao, the minister of mines for Chihli Province (in which both Tianjin and Beijing were located). Chang was Bert's immediate boss, which meant that Bert and Detring would be working closely together. Detring had been employed by the Chinese government in various capacities since 1865, including several years as commissioner of customs at Tianjin, a post that gave him control over much of the trade between China and the West. He was one of the most influential foreigners in China, but Lou did not warm to him. Nor did she care much for his wife and teenage daughters.

She was much more favorably impressed with Edward B. Drew, the Englishman who was presently serving as commissioner of customs in Tianjin. He and his wife, Lucy, soon became good friends. Lou considered Drew a prime example of the "old China hand," and would later use his anecdotes about life among the Chinese as the basis of a series of written sketches that she hoped to publish, supplementing them with her own observations and experiences.

Minister Chang Yen-Mao's wife, who lived in the family's palace in Tianjin, Lou found charming—"one of the most interesting and intelligent women I have met in China—altho' she speaks no English." Mrs. Chang invited Lou to her home for "tiffin," or lunch, where her daughter, Mrs. Chow, who spoke English "very prettily," interpreted for her mother. To Lou's disappointment, the "tiffin" was European-style, "with knives, forks, spoons, etc.—in ten or 12 courses, and each served just as correctly as you could find anywhere." It was even held in a European-style building in the palace compound. But, she reported in a letter to her Aunt Jennie, "they promise me another invitation to the Chinese home and a Chinese meal with chopsticks."6

In her diary Lou described a typical day in Tianjin in those early months: errands in the morning, writing letters, or directing her Chinese seamstress; after dinner, sleep for a couple of hours; then tea, calls, or reading; supper; her Chinese lessons at 8 P.M.; to bed around ten and up again the next day by 7:30—"not uninteresting, even though it would be so in time," she concludes.7 Bert was gone a good deal of the time, but the Stanleys were considerate hosts. In May, they took Lou with them for a short holiday at the coastal resort of Pei Tai Ho.

Gradually, Lou became acquainted with Chinese ways of doing things—including the pervasive custom of "squeeze" (something between a tip and a bribe), that was a part of even the most inconsequential financial transaction. From Mrs. Stanley she learned how to handle a houseful of servants, as opposed to the single cook her mother had employed, or the maid she had hired for the sorority house at

Stanford. Although she found Chinese servants generally honest, Lou was distressed when someone stole her KKG pin, as well as the gold nugget that Bert had kept as a souvenir of Australia.

In early June Bert invited Lou to accompany him on one of his trips to Beijing. She kept careful notes in her pocket diary of her impressions of China's capital city. The train station was four miles from the city, but they had brought their own ponies so that they could ride the rest of the way in comparative comfort. The city was built of gray brick, or occasionally stone. Its streets were dirty and so crowded with stalls, booths, pedestrians, and coolies with heavy loads that Lou and Bert could only see what was around them while they were on horseback. Lou was delighted with the gaily decorated signs, the gilding on the more prominent storefronts, and the trees and flowers growing everywhere.[8]

While Bert talked business with Minister Chang, Lou stayed in a "very good little French hotel—only foreign one in [Beijing]."[9] It was "a Chinese with foreign hybrid surrounding a little court into which no breath can penetrate,"[10] which caused some discomfort during the hot summer nights. William Bainbridge, the United States secretary of legation, and his wife Mary came to dinner their first evening in the capital city. Mary Bainbridge, a lonely woman with two sons who had married Bainbridge a few years earlier after the death of her first husband, found Lou a congenial guest. "You are my best friend on this side of the Pacific," she would write Lou wistfully some months later.[11]

Since the Chinese officials preferred to do business late in the evenings (often working through until 4 or 5 A.M.), Lou spent her mornings sightseeing, escorted by servants. One day she accompanied Bert on his way to Chang's palace, owned by the father of the Emperor, where she was invited in to see the grounds. She was amazed to see how much the palace resembled the Chinese paintings she had seen on fans. As she started back to the hotel, Chang sent a servant after her to invite her inside to see his curios, but the boy was unable to catch up to her. She deeply regretted this lost opportunity.

On their last day in town, however, she and Bert were honored by a visit to their hotel from Chang Yen-Mao himself. "State occasion!" Lou wrote in her diary. Chang arrived "in his official chair with full retinue at 6 P.M. He drank foreign tea and smoked foreign cigars for over an hour,"[12] and expressed great delight at meeting the "American Lady Engineer." "He spoke a *little* English, I a little *more* Chinese, but Yueh [Bert's interpreter] did most of the talking."[13]

On her return to Tianjin, Lou found a furnished house that she and Bert could rent for the summer. Hospitable as the Stanleys had been, it must have been a relief for Lou to have a place of their own at last. By the end of September they had acquired more permanent quarters on Racecourse Road, at the edge of the Settlement near the wall overlooking the plain. This was a two-story, blue-brick house with fifteen rooms, requiring a staff of nine servants to run. Servants' quarters, kitchens, storerooms and the like were in another building across the interior courtyard. In a letter written in 1939 Lou described it as "a rather small [house] for foreigners," but added that she and Bert preferred it to a larger dwelling "because we stayed in it so little, on account of travelling much in the interior."[14]

The house was unfurnished, so at the first opportunity the Hoovers took a short trip to Shanghai to purchase the necessary furniture. They also wrote home, asking their relatives to send things they could not find in China—a solution that had its drawbacks. A letter from Bert to Lou's sister Jean in January 1900 complains bitterly about the dishes his brother Theodore had sent from California—"They were exactly what we did not want."[15] Lou quickly added a caveat: "Please don't mention the dishes to anyone. If Mrs. Theo asks about them, you can tell her we have *said* nothing about them. (We have only written.)"[16] Apparently the pattern, of large multicolored roses, struck Bert and Lou as tasteless. A high-backed cart that Theodore also sent received a more cordial welcome. A few years later, Lou unintentionally got her revenge when she gave her sister-in-law Mildred a rug. It was a bright pink, with a pattern of large roses, perhaps inspired by the pattern on the dishes. "It dismayed her, but later found a happy home with me," Mildred's daughter Hulda notes in her own memoir.[17]

In October Lou went with Bert on a trip into the interior to examine the Chow Yuen gold mine. The Hoovers traveled in style in a caravan that included two ponies, thirteen pack mules, a mule litter, a *mafoo*, or groom, and "boys and mule drivers without number." Near the end of the expedition, Lou's pony went lame, and she was left for four days in a hotel in Chefoo while Bert continued his tour. They then returned to Tianjin by boat—"the Chief Engineer of the Empire and all his vassals with 58 pieces of luggage."[18]

Both Hoovers found the Chinese attitude toward Bert's official position awkward. "Being a mining engineer," Lou wrote her Aunt Jennie, "they think he only needs to come within a few miles of the mines, be entertained in the officials' homes, take a cursory view of the distant landscape, and then tell them all about the mines. They are absolutely shocked at the idea of his wanting to go underground and explore the shafts & tunnels."[19] Surprised at Bert's insistence on going into the mines, the Chinese miners were aghast when Lou did so as well. After she came back out, the miners went through an elaborate ceremony, complete with drums and firecrackers, to chase away any evil spirits who might have followed this presumptuous female into the mine.[20]

Bert soon realized that Chang Yen-Mao's concept of his role differed materially from his own. He had been asked originally to map the country's coal deposits, advise the government on technical and administrative improvements, and suggest a code of mining laws. Chang, however, seemed to want him to concentrate on finding new gold mines. "The main principle" of the mining industry in China at that time, Lou would write to Theodore some years later, "was to extract as much of the proceeds for the Royal Treasury as possible, and for all the officials along the route to 'squeeze' out what they could on its way."[21]

Nevertheless, Bert buckled down to his job with enthusiasm. Returning to Tianjin, Lou resumed her social duties and her Chinese lessons. "Hsien Sheng [an honorary title for her tutor, Chu'an Yueh-tung] and I are getting out a dictionary," she wrote in her diary one day.[22] She told her mother about the lovely silks her dressmaker was stitching for her, and asked for patterns of the latest styles.[23] Pajamas, she said, were much more comfortable to sleep in than nightgowns, and she recommended them to her sister Jean, who hoped to come for a visit.[24] One evening, Lou held a dinner at her home on Racecourse Road to mark the formation of a Stanford alumni chapter in Tianjin. Seven Stanford graduates—many of them engineers brought to China and employed by Bert—attended.[25]

Lou began collecting Chinese porcelain, chiefly blue and white ware of the Ming (A.D. 1368–1662) and K'ang Hse (A.D. 1662–1720) dynasties. The collection continued to grow over the years, even after she left China, and became one of her proudest possessions.

While she was in China, Lou kept a diary in small notebooks, which she sent home monthly to her parents. She supplemented them with long letters to her parents, her Aunt Jennie and Jean (now seventeen and about to graduate from high school). Bert charged Jean with sending periodic shipments of magazines and books; he insisted that he would not pay her for them unless she also bought herself a box of candy every month. His letters described their daily routine in a humorous style that his wife found exasperating.

"Have just been reading that idiotic boy's stupid letter," she wrote her sister in January 1900. "It's true we *don't* have breakfast at 8:00 (except ideally)—but you never expected I would. . . . And only *twice* have I been late dressing to go places, and those times we arrived early after all. . . . So of course any time we are late now *my dressing* is the reason!"[26] Another letter claimed that Bert had thought a tie he received for Christmas was too bright, until Lou started to wear it; the next thing she knew, it was back around his neck. Sometimes he appropriated ties she had chosen for herself! She complained that he had even copied the frilled collars and cuffs she had put on her pajamas, so the washman would be able to tell hers from Bert's, "so now we can't tell them apart!"[27]

The light, teasing tone of these letters testifies to the warmth of the relationship that existed between the young Hoovers, a relationship based on mutual respect and sheer pleasure in each other's company. Bert once told his cousin Harriette that Lou was "the only real *comrade* I could ever have in a woman."[28]

Acquiring a typewriter, Lou taught herself to type, and by April 1900 was at work on a scientific article on coal mines in China. Bert was also writing articles, which she helped him edit. In December 1899 she had written to a literary agent in New York, asking whether he thought there would be a market for a series of articles on her experiences in China. When he gave her an encouraging reply, she began a series of "character studies" intended as a basis for these articles.[29]

While Lou found many individual Chinese admirable and deserving of respect, she was not immune to her generation's fondness for stereotypes. Her impressions of the Chinese people were undoubtedly colored by the negative attitudes toward them prevalent in California during her years there and reinforced by those of the

European community in Tianjin. These sketches (which were never published) are engagingly written, but condescending. They tend to show the Chinese as a quaint, peculiar people whose morals were not quite up to Western standards—a common opinion among Western observers at that time. In a letter to Professor Branner, Lou bemoans "the utter apathy of the Chinese to *everything*, their unconquerable dilatoriness . . . sometimes near heartbreaking to an energetic Yankee."[30]

From her mother, Lou received news of her family. While she was still at Stanford, Grandpa Weed had died in 1895 and Grandma Weed in 1896, but her Grandma Mary Ann Henry was still going strong in Wahpeton, North Dakota, at the age of seventy-two. Uncle Will Henry, who was an officer in the Wahpeton bank, lived with her. Uncle Addison Henry had left the army for the business world, and was living in Oakland, California, with his wife Ann (Aunt Nannie) and their two children. On her mother's side, Aunt Jennie had recently moved to Cortland, New York, to become companion and caretaker for an elderly aunt. Aunt Jessie was living in Waterloo, where her husband Ed Jones was a merchant. Uncle Wallace Weed and his wife, Lill, had taken over Grandpa Weed's farm in Shell Rock.

Lou also corresponded with Bert's sister and brother, both of whom had married within months of Bert and Lou. In March 1899 Mary (generally called May) had married Cornelieus Van Ness Leavitt, a plumber from the San Francisco area whom neither of her brothers thought worthy of their beloved little sister. They were particularly disappointed that she had given up her studies at Stanford in favor of marriage. In June, Theodore, who was still studying at Stanford, had married his childhood sweetheart, Mildred Brooke.

While they were in China, the Hoovers continued the informal scholarship program Bert had begun during his years in Australia. In addition to helping Theodore and May, Bert was paying the college expenses of his cousin Harriette Miles, who had lived with him and his siblings for a time in San Francisco. He also anonymously assisted several Stanford friends, including Ray Lyman Wilbur, who later became president of Stanford and would be secretary of the interior when Bert became president.[31] Lou wrote to her father, "We're going to have to be careful with our money, because we have five people in college and we're helping two others."[32] These "loans," as Bert called them, were then costing the Hoovers nearly $3,000 per year.[33] Lou had no objection to this expense. She shared her husband's belief in both the importance of education and the need to share wealth. Throughout her life, she would always be ready to pay the educational expenses of people she considered deserving.

In the early spring of 1900 Lou accompanied Bert on a trip up the Yellow River by boat to study the flood control system. (Although Bert had protested to Chang Yen-Mao that he was not a hydraulics engineer, the minister wanted his opinion on the subject.) "She got much joy out of the teeming life all about us," Bert's *Memoirs* report.[34] Lou sketched scenes of life along the way, and sent them home to her family.

In April, soon after their return to Tianjin, the Hoovers received a visit from Algernon Moreing, senior partner in the firm of Bewick Moreing, and his wife. Moreing had come from London to discuss arrangements with Bert, Chang Yen-Mao, and Chang's German adviser, Gustav Detring, for a loan the firm was trying to arrange to build a pier at Chinwangtao, to would serve the immense coal fields at Kaiping. Bert had reported that the Kaiping coal fields were the most promising in China, if they could be operated in an efficient manner. He suggested to Bewick Moreing that they try to secure Chang's approval for their firm to assume administrative control of the mines in the area.

Lou did her best to entertain the Moreings during their three-week stay. Gustav Detring gave a dinner in their honor. "Rather a stupid time," Lou noted sourly in her diary. Of Detring's teen-aged daughters, she observed, "German girls are infinitely inferior to the American article."[35] Although she was obliged to treat Moreing and his wife with the deference due from a junior partner to a senior one, Lou seems to have found them difficult guests. When they departed at last on April 20, Lou wrote, "in lead pencil, I was glad to see the last of them."[36]

Lou's relief at the Moreings' departure may have had more behind it than simply an overload of hospitality. During the spring of 1900, China's foreign community was finding itself under increasing psychological pressure. The conflict between progressive and reactionary forces in government had spawned a violently anti-foreign movement among the people of the country. It was spearheaded by a group calling themselves I-ho-ch'uan, or Righteous Fists—loosely translated as "Boxers."

As early as June of the previous year, Lou had reported that a Chinese shipping firm called the E&M Company had been burned "by devils." By May 1 Bert was forced to call in his surveying teams, which had been mapping anthracite coal fields west of Beijing. He went to Beijing a few days later, to investigate the situation, and Lou went with him. While there, she developed a severe sinus infection. No doctor was available, and Bert was frantic. He rushed her back to Tianjin. Mary Bainbridge from the Embassy accompanied her, arriving in Tianjin on May 11. Lou recovered quickly, and Mary Bainbridge returned to Beijing on the 22nd. On May 28, the Boxers burned a railroad bridge on the Beijing-Tianjin line, cutting off all communication between Tianjin and the Chinese capital. The troubled period the foreign press dubbed the Boxer Rebellion had begun.

On June 1 Lou wrote in her diary that "the Chinese Dragon Festival on which we were all to be massacred by 8 million heavenly soldiers" had "passed quietly,"[37] but by June 4, reports of Boxer forces converging on Tianjin were substantiated. "*Mafoos* and coolies evade going out of the settlement on errands," wrote Lou. Military patrols were everywhere.[38] On June 10 some "bad native children" harassed her as she rode her bicycle through the streets.[39] Her number one boy, Kuoh, argued very convincingly that she and Mr. Hoover should take this opportunity to go to Japan for a short vacation, until things quieted down.

"I told him that of course I would talk to the master about it but that I did not think he would go, because if all the things Kuoh thought were true, he would all the more have to try to take care of those who were under him."[40] This referred not only to the foreign engineers under his direction, but also to the numerous Chinese involved in the project. The Boxers had a particular animosity toward those of their fellow countrymen, especially Christians, who cooperated with the "foreign devils" or worked for them.

Kuoh then asked permission to take his family to a place of safety in the north, promising to return before the trouble started. He arranged for part of the staff—his eighteen-year-old nephew, two coolies, a Christian refugee who had attached himself to the household, and the head *mafoo*—to remain behind and look after the family, which they did. "We were therefore infinitely better off than most of our neighbors . . . as the whole force of servants to the foreigner cleared out almost to a man," noted Lou in her narrative of the Boxer Rebellion.[41] Bert tried to get Lou to leave, "but there was too much pleasant excitement bustling about the neighborhood to let me think of missing anything that might happen."[42]

The seriousness of the situation was underlined by the sudden return from Beijing of Chang Yen-Mao, who had fled the capital after several attempts on his life. The diplomatic corps in Beijing was on the verge of panic as well. Frantic wires arrived daily from the ministers of various foreign countries. On June 10 a relief force of 2,400 men was despatched from Tianjin under British Admiral Sir Edward Hobart Seymour to protect the foreign diplomatic community in Beijing.

In Tianjin on June 15 fires broke out in the French settlement at the northern edge of the Concession area; the Catholic cathedral was gutted. Many of the foreign inhabitants of Tianjin sent their children away by boat to Shanghai for safety. The Detrings moved into town from their villa in the hills. Charles D. Tenney, president of Tientsin University, which lay exposed a mile beyond the settlement walls, sent his family in to stay with the Hoovers until the danger should pass.

"We took a bicycle ride all around the outskirts of the settlement on the afternoon of Saturday the 16th of June," Lou's narrative reports. "Ominous quiet was everywhere."[43]

What the foreign community did not know, but would soon learn, was that on the morning of June 16, Allied forces from Germany, France, Britain, and Japan had destroyed the Chinese forts at Taku and Tongku harbors, some thirty miles away at the mouth of the Pei Ho. By the next day some thirty thousand Boxers had gathered in Tianjin's Old City, looting foreign property and attacking anyone they thought might be connected with the foreigners in any way. Some of the Chinese troops stationed in the area allied themselves with the Boxers and began shelling the foreign settlement. An attack on the railroad station was held off by the small European guard force of some 2,300 soldiers—most of them Russian, but with small units from various other countries—augmented by civilian volunteers. The defenders set up barricades made from bales of wool and rice from the warehouses along the Bund, and formed an ad hoc military force to man them.

Most of the Boxers were young men in their teens who believed that their zeal had made them invincible to bullets fired by foreigners. The alliance between them and the regular Chinese army forces was not as solid as it appeared on the surface. The Chinese troops had little respect for the undisciplined Boxers, who could not be relied upon in battle and sometimes seemed more interested in plundering the city than in fighting. Many of the casualties among the Boxers were caused by fire from their supposed allies. This was little comfort to the defenders of the settlement. It was the artillery of the army units that caused the greatest damage, and the Western-trained government troops who presented the greatest threat.

The next six days were terrifying for those who remained in the besieged Concession. The Hoovers' house was one of the first struck by the shelling. The Tenneys decided to leave and take shelter in Gordon Hall, the administrative center of the British Settlement, where some 280 refugees were already holed up. Lou took her remaining Chinese staff and moved in with the family of their good friend Edward B. Drew, the English commissioner of customs. The Hoovers brought along the food they had been stocking up for a proposed trip to Mongolia: canned California fruit, crackers, canned meat, and vegetables. The food was very welcome, as were the servants, since the Drews had only two elderly men left of their staff. Bert's young engineers kept them supplied with water from the river and rice from the barricades. One of these young men had found eleven cows wandering about on the plain outside the city shortly before the shelling began. He brought them into the settlement, where their milk was highly valued. Lou delivered the milk to the makeshift hospital at Gordon Hall on her bicycle. She also volunteered her services at the hospital as a temporary nurse.

"Mrs. Hoover had a small rifle that she knew how to use," observed Mrs. Drew in her own diary of the siege, "and she used to walk quietly all about the garden . . . in the darkness"[44] during her 9–11 P.M. shift. The outbuildings were full of Chinese refugees, many of them Christians.

Hard as life was for the foreign community, it was much worse for the three to four thousand Chinese people stranded inside the Concession area. Many of them had little to eat. Some of them saw their homes destroyed by the defenders, who feared that these quarters would provide cover for the attackers. And it was difficult for the besieged foreigners to differentiate between "good" and "bad" Chinese. "There were executed 10 or 12 Coolies who were suspicioned and convicted on evidence that merits rank with the Salem witchcraft," Bert's account states.[45] Chang Yen-Mao himself was arrested, but later released on the protest of his friends in the foreign community—primarily Herbert Hoover.

On June 23 a 4,000–man relief force arrived from the allied fleet in Taku. Two thousand of them were detached and sent after Admiral Seymour, whose relief column had disappeared somewhere between Tianjin and Beijing. The rest set about relieving the siege and driving the Chinese forces from the city. The "black fear," as Bert called it, was over,[46] but it would be another two weeks before the crisis ended.

The Hoovers returned to their own house on June 24. "It was a joy," Lou would recall, "to snap one's fingers at a close 'whi-i-iz-z-z' and say 'just wait till tomorrow old fellow.' "[47] With the relief force came the press, including *Collier's* writer Frederick Palmer, whom the Hoovers had first met on their honeymoon cruise a year earlier. Palmer, who stayed with the Hoovers, described Lou playing solitaire in her house when a shell came through the door. Unfazed, Lou calmly went on playing, saying only, "I don't seem to be getting this."[48]

Bert again tried to talk Lou into leaving, now that the road to Taku was open. Palmer quoted their exchange:

"You will go out," Bert said.

"I will not," Lou replied.

"You will."

"I will not go unless you go."

"Hum-m-m," he grumbled, and walked away.

"All right, Bertie," she called after him.

"All right, Lou."[49]

Although the foreign community in Tianjin was relieved to have military protection again, relations among the various national units were not always harmonious. Lou complained bitterly about the loss of Christmas gifts from home that had been destroyed or stolen when Russian troops looted the train station. One day, one of the cows vanished. The "old coolie" suggested taking her calf through the streets to search for her. He and Lou set off, leading the calf on a rope. At last, outside the German barracks, the calf's bawl was answered by a maternal lowing. Lou knocked on the gate, and tried to explain to the German sentry that she wanted to take the cow home. This was its calf, she pointed out. The young soldier nodded, took the calf inside the gate, and thanked her for returning the calf to its mother.[50]

Despite the dangers and the irritations, Lou had found the experience exhilarating. "You missed one of the opportunities of your life by not coming to China in the summer of 1900," she wrote to Evelyn Wight, now teaching in New York, "you should have been here,—at the most interesting siege of the age."[51]

On June 26th the remnants of Admiral Seymour's column returned, tattered and wounded. They had been cornered only thirty-eight miles from Tianjin and forced to entrench and wait until they were rescued by the relief force. "They were a sad, worn-out lot of men," Lou recalled in her memoir.[52] As recriminations flew regarding the quality of the force's leadership, the injured survivors were taken to the hospital for treatment.

In Beijing, the Hoovers learned, the German minister and the Japanese chancellor of legation had been killed and much of the city around the diplomatic enclave burned. By the time a relief force arrived on August 14, casualties in the foreign community had reached 68 dead and 167 wounded, mostly among the guard force of five hundred men from the various embassies. The Hoovers' friends the Bainbridges were unharmed. In Tianjin's foreign community, the civilian casualties were 2 dead and 5 or 6 wounded out of 900; of the 2300 foreign troops who had been in the city at the beginning of the seige, about 300 were either dead or wounded by the time reinforcements arrived on June 23.

Lou finally agreed to leave Tianjin for the coast on July 11, but she returned on August 3 to pack her belongings and take photographs of the "forts, etc." It was probably at this time that she acquired the rifles and other weapons that formed the nucleus of a small arms collection that she took back with her to Monterey.

On August 4 she and Bert left for London to report to headquarters on the effect the Boxer Rebellion would have on Bewick Moreing's business arrangements. Bert believed that a new opportunity might be opening up, through which—if the company acted quickly and firmly—Bewick Moreing might acquire sole control over the Kaiping coal fields.

"Japan is lovely and *clean* and peaceful after China," Lou wrote of the week she and Bert spent in Nagasaki.[53] From Japan they sailed for Shanghai, Hong Kong, and on to England via Suez. The ship, the German mail ship *Weimar*, was "horrid," but London, where they arrived at last on October 1, was everything she had imagined it to be—"quite like all the books, and *so* English!"[54]

The Hoovers stayed with the Moreings in their country house in Surrey, thirteen miles from London. "I am getting ever so much better," she wrote in her diary, "both from the cold [which she had caught shortly after her arrival] and regaining the pounds I lost on the Weimar. . . . England is a lovely country - just a garden as people say."[55] When she and Bert moved to the Savoy Hotel in London a few weeks later, she was able to spend her spare time "reading in the British Museum."[56]

The Hoovers started back for China in November, traveling this time by way of the United States. They stopped in New York, where they tried unsuccessfully to talk Evelyn Wight and her fiancé Mansfield Allan into advancing their wedding date by six months, so it would take place while they were there. They visited Grandma Henry and Uncle Will in North Dakota, and stayed briefly with Lou's parents in Monterey. When they sailed for China in December 1900 on the *Nippon Maru*, young Jean Henry joined them for her promised visit to the Orient.

The Boxer Rebellion had provided foreign interests with a perfect excuse to increase their commercial investments in China. Concessions were being gobbled up by a variety of new companies with European connections. The Chinese government feared that it might lose all rights in the Chinese Mining and Engineering Company. At its request, Bert had arranged before he left in August for Bewick Moreing nominally to take over the company. For several months, the company was listed in Bert's name, to prevent its being confiscated by some foreign government as reparations. Later, it was registered as an English corporation, with some shares held by the Chinese government and the rest sold to English, Belgian, and Russian investors. Bert was appointed the new company's general manager, at an increased salary.

This transfer of control of the company led to problems, however. By Chinese law foreigners could not own businesses in China unless they had Chinese partners. Moreing, having found it difficult to arrange the necessary funding for the deal in England, had been forced to bring in Belgian investors. It soon transpired that these European investors—British and Belgian—had a very different concept than that held by Chang Yen-Mao and his colleague, Gustav Detring, of the role that the Chinese partners would play in the organizational power structure of the newly formed company. The Belgian investors appointed one of their country-men, Emile Francqui, as managing director of the firm. Francqui had made a name for himself in the Belgian Congo as an adventurer and a financier. His ideas on running the company differed from Bert's, and there was frequent friction between the two men as Bert attempted to reorganize the administration of the coal fields. In September 1901 when his provisional term as administrator ended, Bert gladly turned over the management of the firm to Francqui. He then returned to London, where he had been promoted to senior partner in the firm of Bewick Moreing.

Chapter 4

Rolling Stones

While Bert was dealing with company matters in Tianjin and Beijing, Lou and Jean spent the first few months of 1901 in Japan. In part this may have been a natural caution about returning too soon to a country so recently the scene of violent turmoil, especially when they had eighteen-year-old Jean's safety to consider. Lou, however, was not well. Some months before the siege began, she had injured her tailbone when her foot slipped off the pedal of her bicycle, causing the saddle to strike her sharply at the base of her spine. The pain eased within fifteen minutes, and she continued on her way, thinking no more about it, but for the next year and a half she was plagued with backaches. Typically, she never complained. "Mrs. Hoover would never admit she was sick," one of her secretaries would remember of her years later.[1] By the time she reached Japan in January 1901, the pain had gone from chronic annoyance to serious distress.

She consulted a doctor in Tokyo, but he could find nothing wrong. However, while in America, she had heard about an operation that her Aunt Nannie Henry had undergone to remove a broken coccyx. Aunt Nannie's symptoms sounded much like Lou's own. Lou said nothing at the time, not wanting to have to stay behind while Bert went back to China. But when the condition persisted, she consulted a Dr. Hall, who lived in Yokohama. Dr. Hall confirmed that her coccyx was indeed broken. He suggested an electrical treatment that he thought might relieve the pain, and to some extent, it did. At last, however, on March 5, Dr. Hall operated to remove the broken coccyx. The operation was successful, and Lou recovered rapidly. By the time her twenty-seventh birthday arrived on March 29, she was taking meals in the hotel dining room. She was even able to enjoy a carriage ride.

On April 4 she and Jean left for Tianjin. "Our only sadness now—aside from leaving some of the nice people we had gotten to know in Yokohama—was dear little Yoshi," she wrote. Yoshi was her Japanese maid, whom she had hoped to be able to take with her to China.[2] Although Yoshi was willing to go, her parents objected, and even though she was nearly forty years old, Yoshi felt obliged to obey their wishes.

Lou and Jean arrived at last in Tianjin, where they found that the xenophobic mania of the previous year had almost completely dissipated. Lou was able to share some of her favorite sights with Jean. In May they visited Mary Bainbridge in Beijing, where they toured the Summer Palace, the Forbidden City, the Great Wall, and other sights previously unavailable to foreign tourists.

Letters from home brought good news from Theodore Hoover, who had earned his A.B. in engineering from Stanford in June. He was now working at a mine in Amador, California. In May, he and Mildred had been blessed with a daughter, named after her mother but generally called Mindy. Aunt Jennie, with whom Lou had corresponded frequently while in China, had remarried, and was now the wife of George Mager, a bank president, in Cortland, New York.

In September 1901 the Hoovers left China for good. They traveled to London via California, taking Jean home so that she could start classes at Stanford. While they were in Monterey, Bert arranged to build a new home for Lou's parents, which Charles Henry christened Henry Croft. The house was registered in Florence Henry's name. Set on a large lot, with a smaller cabin in the back for guests, Henry Croft would be the Hoovers' refuge in California, as Bert's engineering career took on a global scope.

The next six years were busy, active, and profitable for the Hoovers. They traveled extensively. Bert was one of four partners in Bewick Moreing; he had a 20 percent share in the firm. The others were G. Algernon Moreing, the senior partner, who owned 50 percent; A. Stanley Rowe (a clerk and accountant), who, like Bert, owned 20 percent; and Thomas W. Wellsted (a mechanical engineer), who owned 10 percent. Bert's chief responsibility was the operation of the company's mines—administration and engineering. He was charged with locating suitable locations for mine development, arranging for the formation of a company to develop the mines, and overseeing the work itself. His work took him to such far-off locations as New Zealand, Burma, Korea, Russia, and South Africa, as well as France, Italy, the United States, Belgium, and Wales. As often as possible, Lou went with him.

In Kalgoorlie, Australia—where she toured a gold-processing plant in January 1902—she joined Bert and his colleagues in their discussions around the dinner table, her background in geology and banking enabling her to participate on an equal basis with the men. And later, "when we were alone I would get more of the details than could be divulged when the guests were present," she later wrote in a memo for her children.[3] Among the men who attended these dinners were Australian engineers John Agnew and Wilfrid Newbery, who had been with them in

China. Stanford University graduates Deane Mitchell, in whose mother's home Lou had lived during her sophomore year, and William Pritchard, who had given Theodore Hoover his first job in mining, were also frequent guests. Lou considered these talks "the subject of the greatest intellectual interest of all the many things that came within our purview,—as well as embodying the most romance of anything we knew or came across."[4]

Despite Bert's comparative youth—he was now twenty-seven—and the rapidity of his rise in the firm, neither he nor Lou had any doubts about his ability to achieve the goals set by the company. In Lou's diary she tells about a young American couple she had heard of who had come to Australia intending to make their fortune, but who were now broke. It was "sad and amusing," she observed, "—'amusing' to think of mature college graduates being so ignorant and dependent."[5] She could not imagine herself or Bert finding themselves in a similar situation.

While Bert was in the field Lou spent her spare time at her new typewriter composing articles about her experiences in China. Expanding on the character sketches she had written earlier and including details of the siege of Tianjin from her own notes and those given to her by others, she produced a twelve-chapter manuscript. There is, however, no evidence that she ever attempted to have it published.[6] The only article she ever published from her China years was a study of the Dowager Empress (whom she never met) that appeared in 1909.

On their way back to England in April, the Hoovers stopped in Paris, where Lou spent a week shopping and sightseeing while Bert went on to London. It would be helpful to have her comments on Parisian society at the turn of the century, but she has left us no record of this holiday. Her diary-keeping was sporadic, designed mostly to keep her family informed about events in her life, and her mother was not one to keep correspondence for long. Like her daughter, she tended to burn letters once they had been read and answered. Only a few letters from the China years and shortly afterward would be found in a box in Monterey in 1930, and retrieved by Lou for her own files.

Clearly, however, the young Hoovers were beginning to enjoy their new wealth. Lou was now able to buy whatever she wanted, including the services of a French maid, Thérèse, a skilled seamstress whom Lou brought back with her to London.

While in France that spring, the Hoovers also had purchased a motorcar, a French Panhard, which they took with them to England. Automobiles were a relatively new phenomenon, and not always reliable. In his *Memoirs* Bert observed that "it ran some of the time."[7] The Hoovers hired a French chauffeur, but the young man proved unreliable. When he took the car to London for repairs in mid-July, he took it on a joyride, damaged it, paid the resulting fine with money from the purse Lou had put in the car to pay for the repairs, and then claimed that the car had been stolen. When he returned to Walton to collect his luggage, Lou confronted him, and he confessed his guilt, returning her purse. Lou refused to press charges, sending the youth back home to his mother in Dieppe.[8]

Shortly after they reached England in May 1902, the Hoovers rented a summer home, prophetically called the White House, a few miles southwest of London in Walton-on-Thames. Lou spent the summer there, while Bert returned to the United States on a two-month tour of inspection of his firm's properties. Her friend Evelyn Wight, now Mrs. Mansfield Allan, came to visit, and Lou took her on a grand tour of England and Wales. They visited both Oxford and Cambridge. Lou noted in her diary that Cambridge's Girton College, established in 1869 "for six girls," was England's first institution of higher education for women. Lou and Evelyn were back in London by August 9, 1902, when Edward VII was officially crowned King of England, but they stayed home "to avoid the crowds."[9]

In addition to entertaining Evelyn, Lou was hunting for an appropriate house to rent in London. Eventually she located an apartment, or flat, at 39 Hyde Park Gate in the Kensington area, which she leased beginning in September. Its redecorating kept her occupied until Bert's return on September 4. She may also have taken a few courses at the London School of Mines during this period.

Bert was discovering that there were unsatisfactory aspects to his partnership arrangement with Bewick Moreing. These difficulties are spelled out in a summary of the situation that Lou later wrote for her children's edification, in which she observed that "being partners with a man did not imply any spirit of loyalty toward him."

Algernon Moreing, the firm's senior partner, according to Lou, tended to take the most promising projects under his personal control, allocating only the more doubtful ones to the firm as a whole. "In the latter case," Lou explained, "if it turned out successful, it managed to get bought up by the older man in some form or other while it was still very cheap,—but if it was a failure, as a large percentage of mines must be, it remained on the firm's books."[10]

Moreing also had a power of attorney from his junior partners to attend to "such small matters" as investment in syndicates set up to develop mines owned by the firm, while the junior partner was out of the country: "In one of the early absences, before the shares had really reached any value . . . the senior partner sold out both their shares at a ridiculously low figure. Later on it accidentally transpired that he had sold them to another syndicate of which he owned practically all the shares, so that the youngster [meaning her husband] was left with some $10,000 (or was it pounds) as his entire profits out of three years hard work, while his own senior partner pocketed the fortune (a little one) to which he had no right whatever,—and which he accepted with what might be termed jaunty grace and in a jocular mood, when he was discovered!"[11]

Bert found the two other younger partners more agreeable to work with. When Moreing decided to go himself to China in late 1902, the three young men became better acquainted. In Lou's words, "the American appreciated the mechanical efficiency . . . of the office director [Wellsted] and the absolute financial genius" of Stanley Rowe.[12] From them Bert learned the financial side of his business, which he had previously considered subordinate to the engineering aspect. Rowe especially showed him how corporations were financed and shares floated in London's business world. Bert became fascinated with the interrelationship between the financing and the development of profitable mines, and quickly grew expert at putting together packages for projects he thought deserving of investment. He discussed his plans with Lou, whose background in banking helped her to understand what he was doing.

Shortly after Christmas in 1902, however, disaster struck. The Hoovers had had dinner with the Rowes on Boxing Day, Britain's traditional post-Christmas gift-giving holiday. The next morning, Rowe failed to show up for work. His wife telephoned, in tears, with the news that Rowe, who kept the company books, had left town during the night. He left a letter confessing that he had been speculating on the market with the firm's funds, and an unexpected slump made it impossible for him to replace them. The embezzlement totalled nearly a million dollars. "It was widely known," Lou's account to her children declares, "as the most clever piece of rascality that had occurred in the city for twenty years,—and it transpired that it had been going on for the past ten years."[13]

Bert's first instinct was to figure out what his share of the losses would be, and then withdraw from a partnership that had become thoroughly distasteful to him. But he was concerned that if the firm did not make good its debts, thousands of small investors would lose their whole investment. He therefore made a public announcement stating that the firm would make good any losses resulting from Rowe's embezzlement. Moreing, when he heard, was furious, but agreed to support his junior partner's decision. He made it clear, however, that Hoover would have to find the money on his own. According to his brother Theodore, Bert found himself with "a legal obligation of $50,000 and a self-assumed moral obligation of $500,000, all of which was paid off before he called a penny his own."[14] It took him six years.

Rowe eventually surfaced in Canada. He was tried for fraud and forgery and sent to prison for ten years. This was not, it turned out, his first offense. During the years that Rowe was in prison, the Hoovers helped to support his five young children.

Other troubles followed, some of them arising out of Rowe's defalcation, some from other investment problems. In 1902 a man named Edgar Storey sued the firm, and Herbert Hoover personally, claiming he had not received payment for three thousand shares of stock in the Great Fingall mine, one of Bewick Moreing's Australian properties. Bert insisted that he was not involved in the deal, and although the initial lawsuit went against him, he won on appeal. In November 1903 another firm sued Bewick Moreing, claiming it had been given forged shares in Great Fingall as security on a loan. This suit also went initially against Bewick Moreing, but in 1905, in an appeal before the House of Lords, Bert was cleared of all responsibility. And in May 1903, Chang Yen-Mao arrived in England with Gustav Detring to file a lawsuit against Bewick Moreing concerning the Chinese Mining and Engineering Company. Chang's chief complaint was that, contrary to the original agreement, the Chinese government had no effective power over the company's board of directors. The transfer of the company to European hands in 1900, he claimed, was illegal and obtained by fraud. The trial opened in January 1905. "Everyone's lawyer tore everyones else [sic] reputation to shreds," wrote Lou in a subsequent memoir.[15] While the initial verdict favored Chang, on appeal Bewick Moreing was cleared of responsibility for Chang's loss of control over the company. In a small footnote, the court judged that "Herbert C. Hoover had acted scrupulously within the confines of his authority."[16]

Despite these difficulties, Bewick Moreing flourished. Bert's own reputation grew steadily as well. American-trained engineers were believed to be the best in the world, and were highly valued by British firms, which competed for the honor of listing an American engineer on their business letterheads. As a full-fledged partner in Bewick-Moreing, Bert's 20 percent of the profit amounted to a princely sum (estimated by an American reporter at over $150,000 a year), not counting the additional fees he earned from the various enterprises he developed as independent companies in which Bewick Moreing was a senior partner. Bert told his brother Theodore in 1904 that when he left China, he was worth $250,000, and though this nest egg was diminished by the Rowe affair, the Hoovers no longer had to worry about financial security.

Such wealth had its advantages. "Pre-war England was the most comfortable place in which to live in the whole world," Bert observes in his *Memoirs*. "That is, if one had the means to take part in its upper life."[17] The Hoovers had the means, if not the inclination. British high society didn't appeal to either of the Hoovers. This was the height of the Edwardian era, a period noted for its ebullience and excess. British society was tightly organized, with each member, from the 650 peers of the realm down to the lowliest street sweeper, implicitly aware of his or her proper position. It was a mindset that grated on the Hoovers, who recognized no such limitations on ambition. The British Empire spanned the globe, and British national pride was at its zenith. British arrogance clashed with the equally intense national pride of Americans. In Australia, Bert had been nicknamed "Hail Columbia" Hoover. His wife shared his patriotic outlook. While she was gracious to everyone she met, her closest friends were all Americans—and usually from California.

In March of 1903 Lou's sister Jean came to spend a few weeks in England. Jean had spent a little over a year at Stanford, studying geology like her older sister, but gradually she had come to realize that her own interests lay in the field of music. She was now on her way to Germany, where she would spend a year studying violin at a music conservatory in Berlin—most probably at her sister's expense. The Hoovers had replaced the Panhard with a new car, big enough for five, in which they could travel around the countryside. Now they could take friends along on their jaunts without feeling crowded. Independent as ever, Lou learned to drive the car herself, although they still employed a chauffeur. She and Jean accompanied Bert on a two-week trip to Italy during Jean's stay in March, visiting Cannes and Monte

Carlo while Bert negotiated with Italian mining interests. It would be Lou's last trip for several months. She was now pregnant.

Herbert Charles Hoover was born on August 4, 1903. He was a strong, healthy baby, and Lou saw no reason why she should not accompany Bert to Australia in October, bringing the baby along. Other women in her situation, daunted by the tactical demands of traveling thousands of miles by ship with an infant, might prefer to stay comfortably at home in London, but not Lou. She hired a nurse to help her with the baby, and was joined by one of her old Stanford classmates, Emma Martin, who was taking a world tour. "Traveling with babies," Bert later said in his *Memoirs*, "is easier than with most grown-ups."[18] The Hoover entourage—including the new automobile, which Bert claimed was far superior to a horse and buggy, despite its frequent breakdowns—spent two months in Kalgoorlie. They then sailed on via Honolulu to California to introduce young Herbert to his grandparents.

Lou's diary from this period records a typical new mother's delight in her child's progress: November 4: "Two great events—the boy put into short frocks and Bert came back from the North." December 25: "The boy's first Christmas tree. Spirited from the hotel hall [the Grand Hotel in Auckland], decorated with last night's purchases." January 1: "Boy put *entirely* on bottles today." January 4: "First tooth."[19]

In February, the Hoovers returned to London. Lou remained in England for most of the year, not accompanying her husband on a trip to South Africa in July and August. According to Hoover's biographer George Nash, Bert was suffering from the heavy stress of the past several months and had come close to a nervous breakdown. He told Theodore that he was "slipping in Memory and unable at concentration of thought—and being able to sleep but 3 to 5 hours the Doctor ordered me off."[20] The cruise to South Africa was to be a form of rest and recreation. Apparently the doctor felt that even the presence of an active year-old son might be too much stimulation for his patient, and he insisted Bert go alone.

How Lou felt about being away from her husband's side at this difficult time is not known. If she was upset, she neither committed her feelings to paper nor confided them to her friends. Certainly a toddler is more difficult to travel with than an infant in a basket, but the Hoovers could have hired a nanny to watch young Herbert and keep him from disturbing his father's rest. It is tempting to speculate about Lou's own health at this time. Her penchant for privacy could conceal any number of things. Was there another pregnancy, one that ended in miscarriage? Did her husband's nervous condition cause her to worry about her son's safety? There is no evidence, however, that Herbert Hoover was ever anything but the most doting of fathers, a man who delighted in the presence of young people and thoroughly enjoyed playing with his sons and nieces. Perhaps she just felt that for her husband's own good, it would be best to follow the doctor's orders.

When Bert returned from South Africa in September, he was refreshed and ready to resume his intense work schedule. He thrived on challenge and loved nothing more than to take up a problem, work out the most logical solution, and then put that solution into action. His uncanny ability to concentrate on the job at hand often irritated those around him; he could walk right past an old friend without speaking. He was, however, highly sensitive to criticism, especially when his moral status was called into question. Although he would eventually develop a thicker skin, in 1904 he was only thirty years old. The allegations of misbehavior involved in the lawsuits he faced in these years, and the misgivings he felt about the moral rectitude of his senior partner—which would inevitably reflect upon him as a member of the firm—hurt him deeply. He was increasingly anxious to reach a financial position that would permit him to leave Bewick Moreing and strike out on his own.

Lou offered her support on several fronts. "She was his buffer against the distractions and petty claims of the world," asserts her niece Hulda in a later memoir.[21] Lou was always ready to listen if Bertie wanted to talk. Knowing that behind his shy appearance was a man who loved company, she maintained an open house where friends always felt welcome. Sunday dinner at the Hoovers' became a popular institution among the engineering community in London.

In 1905 the Hoovers reversed their round-the-world journey, visiting California in the early summer. The Rowe defalcation debts had finally been paid, and the lawsuits ended, with Bert's reputation intact. He and Lou were able to relax and enjoy the trip. In June, they took Theodore and Mildred camping in Yosemite Park before sailing the following month from San Francisco for New Zealand and Australia. Lou, whose interest in geology had never flagged, arranged for rock samples to be sent from there to Dr. Branner at Stanford for his collection. While Bert was busy with his mining work, she also took a short trip to Tasmania, collecting additional rock samples for the Stanford geology department. The Hoovers were back in England by mid-January. In March 1906 Lou sent Dr. Branner some notes she had taken on the geology of the Red Sea, where she had spent two weeks consulting with local geologists as her ship passed through the Suez Canal.

Then, in July, the Hoover family was off again, this time to the United States. Lou and young Herbert spent a month with her parents in Monterey while Bert traveled around, inspecting his firm's enterprises in the Rockies and Canada. When he had completed his tour, Lou joined him in New York, and they took time for a brief sightseeing excursion to Lake George before sailing back to London.

While they were in California, Lou learned that her brother-in-law and his family would be coming to London, too. Theodore Hoover had been hired earlier that year as an engineer by Bewick Moreing, spending several months in Mexico on the firm's behalf. In August 1906 a few weeks after the birth of his second daughter, Hulda, he and his family sailed for London, where he would be employed by Minerals Separation Ltd., a Bewick Moreing subsidiary. Bert made it clear that it was Theodore's own ability, and not his relationship with a partner in the firm, that led to his hiring. Bert was "absolutely opposed to nepotism," Theodore declares in his own memoir.[22]

For the next ten years, the two Hoover families were exceptionally close. Theodore and his family lived for a short while with Bert and Lou in the Hyde Park Gate flat until they found a place of their own at St. James Court, Buckingham Gate. In an oral history interview, Theodore's daughter Mindy recalled the strict Nurse Thomas who looked after her, Hulda, and young Herbert. It was the fashion for the children of the middle and upper classes to be kept under close supervision at all times, leaving the house only for specially planned outings or school. The Hoover children enjoyed trips to the nearby Kensington Gardens, where they sailed boats on the pond.

About this time, the Hoovers met another couple who would become lifelong friends. Edgar Rickard had taken his engineering degree from Berkeley and was editor of a technical journal on mining. A few years earlier in San Francisco, Bert had met Edgar and his cousin, T. A. Rickard, whose *Mining and Scientific Press* was the leading American journal in its field. Bert encouraged Edgar to come to London in 1905. There Rickard founded the *Mining Magazine*, an independent publication that soon acquired a solid reputation. Rickard's wife Abigail was a native of Oakland, California. In the Rickards, the Hoovers found perfect foils to their own personalities. Bert excelled at conceiving large schemes; Edgar was a master of details. Abbie Rickard was a cheerful, competent woman who was as willing as Lou was to try something new—and willing also to let Lou take the lead in their endeavors.

On July 17, 1907, the Hoovers welcomed a second son, Allan Henry Hoover, to their family. When he was five weeks old, his mother put Allan in a basket similar to the one she had used for young Herbert four years earlier and the family took off for Burma, where Bert was trying to revive an ancient silver mine. Lou's sister Jean went with them. During this trip, Bert's *Memoirs* recall, Lou "added much Asiatic lore to her stock, but both of us contracted malaria which took months to get rid of."[23] The boys and Jean, however, were not affected. Lou would later tell a reporter that young Herbert had circled the globe three times before the age of four, "and not once had he missed a meal or his sleep or been ill during these long trips by land and sea."[24]

The close relationship between Lou and her husband was now extended to their two sons. The Hoover family became a unit in which each member was treated with respect and consideration. For Bert, this was a realization of the dream of family he had had as a lonely orphan. For Lou, it was a development of the relationship she had known with her own parents, especially her father. The sense of family was reflected in the way that Lou and Bert began to refer to each other as "Mother" and "Daddy," a habit that would stick with them throughout their lives.

Chapter 5

The Consulting Engineer's Wife

The flat in Hyde Park Gate had by now become too small for the Hoover family. When they returned to London shortly before Christmas 1907, they moved into a house on Hornton Street in the Campden Hill region of London's Kensington district. The Red House—so called because of its large red door—was "a delightful old but small house with a garden,"[1] in Bert's words. Built in the 1830s, it was one of four houses on what had been a large estate before Kensington was swallowed up by the growing metropolis. (The original lease was so old that it required the lessees to prevent their cows from wandering on the High Street, and not to hang their laundry where the neighbors might see it.)[2] It rented for $2,000 a year—a significant sum for the time.

The house was a rambling, two-story structure with steam heating, one large bathroom, and an oak-paneled library with a fireplace and leaded glass bookcases. The walnut-paneled dining room had a raised dais at one end, where theatrical performances could be given. The big garden, with its century-old mulberry tree, was one of the house's chief attractions, providing the boys with a safe playground. Bert frequently joined them, romping with Rags, the family's Irish terrier, or showing the boys how to pan for gold in the fish pond. In addition to the usual Sunday evening dinners, house guests often came to stay for varying lengths of time. A full complement of servants—maids, butler, cook, and nanny—assisted Lou in running the house.

In her memoir, Theodore's daughter Hulda Hoover McLean recalls the fragrance of damp ferns from the indoor goldfish fountain at the Red House, and the strong scent of her Uncle Bert's cigars. She, Herbert Jr., and her sister Mindy would hang over the bannisters in the evenings to catch sight of her mother and Auntie Lou, dressed in satin, lace, and jewels, ready to attend the theater with their husbands. There were trips to the zoo to see the bear that her father had brought back from Russia as a cub, and picnics in the country where the children flew kites, picked up beechnuts, and caught minnows in roadside streams.[3] If Uncle Bert was along, they might build dams in those streams with twigs and mud.

In the summer of 1908 Herbert Hoover left Bewick Moreing to set up his own firm as a consulting engineer, with offices in London and San Francisco. Bert no longer felt any obligation to the firm that had brought him wealth and prestige, but kept him constantly on edge by its sometimes dubious financial dealings. After selling his interest in the firm to another American engineer, he signed a formal agreement promising that he would not compete with his former partners in matters of mine management and development anywhere within the British Empire.

This still left him plenty of scope for operation as an independent consultant. "We would serve as engineering doctors to sick concerns," he explains in his *Memoirs*, examining mines that were not producing properly and finding ways to make them profitable.[4] He opened an office at 62 London Wall, near the office of his friend Lindon Bates, a prominent civil engineer who had designed harbor facilities around the world. Within the next four years his brother Theodore, John Agnew, Deane Mitchell, A. Chester Beatty, and Amor Kuehn (all long-time friends and associates) had opened offices nearby. These men worked sometimes independently and sometimes together on a wide range of engineering projects.

"Mines came to him from all over the world," Lou noted in a 1918 memo for her family.[5] Over the next six years, Bert's work took him to Burma, Korea, Nicaragua, Newfoundland, Siberia, California, the Caucasus, and Peru. He established a mining operation in Kyshtim, Russia, that was a model of efficiency and set a new standard in facilities for the comfort and well-being of workers and their families. Lou accompanied him whenever she could, traveling by steamship, railroad, horse-drawn carriage, or newfangled automobile. No degree of inconvenience ever discomfited her.

Much of the Hoovers' traveling took place on the steamships that were becoming ever more numerous, and ever more luxurious, especially in their upper-class sections. The Hoovers always traveled first class, with a nurse or nanny to keep an eye on the children. A letter Lou wrote some years later to a friend who was planning a trip by steamship to South America gives a vivid picture of her life on these vessels. "There is nothing I know so comfortable as to be able to have your own dainty tea things on some pleasant spot of the deck, where you can have two or three friends stop by for a visit."[6] She suggested buying a cheap Japanese tea set and a tablecloth, kept in a small box "with two or three well-keeping cakes and some tins of different kinds of wafers and cookies and candy . . . arrange them in a long flat box which will strap on the side of a cheap folding card table, which acts as card, tea and writing table as required." It would be necessary, of course, to saw the legs off the table so that it would fit the low deck chairs provided by the shipping company. Reading also helped to pass the time on these voyages, which could last for several weeks.

The Hoovers spent the summer of 1908 in Brighton, a resort area on England's Sussex coast. They went back to California in December to spend the holidays with Lou's parents. While he was there, Bert opened an office in San Francisco. He planned to stay in America for several weeks, giving a series of lectures at Stanford and Columbia universities.

In order to have their own living quarters during this period, Lou rented a six-room cottage on Salvatierra Street on the Stanford campus in January 1909. The house, which Lou rented for six months, belonged to her longtime friend Evelyn Allan, Stanford's first dean of women. Evelyn's husband, Mansfield, had committed suicide in May 1903, less than two years after their marriage. After his death, Evelyn returned to teaching at a Brooklyn high school until she was offered the Stanford position in 1907. She would serve as dean for the next ten years. Lou was glad of the opportunity to spend time with her old friend, and pleased that Stanford had recognized Evelyn's abilities.

Lou accompanied her husband to New York for the Columbia lectures in February, and then went with him to Washington in March to attend President Taft's inauguration. They left the two boys and their nursemaid with Lou's parents in Monterey. Jean wrote her sister daily accounts of the children's activities. Six-year-old Herbert Jr. was already taking an interest in engineering. "He dug a good sized ditch right across the drive for his waterworks,"[7] Jean reported one day. Another time, she wrote, "Herbert has just dug up a lot of sand and come in and dumped it into the kettle on the fireplace. He says he is going to cook it down and get iron. He thinks if it cooks a week it ought to be hard."[8]

From Washington, Bert left for London, and then on another business trip through the Far East. Lou returned to her sons in California. In May she took the boys back to England, accompanied by her friend and former schoolmate Edith Starr Jordan, daughter of Stanford's president. Edith spent much of the summer with Lou in a rented cottage at Swanage on the Dorset coast. The boys both had whooping cough, but recovered with no apparent ill effects. In August, Lou and Edith took a sightseeing trip to Ireland. Bert was home for several weeks, then left again in September for New York, where he opened another office on Broadway in partnership with his colleagues Lindon Bates and Chester Beatty. In October Lou brought the boys back to the Red House, arranging to send authentic plum puddings to all her friends in America for Christmas.

A project that would become one of the Hoovers' proudest achievements began with Lou's gift to her brother-in-law at Christmas of 1907 of a copy of *Essays about Origins and Virtues of Gems*, by Robert Boyle, published in London in 1672. Theodore, Bert, and Lou had all become fascinated by the availability of such venerable works in London's second-hand bookstores. Over the next several years, they acquired a fair-sized collection of sixteenth- and seventeenth-century volumes on scientific subjects. One of these was *De Re Metallica* (On the Matter of Metals), by

Georg Bauer, a German philosopher who wrote under the Latinized form of his name, Georgius Agricola.

Agricola's book, a compendium of sixteenth-century knowledge on the subject of metals and minerals, had never been translated satisfactorily into English because of the difficulty of its language. Agricola wrote in Latin, then the *lingua franca* of the literate world, but because so many of the processes he was describing had no Latin equivalent (at least not in the church Latin of the day), Agricola had made up his own terms. Lou wrote to Dr. Branner in December 1906 about her frustration in being unable to find an adequate translation of the book in the British Museum. She might, she said, have to translate it herself.

The project became a cooperative venture, using Lou's knowledge of Latin and German and Bert's fluency in the various processes used to extract metal from ore. Over the next five years they puttered away at the task, in Bert's words "a sort of detective job," sitting on opposite sides of the big secretary desk in the library. They even carried the book with them on their travels, decoding it sentence by sentence in their spare time. Sometimes Theodore and Mildred would join in on the fun. By 1911 they had hired four additional translators to work on collateral texts, to be used in the copious footnotes. But while many people contributed to the work, the final product was the work of only two: Lou and Herbert Hoover.

The translation was completed in 1912. The final volume included not only a translation of Agricola's work, but also a translator's preface, a biographical sketch of Agricola, a bibliography that included all significant mining literature written prior to Agricola's time and lengthy historical notes concerning the development of mining and metallurgy from prehistoric times to that of Agricola. The authors dedicated their book to Dr. Branner, "the inspiration of whose teaching is no less great than his contribution to science."[9]

Edgar Rickard published the book through his *Mining Magazine*. Believing that the venerable work deserved only the finest paper and binding, the Hoovers put out a very limited edition, only 3,000 copies, bound in white vellum like the original and printed on paper that had been manufactured using sixteenth-century methods. Because they did not want it to be beyond the reach of "interested parties," they set the price at only one-fifth of the printing cost. Half of the copies were donated by the Hoovers to friends, libraries, museums and universities around the world. Theodore Hoover estimated that the whole project cost its authors over $20,000.

In their spare time, both Hoovers worked on other writing projects. During 1908, Lou did research at the British Museum on Chinese history, with a special emphasis on mining. Lou's article on the Dowager Empress of China was finally published in London's *Contemporary Review* of January 1909. Bert's first book on modern mining principles, entitled simply *Principles of Mining*, was published in the United States in April 1909. Lou, whose mastery of the written language was much superior to her husband's, did much of its copyediting, spending several weeks in New York for that purpose while Bert returned to London.

Bewick Moreing, which had lost a good deal of its momentum after Bert's departure, filed suit against him in April 1910, contending that the oil investment company he was setting up in the Caucasus with Lindon Bates was a breach of the agreement he had signed when he left the partnership. The case was settled out of court. The Hoovers seem to have regarded this lawsuit as a nuisance rather than as a serious threat to Bert's reputation, as the earlier lawsuits had been. Lou doesn't even mention it in the memo she prepared for her family on her husband's activities during this period.

Bert was off to Paris on business in July, and to Russia in the fall to investigate the possibility of reviving a large copper, gold, and iron processing business in Kyshtim. Lou and the boys remained in England, where she played hostess to Stanford University's President David Starr Jordan. Jordan was on his way to Berlin for a meeting of the World Peace Conference, an organization he served as director from 1910 to 1914. Lou took him on a brief tour of England and Wales. Jordan came back again on the same mission for the next three years, until World War I put an end to his peace efforts. Each time, he stopped in London to visit the Hoovers.

Bert was at home in August 1910 when his friend, Ray Lyman Wilbur, came to visit with his wife Marguerite. Wilbur was still unaware that it was Bert who had anonymously financed his years of graduate study in the field of medicine. He and Marguerite were on their way home from a year's study in Germany, returning to Stanford, where Wilbur hoped to join the faculty. The Hoovers took them on a two-week tour of Scotland before they left for the United States.

Lou seems to have enjoyed this steady stream of visitors from home, and the opportunities they provided for travel around the British Isles. It was understood among their friends and relatives that whenever their travels took them to London, the door of the Red House was always open.

"Mining engineers," Lou once wrote, "are like members of a big club. They all know one another."[10] American engineers and their wives were frequent visitors at the Red House, as were such people as Francis Hirst, editor of London's *Economist*.

The Hoovers' Sunday evening suppers were noted for their lively conversation and good fellowship. Although Bert was never good at small talk (the children would sometimes hold contests to see who could get him to respond first to a question), he could talk fluently and intelligently about matters that interested him. His colleagues admired his ability to analyze a situation clearly, without being distracted by unnecessary data. In his biography of Hoover, classmate Will Irwin claims Bert could tell a story "without adornment and yet with all its picturesque and dramatic values."[11] But it was Lou who kept the conversation flowing. She was a "delightful raconteur," with a knack for putting other people at ease. Lou's energy and enthusiasm were contagious. Her obvious interest in other people made her the center of any group. Irwin calls her "one of those women who thrill to intelligence."[12] Table conversation at the Red House focused more on scientific and intellectual matters than gossip and fashion, which Lou found boring. "There are so many perfectly worthwhile and interesting things to do in the world," she wrote in 1929 to her son Allan, "don't waste time doing dull things unless they are real duties."[13]

Her flexibility became a hallmark. She could entertain twenty guests as easily as a dozen, and was not distressed by the sudden addition of several unexpected arrivals. This was fortunate, as her husband had the habit of frequently inviting people without consulting her. "I have often said he thought I had some sort of mental syphon that carried information from his mind to mine," she observed some years later.[14] Friends were encouraged to drop in at any time—even when the host and hostess were not at home. The servants had instructions to look after them as if the Hoovers were there.

The Hoovers' habit of philanthropy had not lessened. In April of 1908, Lou learned that her old friend from China, Mary Bainbridge, was in serious trouble in Paris. Mary's husband, attached to the American Embassy there, had died suddenly, and for some reason Washington would not provide funds for Mary and her two sons to take his body home for burial. Lou arranged to lend the widow the money she needed to get home. The arrangement was made anonymously, in typical Hoover fashion, but Mary Bainbridge had no doubt as to whom she should thank for this gift.[15]

In September 1910 Mary Austin, an American author whose "naivete" Lou had found "most refreshing,"[16] needed money to pay for passage home to America. Lou considered her "an extremely conceited, egotistic woman who bored [Bert] desperately. But there was no doubt a streak of genius about her that was very entertaining to me."[17] Mary was a frequent visitor at the Red House. A friend of the American authors Ambrose Bierce and Jack London, she had written several books between 1903 and 1909 about life in the American Southwest that had been very well received. Lou loaned her the money to return to New York, and in 1911 contributed $750 toward the expenses of producing her poetic play, *The Arrow Maker*, in New York.

A closer friend to whom Lou also loaned money in 1911 was her Stanford classmate Anne Martin. Anne, who was active in the British suffrage movement, had been arrested for striking a British policeman during a rally for women's right to vote. Though she didn't share Anne's enthusiasm for the cause, Lou paid her fine and helped her get back to the United States.

In London Lou had joined an organization called the Friends of the Poor, whose members pledged "by personal service to assist deserving families in times of distress,"[18] and "to place poor boys and girls in satisfactory situations upon leaving school." This goal coincided neatly with Lou's belief that young people deserved encouragement from those who were in a position to help them. Lou recommended several deserving poor people for employment, and sometimes provided needy families with financial assistance on a temporary basis.

Lou's open-handed generosity was reflected in her sincere concern for the well-being of her servants. She invited their children to holiday parties and took an interest in their personal lives. When she heard that some members of the large family of her charlady, Mrs. Beale, were ill, she sent them money to pay for food and medicine. Two years later, in 1911, she paid for the whole family to take a holiday at the seashore, and in 1912 she paid Mr. Beale's hospital expenses. Even after the Hoovers left England for good in 1917, Lou asked a friend in London to send Mrs. Beale a few pounds now and then on her behalf, and to do what she could to help the Beale children find jobs. "She has made such a splendid fight to keep [her family of eight children] all together," Lou wrote.[19] Mrs. Beale was then the sole support of her family, as Mr. Beale had been seriously wounded in the war and was again hospitalized; he died in 1921.

Now that she was spending more time in London, Lou joined several clubs. The most important of these was the Society of American Women in London. The Society had been founded in 1899 as a club for American women who had made London their home, either because they had married Englishmen or because their husbands, like Lou's, had their business headquarters there. It was affiliated with the General Federation of Women's Clubs in America. Its purpose, stated in its constitution, was "to promote social intercourse between American women, and to bring together women who are engaged in literary, scientific and philanthropic pursuits." Lou joined the club in 1908, and later registered her mother as a "foreign" member.

The end of the Civil War in America had seen an upsurge in club membership among both men and women. Seeking to maintain the sense of fellowship and purpose they had discovered in the army, men formed fraternal organizations at a steady rate, until by 1900 over three hundred orders had been founded, with a total membership of more than six million men.[20] Women felt a similar urge to band together. The church-sponsored charitable organizations and Chatauqua-inspired literary societies had by 1890 spawned the woman's club, dedicated to the improvement of both the individual and society. The General Federation of Women's Clubs was founded in April 1890 in New York, bringing together representatives of nearly one hundred women's groups from around the country. By 1897 it boasted a membership of over eight hundred clubs in twenty-five states, representing more than 100,000 women. Satellite clubs had been established in five foreign countries. The Federation considered itself "a new force in progressive womanhood, that of the home-keeping and home-making woman . . . alive to means of culture, interested in all means of progress, and eager to seize and multiply opportunities for individual and collective advancement."[21]

Lou served on the Society of American Women in London's Education and Philanthropic Committee, first as a committee member and later as its chairman. The committee administered a scholarship fund for needy schoolchildren and helped to support the Browning Settlement, a home for the indigent, and other worthy causes, including an Easter Sunday dinner for the poor of East London's slums. It also arranged luncheons and salon lectures on a variety of subjects ranging from Bergson's philosophy to the political unrest in the Balkans to the progress of the women's suffrage movement in the United States. At one of these luncheons, Hilaire Belloc gave a talk on the causes of the French Revolution. In 1913 Lou sponsored a dramatic reading by Katherine Everts, an American drama teacher whom she had met through Evelyn Allan.

Lou also belonged to the Lyceum Club, an international organization that sponsored a wide range of lectures, concerts, and debates. In 1908 she sponsored Lindon Bates' wife Josephine for membership. Not only was Lindon Bates a business associate of Bert's, but he and his wife were also friends of the Hoovers. Lou and Bert were especially fond of the Bateses' son, Lindon Jr. They enjoyed reading his travel book on China, published in 1910. Josephine Bates spent several weeks as a guest at the Red House in 1911.

Seven-year-old Herbert Jr. was now old enough to attend school, and the subject of his education posed a problem for his parents. A governess had taught both Herbert and his cousin Mindy during their early years. But now he needed a more formal education. The Hoovers had no intention of sending their boys to boarding school, as the English upper and upper middle classes did. They wanted them to have an American rather than an English style of education. But Lou was not willing to remain in America while her husband went traipsing around the world tending to his business affairs. Young Herbert's schooling, therefore, consisted of a mix of private tutoring and attendance at British grammar schools or American schools, depending on where the family was living at the time. His parents kept a close eye on his progress, encouraging him in his scientific adventures by joining in enthusiastically, providing him with tools to dismantle mechanical toys and reassemble them, and providing plenty of space for his collections of rocks and bones. The Red House had a large sandpile in the garden for excavating and building roads. A wide variety of animals shared the family's living quarters—parakeets, cats, rabbits, turtles, frogs, and Rags, the Irish terrier, who sometimes accompanied the Hoovers on their travels.

Lou was concerned that her boys not be spoiled by the comfortable lifestyle that Bert's wealth had brought them—and that Bert thoroughly enjoyed. She worried about how they would cope if they were suddenly forced to "work literally . . . for our bread and butter, or bacon and beans." They were given small but adequate allowances, for which they were expected to present a full, regular accounting to their parents. But the best way to teach them self-sufficiency, Lou thought, was to take them camping, as her father had taken her, and to teach them how to "make-do" in a primitive setting. That she enjoyed "pioneering," as she called it, was of course a bonus. "I have been rather amused," she was to write later, when they were grown, "that neither of you . . . cared about keeping up the practice of pioneering for recreation."[22] But she felt that the effect of her efforts on their characters was satisfactory.

In February 1911 the Hoover family spent several months in New York, where Bert was occupied at his branch office. Lou and the boys lived in an apartment on East 60th Street. Herbert Jr. attended Buckley School and joined the Boy Scouts, which had just started in the United States the year before. Friends who lived in the area introduced Lou to New York's social scene. Her parents came for a brief visit.

When the Hoovers returned to London in April 1911 on Cunard's popular luxury liner, the *Lusitania*, Great Britain had a new king. Edward VII had died in 1910 and his son George V was to be crowned officially on June 22, 1911. The Hoovers showed little interest in the pomp and ceremony surrounding the British monarchy, which was becoming increasingly distanced from the political process. Once again, they made a point of being out of town on Coronation Day. Lou and the boys spent the summer at the cottage in Swanage, Dorset, that they had rented the previous summer. In between business trips to Berlin, Moscow, Warsaw, and Kyshtim, Bert joined Lou for a motor tour of York in July and another to Kinlochrannoch, Scotland, with Evelyn Allan in August.

That summer Lou received the news that her sister, Jean, was to be married. Jean, now twenty-nine, had become active in volunteer work at a settlement house in San Francisco. There she had met Guthrie Large—"Bo," as he was called by his friends—a Stanford graduate who was the son of a prominent New York attorney and grandson of a banker from Dubuque, Iowa. The wedding was held in Monterey in September 1911. Busy with her own family's affairs, Lou was unable to attend, which must have disappointed her, as she and Jean had always been close.

Although Guthrie had a degree in civil engineering, he thought that he could earn more from agriculture. Constant improvements in rail transport had made California a major producer of fruits and vegetables for the rest of the nation. Truck farms were proliferating in the Sacramento and San Joaquin Valleys, as well as along the Salinas River south of Monterey. Guthrie was eager to become a part of this developing industry. With Charles Henry's assistance, the young couple bought a ranch near Monterey and began cultivating fruit trees and grain.

From California that summer also came the news that the Hoovers' longtime friend Ray Wilbur had been appointed head of Stanford's new medical department. When Stanford acquired a small medical school in San Francisco, there had been some controversy over whether the university really needed it. Proponents of the scheme won the support of the board of trustees by assuring them that the new department would be largely self-sufficient, requiring no more than $25,000 out of the university's annual budget. This was not a realistic estimate, as Wilbur would soon discover.

Lou was still finding time in her increasingly busy schedule to write the occasional scientific article. In addition to *De Re Metallica*, which was well-received by members of the engineering profession, she published an article in the March 1912 issue of the *Bulletin of the Seismological Society* on Professor John Milne, a leading seismologist. Far more common, however, were the light-hearted bits of verse she dashed off for the entertainment of house guests.

In February 1912 the Hoovers and the Rickards treated themselves to a seventeen-day tour of Paris, Rome, Venice, Florence, Cannes, and Vienna, financing it from what they called their "Seeing Cairo Fund"—money set aside for ad hoc excursions whose destination frequently would not be decided until the last minute. This trip was unusual for the Hoovers in being taken strictly for pleasure. For once, Bert had no business meetings to attend, no mines to inspect. The Hoovers visited many of the sites included on the Grand Tour that had become *de rigueur* for wealthy Americans, who were visiting Europe in increasing numbers on the luxury liners of the Cunard and other steamship companies.

Friends from America continued to visit the Red House on a regular basis. During the summer of 1912 Vernon Kellogg and his wife, Charlotte, came to stay for several weeks. Kellogg, a zoologist, had been a lecturer at Stanford when the Hoovers were students. Not much older than his students, he had come to be regarded as almost one of them. Vernon had been studying in Leipzig and Paris, and was working at the British Museum Library for the summer before rejoining the Stanford faculty. Charlotte Kellogg, like Abbie Rickard, was from Oakland, California, and she fit in well with the Hoovers' circle of friends in London. Lou especially liked Charlotte's good nature and common sense, recognizing in her a shared love of adventure.

In July Lou took the boys back to California. She rented a house in San Francisco for six months, as Bert, who joined them in September, was considering moving his base of operation to that city. Ever since leaving Bewick Moreing, he had been talking about leaving the business world and taking up some kind of public service in the United States. In part this was due to changes in the profession itself. University-trained Americans had transformed engineering from a trade to a profession. Now the Golden Age of American engineers in foreign countries was ending, as European universities developed engineering programs of their own. But more significantly for Herbert Hoover, the challenge had gone. "If a man has not made a million dollars by the time he is 40, he's not worth much," he once said.[23] He was now thirty-eight, and his personal fortune had long since passed the million mark. He had set himself a goal, achieved it, and now needed something more. He was looking into the possibility of buying one of San Francisco's newspapers. "Hail Columbia" Hoover was becoming increasingly homesick for America. "An American is always an alien abroad," he wrote to his friend George Bancroft.[24]

In October 1912 Bert was elected to Stanford's board of trustees. It was an honor that pleased him. He considered his years at Stanford the happiest of his youth, and would maintain a close relationship with the school for most of his life. Lou was delighted with this recognition of her husband's many years of unofficial service to his school. One of his more substantial efforts had been his proposal in 1909 that the university construct a men's clubhouse for students, which would become the Stanford Union. He organized a fund-raising campaign, to which he personally pledged $11,000. When the campaign began to slacken in 1912, Bert instigated a renewed push to raise the remaining money. Lou, too, felt a fondness for her alma mater, never missing an opportunity to visit during her annual trips to California. Feeling that there was a need for a similar facility for young women, she campaigned to have a women's clubhouse built near the men's building. Like her husband, she sweetened the kitty with several thousand dollars of her own. Both buildings were completed in 1915.

During the family's stay in San Francisco, young Herbert attended public school. Lou was able to visit her parents frequently in Monterey, and to admire her sister Jean's baby daughter, Janet, who was born on September 26. She was in San Francisco on October 3, when Uncle Will sent the news from North Dakota that her paternal grandmother, the redoubtable Mary Ann Henry, had died in Wahpeton at the age of eighty-five. Her father's family now consisted only of Charles Henry and his brother Will. Uncle Addison had died in Oakland in 1906, leaving his widow, Aunt Nannie, and one child, Lou's cousin Dorothy Matthews.

Although Lou now spent most of her time tending to the needs of her two boys or entertaining friends and colleagues, rather than accompanying Bert into the wilderness to examine mines, her sense of adventure was not dulled. Years of travel had taught her how to pack up on a moment's notice, and how to establish a "home" in a short period of time at any place that was convenient to her husband's needs. Thirteen years of marriage had only strengthened the bond between her and Bert. His frequent absences placed no strain on a marriage that was still a partnership in many ways. All major decisions, from the children's schooling to Bert's career moves, were fully discussed and jointly made. If Lou rarely opposed her husband's wishes, it was because she trusted his judgment and sympathized with his motives. They were now wealthy enough never to have to worry about where their next meal was coming from. Perhaps it was time to put Bert's talents to work for the good of others.

The Hoovers returned to London with the boys after the New Year. Bert went back to Stanford in April for meetings of the board of trustees, but Lou remained in London because young Herbert needed to have his adenoids removed. When Bert returned in June, the family went to Stratford-on-Avon, where Lou had rented a cottage for the summer called the Dower House, a charming old place built around 1550. Bert weekly commuted the eighty miles to his London office, either by train or by chauffeur-driven automobile, spending only weekends in Stratford. This practice, now fairly common, was then considered quite remarkable. Lou often joined him in London, leaving the children at the cottage with their governess and nurse.

When the Hoovers returned to the Red House in the fall of 1913, they were visited by Stanford's president, David Starr Jordan. Now sixty-three years old, Jordan had been president of Stanford since its beginning, and was starting to find the job something of a strain. The trustees—including Herbert Hoover—had become convinced that Jordan was no longer capable of doing the job well, but they were reluctant to demand his resignation, and he was still two years away from the date he intended to retire. During the trustees' meetings the previous spring, Bert had suggested a compromise that pleased both sides. Jordan would resign in September as president of Stanford, and in return would be granted the new title of chancellor. He would maintain his prestige and remain on the university's payroll, but would be relieved of active participation in university affairs. Jordan was delighted with his new status, and the trustees were free to choose a new president.

There was speculation for a while that they might choose Bert. He may have been tempted by the prospect, which would give him the chance he wanted to perform some sort of community service. In the end, however, he suggested that the position be offered to Dr. John C. Branner, his old mentor from the geology department. Branner accepted the appointment, with the stipulation that he be allowed to resign in two years, when he reached the age of sixty-five.

In October 1913 the Hoovers went to Russia with the Rickards to inspect Bert's mining operations there. They visited Moscow and St. Petersburg, and admired the progress made at the Kyshtim complex. In addition to the mine buildings, the company had constructed homes for its workers, as well as schools and other community buildings. Bert was very proud of the success of this experiment in social engineering—as was his wife, whose admiration for her husband's accomplishments knew no bounds.

In December the Hoovers returned again to California. This time they settled in Stanford, where again they rented a house. The next three months, Lou claimed, were intended to be a vacation for Bert: "the first real vacation he was going to have since he left college. . . . We . . . liked the house, adored the country, found the [automobile] (the only relaxation) in good condition."[25] Young Herbert was enrolled in the Palo Alto elementary school. Bert attended meetings of the board of trustees, where he discussed such issues as the raising of faculty salaries and the future of the medical school, whose rising costs led President Branner to propose selling it off to the University of California at Berkeley.

One day, on a visit to San Francisco, Bert encountered some old acquaintances, members of the wealthy Sloss and Lilienthal family, who told him that they were in serious trouble with a real estate development scheme. Bert was distressed. Echoes of his own experience with the Rowe defalcation came to mind. He promptly took control of the situation, and spent the next three months, in the midst of his Stanford policy efforts, sorting things out so that the development project was saved. "He did not get or rather would not take, a penny in any form of recompense for his labors," Lou wrote to her sons some years later. "Ah, well, there are heaps of episodes like that."[26] She was philosophical about the way that Bert had spent his "vacation" time working. She always took great pride in her husband's charitable endeavors, though she rarely spoke of her own.

In March 1914 Lou and Bert went to New York to receive a gold medal for *De Re Metallica* from the Mining and Metallurgical Society of America, leaving the boys and their nanny with their grandparents in Monterey. Bert went from there to London, while Lou returned to Stanford. While he was in California Bert had become involved in the planning for the proposed Panama-Pacific International Exposition, to be held the following year in San Francisco. In June he met Lou and the boys in Boston for a bit of sightseeing before attending some meetings for the exposition in New York. The family returned to London in July.

Lou resumed her social schedule: club meetings, guests for Sunday suppers, picnics in the countryside. She joined with a group of friends to form a club called the American Teachers and College Women in London. A letter from Jean reported that Guthrie Large's peaches were growing well this year. All indications were that another peaceful summer lay ahead.

But there were rumblings in the background. At first the assassination of the Austrian Archduke Ferdinand in Sarajevo on June 28 caused little concern in either London or the United States. But by the end of July, the European business climate had started to deteriorate. The stock market in London crashed. War fever in Central Europe escalated daily, until on August 1 Germany declared war on Russia. Because France was Russia's ally, and militarily a greater threat, German strategy called for a preemptive attack on France in the event of war with Russia. On August 3 the German army marched into Belgium, outflanking the French defenses.

Alarmed by the unstable political situation on the mainland, England's banks had extended the customary three-day "holiday" on August 1, freezing the nation's assets. Banks throughout Europe followed suit.

On August 4 Great Britain declared war on Germany. The First World War had begun.

Chapter 6

War and Relief Work

The events of August 1914 drastically altered Lou Hoover's life. Since her marriage, she had been—perhaps unconsciously—searching for a way to use her education and skills in a way that would be productive and self-satisfying. She had taken a close interest in her husband's work, visiting mines with him, discussing the intricacies of mine financing and development with him and his colleagues. She had written several articles for publication. Her work on *De Re Metallica* had been recognized as a significant contribution by the international engineering community. Following the expectations of her culture, she was also successfully fulfilling her role as wife and mother. Wherever they made even a temporary residence, she insisted that her family should live in a house, surrounded by familiar furnishings and routines. She took considerable trouble to make her home a refuge for her husband, where he and his colleagues could be comfortable. And she took a deep interest in everything her sons did, encouraging them to follow their own interests while instilling in them a strong sense of morality.

But there was still something missing.

After her husband's election to the presidency, a reporter quoted Lou as saying that while she had earned a degree in geology in college, she had been majoring in Herbert Hoover ever since.[1] Certainly for the first fifteen years of their marriage this was true. But as she followed his lead into the world of humanitarian activity in the first years of World War I, Lou discovered that she possessed a considerable organizational ability of her own. The next two decades would give her the opportunity to develop this side of her personality, to the considerable benefit of those organizations with whom she chose to work.

When the Hoovers came back to London in late July of 1914, they intended to stay only a few weeks. They had, in fact, already booked a return passage to New York on the *Lusitania* for early August. On Saturday, August 1, they drove to Westgate for a planned three-day Bank Holiday weekend in the country with the Rickards. They learned that evening of the outbreak of war on the continent, and that Britain's banks would remain closed for a further three days as a result. Concerned about what might happen next, the two families hurried back to London on Sunday afternoon.

The next morning United States Consul General Robert P. Skinner called on Bert. The Embassy, he told him, was being swamped by crowds of American tourists who wanted to go home immediately, but because of the bank closure they were unable to come up with enough money to procure passage on the available steamships. He asked if Bert could help.

Bert called Lou and asked her to bring him the £100 in cash that she had at home. He then contacted his colleagues, asking them to help him provide money for temporary loans to the frantic tourists. Skinner allowed him to use an office in the consulate. Hoover assisted three hundred people that first day.

It soon became apparent that the problem was much larger than it first appeared. American Ambassador Walter Page told Bert that an estimated one to two hundred thousand American tourists, in England and on the continent, would be in need of some degree of assistance to get back to America. Bert and his friends promptly formed a committee—the American Committee—which undertook to find passage to the United States for as many American citizens as possible. The Savoy Hotel offered a meeting room to serve as the committee's headquarters.

Lou had noticed the large number of distraught women among the crowds at the Savoy. Some of them had been traveling on their own, or were temporarily separated from their husbands and fathers. Many of these women were intimidated by the importunate crowds of male refugees. She discussed the problem with Bert, who agreed that a separate women's committee should be formed to deal with women's problems.

The next morning, Lou called on her friends in the Society of American Women in London. The Women's Division of the American Committee was quickly formed, its headquarters set up in a separate room in the Savoy from the men's committee. In addition to helping unaccompanied women find money for their passage home, the Women's Division collected clothing for travelers who had lost their luggage and located suitable lodgings in London for those in transit from the continent and waiting for an available steamship. Members met the trains and ferries to help the refugees through their first confused hours on British soil, and escorted them to the docks when they were ready for departure. In the excitement, Ambassador Page's wife accidentally gave away part of a friend's trousseau that had been left with her for safe-keeping.

The two committees soon found that not all of those seeking assistance were wealthy tourists needing only short-term loans to get them back to their home banks. There were also large numbers of less affluent Americans whose jobs abroad—as clerks in international businesses, as servants in hotels and resorts, as tutors or governesses, and the like—had evaporated when war broke out. These people had few resources of their own, although some had relatives back home who were willing to send money for their passage, if it could be got to them. Congress appropriated funds to assist American citizens stranded abroad, and Hoover arranged with the Hanover National Bank in New York and the London County & Westminister Bank for funds deposited in the one to be transferred by cable to the other at a rate of $5 to £1. For those without funds, the committee purchased third-class (steerage) tickets, on the promise that the money would be repaid after the travelers returned home. By mid-September, 87,000 Americans had taken ship for the United States, of whom 8,637 had required financial assistance. Of these, 1,223 were unaccompanied women aided by the Women's Division. Bert was proud to announce afterward that most of the loans made had been promptly repaid.

To some extent, it was sheer luck that placed Lou in a position from which the Women's Division could be quickly and easily organized. She had been a member of the Society of American Women in London for several years, finding it a pleasant place to meet other American women when she was in England, and enjoying its cultural and philanthropic activities. She had served two consecutive two-year terms as first vice president, and had only reluctantly agreed to run for a third term in March 1914. She was in California when the election was held, and would not return to London until July. In May 1914 American Consul General John L. Griffiths, whose wife was the club's new president, died. Mrs. Griffiths resigned her position and returned to the United States. As first vice president, Lou automatically succeeded her as club president.

Lou thus had a ready-made forum in which to make her appeal, and an organized body of women to whom she could turn for assistance. She made it clear from the start that she was not interested in continuing the social functions which had been the group's previous reason for existence. "The only way I could consent to take on the work as President," she would later explain, was on the understanding that the group would "turn all fees and dues . . . into a philanthropic work. . . . one simply cannot ask anyone to join a social club in these times."[2]

She was not the only club member who felt that way. A tightly knit group of enthusiastic women, most of them wives of wealthy expatriate businessmen, quickly formed, eager to do something to show their support for Britain's war effort. Abbie Rickard was among them. In New York City, Josephine Bates headed a reception committee that met the refugees at the docks.

By the first of October 1914 most of the stranded Americans had left England. Having by this time canceled five separate steamship bookings in a row, Lou and her sons finally sailed for America on October 3. Arriving in New York, Herbert Jr. cabled his father that he had eaten seven cream puffs—a message that confused the British censor, who thought it must be part of some obscure code!

While Lou settled the boys in Monterey with her parents, Bert was beginning a new phase in his philanthropic career. Hoping to destroy the French armies quickly, before Russia and England could mobilize their own forces, Germany had launched an enveloping movement through Belgium and northern France. England promptly declared a blockade of the European coast, attempting to use her naval superiority to bring the Germans to heel. Belgium, a noncombatant in the war, was devastated. Accustomed to importing 80 percent of its food from abroad, the country by October 1914 faced widespread starvation. The Belgian government, through American Minister Brand Whitlock, appealed for help. America's Ambassador to Britain, Walter Page, negotiated with the British government to allow food shipments to pass through the blockade, promising that none of the food would be allowed to fall into the hands of the German armies. On October 22 Ambassador Page asked Herbert Hoover to take charge of this project.

Bert promptly put together the Commission for the Relief of Belgium (CRB), manned in large part by his friends and colleagues, many of them fellow Stanford grads. Edgar Rickard became his deputy. Others who joined the effort were Vernon Kellogg, Will Irwin, and William L. Honnold. Lindon Bates took charge of the commission's New York office, while his wife Josephine undertook to canvass the women's clubs of America in support of the effort.

Bert sent a wire to Lou in Palo Alto: contact as many people as necessary, he told her, to get a shipment of food together from California. "Our commission is largely Californian, and we should have support of our own people."[3]

Although she had never spoken in public before, Lou made several speeches on behalf of Belgian refugees before a variety of groups in San Francisco and Los Angeles. She also contacted as many of her acquaintances as she could, organizing local committees in Palo Alto, San Francisco, and Los Angeles. As in London, she called on her friends—Judge Curtis Lindley and oil magnate Mark Requa in San Francisco, Charlotte Kellogg and Evelyn Allan at Stanford—to help. Telegrams flew back and forth between Lou in California and Bert in London, as she endeavored to keep him up to date on her progress.

Her efforts were successful. By November 25, the first relief ship was ready to sail, leaving San Francisco harbor for Europe by way of the Panama Canal. Over the next twenty-eight months, thousands of tons of grain, along with canned fruit and vegetables, and in the later months heavy clothing, made their way across the Atlantic, through the mine-fields of the North Sea to Amsterdam, and then overland to Belgium, where they were distributed by Hoover's efficient corps of young American men. (American women were dissuaded from serving in the CRB abroad. There were plenty of Belgian women available to do the "women's work" of preparing and distributing food, Hoover explained.) Incredibly, almost none of this food found its way onto the black market, or to the German army, which kept its promise not to interfere in the CRB's work. The efficiency of the CRB won the admiration of most of the governments involved, few of whom could have matched it.

Donations poured in not only from America, but from Canada, Australia, and Argentina as well. Lou supported efforts by other allied women to earn money for the cause. In late 1914 the Red Cross, as a fund-raiser, printed calendars in memory of the late Consul General Griffiths, whose wife had preceded Lou as president of the Society of American Women in London. Lou asked Laurine Anderson, Bert's secretary in San Francisco, to try to sell as many of these calendars as possible while she was soliciting money and goods for the CRB. In 1916 Mrs. Brand Whitlock, wife of the American Minister in Brussels, appealed to Lou for help in marketing the fine lace made by Belgian women. Belgian lace was a cottage industry catering to a luxury market that had been virtually destroyed by the war. Lou asked Charlotte Kellogg to help arrange for the lace to be sold through Altman's in New York and Selfridge's in London. She made a personal plea to her many friends in America, encouraging them to buy Belgian lace. Even after the war, Lou carried samples of lace patterns around with her to show to anyone who expressed interest in them.

Lou returned to London in early December of 1914. She had left the boys in California. Eleven-year-old Herbert Jr. was settled with art professor A.B. Clark's family in Palo Alto, to attend school there. Seven-year-old Allan stayed with his grandparents in Monterey. It was not an easy parting. Aware of the dangers she and Bert faced by returning to the scene of the war, Lou asked Jackson Reynolds, a friend from their Stanford days, to serve as the boys' legal guardian in the event of their parents' death or incapacitation.

"I think a few years as little boys in California,—where they have plenty of outdoors, and *village* life,—" she wrote Reynolds, "might be very good. But I should like them to have a few years in the East,—at a big school as well. . . . The ambition to do, to accomplish, irrespective of its measure in money or fame, is what should be inculcated. The desire to make the things that are, better,—in a little way with what is at hand,—in a big way if the opportunity comes."[4]

She also wrote a long letter to her sons, to be read in the event of her death. In it she expressed her beliefs about God, death, and immortality in words she hoped the little boys would understand: "Now that soul we *know* does not die when our bodies die, or get buried in the ground, or lost in the sea, or burned up. . . . With some it just goes straight back to God, in the place they call Heaven, that we dont [sic] really know very much about. If it has been rather a lazy soul, it may just sort of go to sleep there. But sometimes they go about helping, and if another soul that is still in a body like yours is wanting some help and is praying for some force to come from God, this helping soul may take some along and help. . . . And that's what I want you to be perfectly sure about me. I *know* that if I should die, I can pray my soul to go over to my two dear little boys and to help and comfort their souls . . . you will know I am there, because your own little soul inside you will feel nice and comfy and cosy, because my bigger, older one is cuddling it. . . . And I will ask God not to have me go up in that place he has called Heaven, until it is time for you to come too. I will just wait there and help and love you, until we can all go together."[5]

But her concern for her children did not dissuade her from sharing her husband's experiences, whatever the risk. She accompanied Bert to Brussels twice, and once to Berlin. Lou was deeply impressed by the courage of the Belgians she met. After a special Christmas service at the Cathedral of St. Gudule in Brussels, she asked her husband, "Do these Germans think they can hold a people whose very souls revolt?"[6]

Upon her return to London she threw herself into philanthropic work. She served on the board of the American Women's War Relief Fund, an expatriate American women's organization founded in the early days of the war by a group of wealthy American socialites headed by Lady Paget and including Jennie Churchill, Winston Churchill's American heiress mother. The Fund raised money for a number of war-related projects. It established the American Women's Hospital at Oldway House, the country home of American businessman Paris Singer, in Paignton, Dorset, which accommodated up to 250 wounded allied soldiers and sailors. One of its wards was dedicated to the memory of the late Consul General John Griffiths. The Fund also fitted up army ambulances and supported other philanthropic projects run by American women in England.

The most important of the Fund's efforts was the workshop program run by the Fund's Economic Relief Committee, many of whose members belonged to the Society of American Women's philanthropy committee. The war had caused an upheaval in the British economy, as industry switched from peacetime production to the making of war supplies. A large number of women in the poorer districts of London became suddenly unemployed. Some of these women were from middle-class backgrounds: former governesses, companions, mothers' helpers, music teachers, and the like. Others were factory workers whose shops had been shut down because of the disruption of trade, who had not yet found alternative employment. At the suggestion of one of its members, the Economic Relief Committee opened a knitting factory in a former YWCA building in Islington, one of London's poorer areas, to provide employment for some of these women. In the next few weeks similar workshops were opened in other parts of the city.

The workshops, which employed between thirty and sixty women each, produced clothing and stockings to be sold to the military or donated to charitable organizations. Various donors provided the premises free of charge. In these houses elegant tables and chairs were replaced with more serviceable furniture, along with sewing or knitting machines. The women were paid a standard salary, given a free tea and in some cases either served a low-cost evening meal or allowed to cook their own meals. They were encouraged to find other jobs as they became available in the new war-related industries, so that more women could be helped. At its height in 1915, the committee supported four workshops: one at Woolwich, one at Islington, one at St. Pancras and one in the old American embassy chancellery at 123 Victoria Street. The committee also partially funded a private field hospital in Belgium run by Mrs. O'Gorman, wife of a British officer, who also proposed setting up a maternity hospital there with the American women's donations.

To supervise all of these efforts, in early 1915 Lou recruited the Duchess of Marlborough, née Consuelo Vanderbilt of New York City, to serve as the committee's chairman. The duchess performed her duties with diligence and enthusiasm. As both an American and a prominent member of the British peerage, she gave the club's philanthropic efforts a higher consequence in British social circles than they might otherwise have attained.

The bonds of friendship forged among the women involved in these projects during the hectic early days of the war would last well after the war ended. Some of the women whom Lou recruited to help with the relief effort that autumn would be her allies in other projects later in her life, either in the Girl Scout movement or as part of the private charity network she put together in the dark days of the Great Depression. Like Lou, they discovered strengths and abilities within themselves that they had not realized they possessed. They would look back on this time as a watershed experience, and they gave much of the credit to the Hoovers. Charlotte Kellogg, who had headed the Stanford Committee for the Relief of Belgium, came to London in 1915 with her husband Vernon, whom Bert had made head of the Belgian sector of his operation. Charlotte traveled back and forth frequently between London and Brussels, stopping often at the Red House. In 1916 she wrote to thank the Hoovers for making her life, and Vernon's, "fuller and richer"[7] by including them in the relief effort. The Kelloggs were convinced that Herbert Hoover was a man headed for great things. As early as 1915, Vernon had begun writing a biography of Herbert Hoover, which he would publish in 1920.

As the months passed, the various war-related programs settled into a routine. The Economic Relief Committee handed over the workshop in Woolwich to a British charity in January 1915, but the Islington knitting factory and the Victoria Street workroom, where some forty women sewed clothing for the army, remained under its supervision until 1917. The American Committee completed its initial task of repatriating United States citizens who wanted to leave England, and set about assisting impoverished Americans who had chosen, for various reasons, to remain in Britain. The committee assisted some nine hundred people during 1915 alone.

A report dated December 1916 cites several cases that illustrate the types of problems the American Committee dealt with during this period. One woman's engineer husband had been stranded in Mexico when revolution broke out there, leaving her in England with two children to support and no training to fall back on. Another woman, pregnant with her third child, became destitute after her husband was sent to prison for theft. An elderly black couple, who had come to England thirty years earlier with the Jubilee Minstrels, lost their house and greengrocer's shop in air raids on Scarborough. Another elderly man, who lost his business in Germany because of the war, was now blind, in poor health, and being cared for by his equally elderly wife. An American nurse suffered a mental breakdown from overwork on the front and was cared for by the committee until she recovered enough to return home. Some of these cases required only temporary assistance; others presented more long-term problems.

Though Lou kept an eye on all of these activities, she could never have run them all personally. She had a real talent for choosing her lieutenants. Although they consulted her frequently, she could be confident that the women whom she had put in charge of her projects were capable of making intelligent decisions by themselves. Her contribution was to organize the effort, arrange the necessary funding (often from her own pockets), provide the inspiration needed to galvanize her colleagues, and support their efforts. As a later colleague would put it, "she had the idea and said, 'Here, do it,' and then backed you up."[8] This freed her to travel back and forth to America, where she could check on the boys and assist her husband in his fund-raising efforts for the CRB.

The Hoovers' London home, the Red House, became, in Bert's words a "general commissariat for men coming and going on relief work."[9] Whether Lou was in residence or not, she saw to it that guests were accommodated and fed. "She kept our house on Campden Hill open at all times as a way station for Commission members and for many breakfasts and dinners when people of importance to the Commission could discuss its problems under a most friendly atmosphere. . . . She was deeply interested in the work of the Commission and brought to it a rare intuition and to its members a hopeful encouraging influence when things were going badly."[10]

On May 7, 1915, German submarines sank the *Lusitania*, pride of the Cunard line and one of the Hoovers' favorite ships. Among those drowned was Lindon Bates Jr., son of the Hoovers' longtime friends Lindon and Josephine Bates. Young Lindon had been a frequent guest at the Red House and the Hoovers were extremely fond of him. The death of their beloved only son devastated the Bateses, and soured their friendship with the Hoovers. Josephine Bates blamed Bert for her son's presence on the *Lusitania*. Her husband, who had already clashed with Bert on certain aspects of CRB policy, wrote an article published in the December 1915 New York *Herald* that was highly critical of the CRB and its director. His accusations sparked a Congressional inquiry which concluded that the commission's work was perfectly legal and aboveboard. Bates resigned from the CRB and was replaced as head of its New York office by another Hoover friend, William L. Honnold.

The Hoovers were astounded and hurt by this public attack. Lou, who was always sensitive to any criticism of her husband's work, insisted that grief must have driven the Bateses temporarily insane. "They are not in any sense the people we have known for so many years," she maintained in a letter to Laurine Anderson.[11] Though the furor subsequently died down without damaging the reputation of either Hoover or the CRB, the longstanding friendship between the Hoovers and Bateses was over. Up to the time Bates died in 1924, his bitterness against Hoover would remain undiminished.

At the end of May 1915 Lou returned to the United States to spend the summer with her sons. She took Herbert Jr., Allan, and several of their friends on a camping trip to Yosemite Park. In November, she sailed again for London, bringing her sons back with her. The boys attended Gibbs School, a grammar school an hour's bus ride from the Red House, during the day, and helped provide hospitality at the Red

House on evenings and weekends. Permitted to join the grown-ups at meals, they listened quietly and with great interest to the adult conversations around them. In an article written thirteen years later, Charlotte Kellogg told how she arrived at the Red House late one night, "after one of the worst air raids [London] had experienced. I did not want to ring even the Red House bell at that hour, but I had to. Very promptly the door opened, and a little boy said, 'Oh, how do you do, Mrs. Kellogg?' as if welcoming travelers at three A.M. were [his] chief delight. 'Come in. Mummy and Daddy are asleep. But I know where there's a room for you.' "[12] Seven-year-old Allan led her upstairs, made sure she had everything she needed, and wished her a good night. Another night, the boys were found to be missing during an air raid. After a frantic search, their parents located them on the roof, watching the Zeppelins fly overhead. The family remained to watch the spectacle, and in the morning located the wreckage of a downed Zeppelin not far away from the house. They brought home pieces of the wreckage as souvenirs, adding them to the guns that Lou had brought home from China after the Boxer Rebellion and stored in her parents' house in Monterey.

Busy as he was with his relief projects, Bert no longer had time to give to his business endeavors. He had been thinking previously of getting out of the mining business, and in early 1915 he asked his brother Theodore to take on the task of liquidating all his British business holdings. Theodore, who was not involved in the CRB, agreed. Like Bert, Theodore recognized that the heyday of American engineers in Britain had ended. With the experience and contacts the brothers had gained from their years in London, it should be no problem to establish themselves comfortably back in America. Theodore had sent Mildred and his daughters home in the fall of 1914, as soon as they could find transport. During the next several months, he disposed of the majority of his and Bert's business interests in London. In August 1915 the Theodore Hoovers moved to San Francisco, where Theodore had set up a consulting office in the Mills Building just down the hall from his brother's.

Such a simple change of venue was impossible for the Herbert Hoovers, however. The war relief efforts occupied all of their time. But as 1916 drew to a close the situation began to change. The pro-war party in America was gaining strength, and it appeared to be only a matter of time until America joined the allies as a combatant. If that happened, the relief effort would lose its neutral standing.

Although Lou had been deeply involved in the American women's relief effort, she never considered herself indispensable to its functioning. When her term as president of the Society of American Women in London—now called the American Women's Club—ended in 1917, she refused to run again. She also resigned her chairmanship of the American Committee's Women's Division, turning it over to the competent women who had been acting as her lieutenants for the past three years. The relief work was now organized well enough to function without her direct supervision. Lou wanted to go home.

While Bert traveled to New York and Washington in January 1917 on CRB business, Lou took the boys back to California. Bert complained that his sons were acquiring Oxford accents. He and Lou felt it was time to get them back into American schools.

At Stanford, President Branner had retired, and the trustees had chosen Ray Lyman Wilbur as his replacement. The Hoovers were pleased. Bert had favored Wilbur for the post, but his duties in Europe prevented him from attending meetings of the board of trustees, so he had been unable to cast his vote on Wilbur's behalf. Lou was eager to give the new president her personal congratulations. She was also eager to see her sister Jean's new baby.

Though she did not know it at the time, Lou would never see the Red House in London again. The Hoovers were about to enter the dicey world of American politics.

Chapter 7

Life on the Home Front

Although the United States did not enter the war against Germany and her allies until April 6, 1917, there were already signs of trouble brewing when the Hoovers came back to America in January. Bert's fund-raising tour for the CRB was shadowed by Germany's decision on January 31 to resume unchecked U-boat warfare and the subsequent severing of diplomatic relations between the United States and Germany. When he returned to Europe in March, he began phasing out American staff, replacing them with volunteers from Holland and Spain. While the upper echelons of the CRB would continue to be filled by Americans, the actual distribution of relief would be taken over by workers from neutral nations.

In late April Hoover went back to Washington. As part of the war effort, Woodrow Wilson had asked him to take charge of America's food distribution system. He would have cabinet rank, but only as long as the war continued. Hoover accepted the job, but refused to accept any salary. After some discussion, the new post was given the title of food administrator, a term Bert found less intimidating than the alternatives of food czar or food commissioner.

From his temporary headquarters in the Willard Hotel, Bert wired Lou to come east and join him. While he assembled his staff—including Edgar Rickard as his deputy, Ray Wilbur as chief of conservation, and Judge Curtis Lindley as chief counsel—Lou scouted around for housing. She was assisted by Gertrude Bowman, whose sister-in-law Florence Stewart had worked with her in London, and Alida Henriques, a society matron whom Lou met in her first days at the Willard Hotel. They helped her to find a furnished house on 16th Street that she could rent as a temporary shelter for the forty-some men on Bert's staff, many of whom would only be in Washington for a short time, as their duties would take them all around the country.

For her family, Lou rented a house nearby from Charles Francis Adams, the prominent historian and railroad executive, grandson of John Quincy Adams. When Adams died the following year, his wife sold the house. A harried Lou was forced to move her family a few blocks away to 1720 Rhode Island Avenue. Her new landlord, James S. Harlan, was a former Senator from New York then serving on the Interstate Commerce Commission. Warned that summers in Washington could be stifling, Lou also leased a summer home, "In the Woods," located in Chevy Chase, Maryland, for a weekend retreat.

As in London, Bert used his home as a supplementary office. Colleagues joined him for consultation over breakfast, and again over supper, remaining hard at work often until past midnight. The staff of six servants whom Lou hired to run the house learned to be flexible about things like meals and hours, since Lou never knew in advance how many guests she might have for dinner or to spend the night. Among the guests at the Hoover home in those years were Arthur Balfour, Ignace Paderewski, and Marshall Joseph Joffre. Assistant Secretary of the Navy Franklin D. Roosevelt and his wife Eleanor also came on at least one occasion. Eleven-year-old Allan caused a minor flurry one evening by telling everyone about the engagement of two of the guests before the couple was prepared to make a formal announcement.

All of this entertaining cost money, but while Bert had refused a government salary, the Hoovers' income was still substantial. When the war began in August 1914, Herbert Hoover owned shares in businesses whose capital worth has been estimated at around $55 million. His yearly income (including dividends from stocks, bonds, and income from serving on a large number of boards of directors) was something over $150,000. The hazards of war lowered the value of many of his investments, as governments changed, transportation routes were disrupted, and agreements to develop mineral resources were abrogated, but enough remained to provide the Hoovers with a tidy nest egg. After Theodore liquidated the majority of Bert's international investments in 1915, Bert returned the money to the United States, where he entrusted its management to his old friend Edgar Rickard. From part of this money, Rickard created three trust funds, one each for Lou and the two boys, with Edgar as their administrator. The interest on the boys' accounts was allowed to accumulate until they reached their twenty-fifth birthdays. Lou used her income for housekeeping purposes—domestic finances had always been her domain—and for other personal projects as they occurred.

Shortly after her return to the United States, Lou had begun planning to build a family home on a lot that she and Bert had leased on the Stanford University campus. When Lou went to California in January 1917, she rented a house on the campus, as she had been doing since 1908. She intended to remain there, sending the boys to school in Palo Alto, while she built a home suitable to the expanded lifestyle that her family had enjoyed in London. It was only when she realized that her husband would be in Washington until the war ended that she brought the boys east and settled into the Adams house and the hectic schedule of war-time Washington.

The Stanford home remained a priority, however. After all, the war would not last forever, and she fully expected that when it ended, her husband would return to California permanently. Bert advised her to go ahead. "You can build any sort of house you wish but if it is to be the ultimate family headquarters it should be substantial and roomy. The cost is secondary."[1] Lou warned Edgar Rickard that she would be calling on him periodically for $20,000 until she had accumulated the $60,000 she thought she would need to construct a house large enough for her needs. Then she hired an architect, Louis C. Mullgardt, to draw up a plan.

News of Mullgardt's proposal to build a twenty-one-room, $50,000 house for the Hoovers leaked to the press in the fall of 1917, causing Bert considerable embarrassment. The political situation had changed since Lou first began thinking about building her house. Bert had launched a nationwide campaign encouraging people to cut back on everything that might in any way be needed to support the war effort. For the man whose name had become synonymous with conservation to contemplate building an extravagant family dwelling was clearly out of line.

Lou was distressed by the unexpected storm of criticism her actions aroused. She tried to explain that she had only asked Mullgardt for a plan that could be implemented "sometime after the war," but the damage had been done. She dismissed Mullgardt, whose plan she had found overly pretentious anyway, and resigned herself to waiting until the war was over to begin building her house. In the meantime, she bought the Albert C. Whittaker home on the Stanford campus to serve as her California headquarters. A former classmate, Carrie Goodhue, an artist of limited means, looked after the house in return for room and board.

There was plenty to keep Lou busy in Washington. Although it was the nation's capital, Washington through most of the early part of the century had remained a sleepy little southern community. The city had yet to fill the entire acreage of the ten-square-mile District of Columbia. In the summers, its population diminished drastically as congressmen went home to renew contact with their constituents, and the more permanent residents fled the hot, humid weather and the summer fevers caused by mosquitoes who bred in the swamps along the Anacostia River's junction with the Potomac. Stately houses occupied by government officials and congressmen lined the broad avenues that radiated out from the monument-studded Mall and intersected periodically in elegant circles. The city's chief business was government. Society divided itself into the formal affairs of high-ranking officials and their wives, and the more mundane activities of a relatively small number of lower-level bureaucrats. Paralleling this mostly white community was a large black community that had evolved a separate, equally complex society with its own wealthy and well educated members as well as its poor. Most of the city's servants came from the lower economic levels of the black community.

War altered Washington's nature abruptly. As the government geared up to defeat Germany and her allies in Europe, thousands of civil servants were added to its payrolls. A large percentage of them were women, since the young men who ordinarily filled the lower-level clerical positions had been siphoned off by the draft proclaimed in July 1917. As spring passed into summer, the city's population swelled steadily. Its boarding houses and restaurants were quickly overwhelmed.

Lou and some of her friends—wives of the men her husband had recruited as dollar-a-year volunteers to help run the Food Administration—became concerned about the social implications of this flood of young women arriving in Washington to work. They had no place where they could eat a simple, inexpensive, nutritious meal, make friends, relax in secure surroundings, and perhaps receive advice from a sympathetic older woman. What they needed, Lou decided, was a clubhouse—something like the house the American Women's Club had occupied in London, the Cosmopolitan Club where she often stayed when in New York, or the women's clubhouse of the Stanford Union, which she had helped to finance—but not so exclusive that it was beyond the means of a clerk's salary.

In November 1917 Lou contacted Edgar Rickard and asked him to advance her enough money to rent a house on I Street, four blocks south of the Hoover home on Rhode Island Avenue, to be used as a "rest house" for the three hundred or more young women employed in her husband's rapidly expanding Food Administration. She recruited Edgar's wife Abbie, Ethel Bagg, and Mrs. Ben Allen, who had worked with her in London, and the wives of several of her husband's other colleagues to serve on the club's board of directors.

By early December the Food Administration Club was in full swing. Six months later it had grown to occupy three neighboring houses in the 1700 block of I Street, each of which provided living quarters, a reading room whose library had been donated by the wives of Food Administration officials, and a parlor for entertaining guests. The dining facility, located in the largest of the three houses, served two meals a day, and was showing a substantial profit. Lou persuaded Bert's secretary Laurine Anderson, who had come from San Francisco to work in her boss's Food Administration office, to oversee the club's finances. Abbie Rickard and Adeline Fuller looked after the administrative side of things, while Gladys McDougal, an instructor at Cornell University's Home Economics Department whom Bert had recruited for his campaign, oversaw the dining room. Alida Henriques, who had helped Lou locate housing and servants when she first arrived in Washington, took charge of the club's social activities.

Although she recruited other women to do the day-to-day work of running the Food Administration Club, Lou Henry Hoover retained legal responsibility for all the club's debts. She signed the leases for the three houses on I Street. She furnished the houses herself, using money given her by the men who had stayed at the 16th Street house in the early months of the war. "Some of those men I did not know very well," she wrote in 1919, "and when Mr. Hoover or Mr. Rickard invited them to come and spend their summer with us, some of them were very shy about doing it."[2] The men offered to pay for their room and board, and although Bert talked most of them out of it, some insisted. Lou used the roughly $1,400 they gave her to buy furniture for her club. She also loaned the clubhouses pieces of her own furniture, and got friends to join her in making donations ("loans") to cover running expenses. One observer estimated that Lou herself invested around $34,000 in the project. How much of it she later recovered is not known, but when the club closed in December 1919, she insisted that she was owed nothing.

The Food Administration Club was open only to white women. In 1917 segregation was the order of the day; to have opened the club to black women could have meant that white women would refuse to join. How Lou, who opposed racial discrimination in principle, felt about this is unknown. Perhaps the issue never arose, as there were few black clerks, male or female, in any government offices at that time.

As the war continued, the Hoovers, who valued their privacy above all things, inevitably became public personages in part because of the massive propaganda campaign Bert was waging to win public support for his policies. Even before 1917 Herbert Hoover had become widely known for his work with the CRB. While the CRB publicity focused primarily on rescuing starving children, the program's success highlighted its director's ability by advertising its uncommon efficiency. Now, with Bert issuing countless personal requests to the country to eat less meat, grain, and sugar, his family's eating habits inevitably came under scrutiny. The boys were chastised in the press for eating ice cream sodas at a Stanford ice cream parlor. Lou's cook, who took pride in her reputation for fine cooking, had to be converted to the standards of food conservation. As Lou struggled to live up to her husband's decrees, the boys learned to value invitations to eat away from home.

Lou urged all her friends and acquaintances to comply with Bert's Food Administration policies, using less meat and finding alternatives to wheat and potatoes. She made speeches praising food conservation, and is credited with inventing the slogan "cash and carry," to save manpower by cutting back on home delivery of small parcels. She also created the "Hoover apron," a cotton housedress worn over an everyday dress to make laundry bills lower.

Maintaining a semblance of normal family life in these distracting circumstances was not easy. The boys attended the Sidwell Friends School, a private academy with a solid reputation for excellence. Sunday afternoons were set aside, whenever possible, for picnics in the country, so that Bert could escape from his duties for a few hours to play at building elaborate waterworks in roadside streams. During the severe winter of 1917–18, the family indulged in winter snow sports, sledding, or building snowmen.

As the war entered its second year, the demands on Lou's time increased. The Food Administration Club was rapidly becoming a reality. She had to keep an eye on her sons, and to keep her home ready at all times to entertain her husband's colleagues. Her correspondence grew as people wrote to ask her advice on food conservation. In March the Belgian embassy asked her to help publicize a traveling exhibit that featured the forget-me-not as a symbol of the continuing need of the Belgian people for food and clothing in the wake of the coldest winter on record. In

May Lou spoke on Bert's behalf to the national convention of the General Federation of Women's Clubs in Hot Springs, Arkansas. One afternoon while she was in New York, she met with a group of engineers' wives at Caroline Honnold's apartment and helped to form the Women's Auxiliary of the American Institute of Mining and Metallurgical Engineers. She was also becoming involved with the Girl Scouts as a district commissioner for Washington. The time had come, she decided, to hire a personal secretary to help keep things under control.

During the hectic days of 1915–16, when she was running several major projects in London and running back and forth to the United States to beat the drums for the CRB, Lou had enlisted the help of a young friend, Catherine Fletcher, as an unofficial aide. Catherine had traveled with her in 1914, helping her to deal with details of scheduling. When the Hoovers left England in 1917, Catherine continued to keep Lou informed about the welfare of various former Red House servants in whom Lou took a special interest. In Washington, Lou first borrowed the services of Bert's secretary, Laurine Anderson. But Laurine's spare time was limited.

In the spring of 1918, while she was visiting Stanford, Lou invited Dare Stark, the twenty-one-year-old daughter of Bert's old friend and classmate Herbert Stark, to come to Washington with her as "a sort of general roustabout."[3] Among the chores Dare would take on were handling correspondence, looking after Allan when necessary, even (if Lou was not available) serving as a temporary hostess for dinner or overnight guests. Although she would be paid a small allowance, most of Dare's "salary" would be in the form of room and board, and the opportunity to be a part of the Hoovers' peculiar lifestyle.

Dare Stark was born in South Africa, where her father was employed in the gold fields. Bert Hoover visited the family there in 1904. The Stark family returned to the United States in 1909, and Herbert Stark died a year later in Nevada. His widow brought her three children—Dare, her sister Vaal, and her brother Herbert— back to California, where they grew up in Palo Alto and eventually attended Stanford. The Hoovers had taken a keen interest in the Stark family's affairs since the father's death. A charming young woman with a talent for writing that she never quite had the discipline to turn into a profession, Dare quickly became a part of the Hoover family. Bert was especially fond of Dare, whose light-hearted gaiety entertained him immensely.

Wars often bring hurried weddings, and Lou, who loved to entertain, was always willing to provide a reception for her friends on these occasions. Ethel Bagg, an art teacher who had worked with Lou's relief programs in London, came to Washington in 1917 to work for the Food Administration. Early one morning in July 1918 she appeared at Lou's summer home, "In the Woods," bursting with the news that Arthur Bullard, a journalist serving on the government's Committee on Public Information, had asked her to marry him. Lou immediately offered her garden for the wedding reception. In September the Bullards left for Siberia, where Arthur—a specialist in Russian affairs—would keep an eye on the Russian situation for the United States government.

That same summer, Bert's longtime secretary Laurine Anderson married Stanwood Small, a Stanford graduate who was serving in the army. Because Captain Small was on active duty in Europe, Laurine continued to work for the Food Administration until May 1919, when her husband was reassigned to Rio de Janeiro. Before Laurine sailed for Rio, Lou sent her a long letter filled with practical advice about life on shipboard, including the suggestion that she take along a small electric fan to ameliorate the tropical heat.

Fifteen-year-old Herbert Jr. had suffered a series of ear and throat infections during the winter of 1917–18. Hoping that a summer spent outdoors might restore his health, Lou sent him to a boys' camp in Duluth, Minnesota. Julius Barnes, a prominent grain merchant who worked with Bert in the CRB and the Food Administration, had a summer home near Duluth, and he and his wife agreed to look after Herbert when the camp ended. At the end of the summer, Lou picked Herbert up from the Barneses' and took him to Connecticut, where she enrolled him in the exclusive Taft School. He wasn't there long before the great flu epidemic struck. Lou had taken Allan to stay at "In the Woods" when the epidemic hit his school, and while between one-third and one-half the Food Administration staff became ill, Lou, Bert, and Allan remained well. Lou organized assistance for the stricken members of her husband's staff and their families. In November, shortly before Bert was to leave for Europe with the American peace delegation, word came from Connecticut that young Herbert had contracted the flu and developed a severe ear infection from it. Lou rushed to her son's side. As soon as he was well enough to travel, she took him to California, hoping that the warmer climate would cure him. She left Allan behind in Washington in Dare Stark's care.

Bert had expected the peace talks to take only a few weeks, at most a month. Instead, he was gone nearly a year. He set up his headquarters in a "white and gold mansion"[4] in Paris' Trocadero district, and soon became one of the most respected members of the American delegation. While he lobbied for efforts to feed the starving people in war-torn Europe, Lou tried to keep things under control at home.

Young Herbert's health remained uncertain, and in February Dr. Ned Sewall removed the boy's tonsils at Stanford's new Lane Hospital. The Hoovers' friend Ray Wilbur, Stanford's president, who was himself a physician, stood by during the operation to reassure the nervous mother that all was going well. When the operation was over, Lou was reluctant to leave her older son to return to Washington. Instead, she wired Dare Stark to bring Allan to California. As soon as Herbert was well enough, Lou enrolled him at Palo Alto High School, while Allan was placed in the local elementary school.

In these worrisome times she had the support of Bert's brother Theodore and his wife Mildred, who were living nearby. Theodore had joined the Stanford faculty in 1918, and purchased a large house for his family on the Stanford campus. In April 1919 he became head of the new Department of Mining and Metallurgy. That same spring, he purchased a ranch called the Rancho del Oso on the coast not far from Palo Alto. Lou took her boys to the ranch often for picnics on the beach with their cousins, where they could enjoy the outdoor life she considered so essential to good health.

Now that the war was over, the Food Administration Club faced new challenges. As the government closed down war-related agencies and young men returned to their former jobs, the number of young women working in Washington began to decline. The end of food rationing had led to an upsurge in new, inexpensive restaurants, which cut into the profits from the dining hall, the club's main source of independent funding. In early 1919, to counter a sharp drop in membership, the directors decided to open the club to women from other government departments. The club's leadership was changing, too. Adeline Fuller, Abbie Rickard and others were leaving Washington as their husbands returned to their pre-war occupations. Alida Henriques assumed the club's management. There was a brief period of friction between her and Laurine Small, who was still handling the club's finances, but Abbie Rickard managed to smooth it over before she left for New York in June. Ethel Bagg Bullard, who had returned to Washington when her husband became seriously ill, replaced Abbie on the board. Lou had hoped that the club could continue despite the peacetime cutbacks, but it soon became clear that this was impossible. One by one, the houses closed, and in December 1919 the last house—the one containing the dining hall—was vacated and its assets turned over to the District of Columbia Women's City Club.

As the agencies Bert had set up as part of the war conservation effort were disbanded, Lou hoped that she and Bert could return to being private citizens. She had never liked living in the public eye, and she much preferred California to the East Coast. From Palo Alto, Lou wrote to Laurine Small, asking her, before she left for Rio, to cancel the leases on the houses the Hoovers had rented on Rhode Island Avenue and in Chevy Chase, and to send their personal belongings to California. Lou also asked Abbie Rickard to close down the New York apartment the Hoovers had leased since December 1916.

It was time to start building her dream house on Stanford's San Juan Hill.

Chapter 8

"Washington Ought to Be in California"

The end of the war meant that no one could now criticize the Hoovers for building a $50,000 house on the Stanford University campus. When Lou cabled her husband in Paris, telling him what she intended to do, he replied, "Build house as you planned it yourself. Probably won't use it much for 15 years, but want it right then."[1]

Ignoring Bert's disquieting caveat, Lou immediately set to work. She knew exactly what she wanted. This time there would be no fussing around with prominent architects whose reputation might get in the way of her ideas. She asked her old friend, Stanford Art Professor A. B. Clark, to be her architect. He demurred, claiming that his teaching schedule would not permit him to give the project the time it needed. But he reminded her that his son, Birge, had earned a degree in architecture from Stanford in 1914. The war had prevented Birge from beginning his career, but now that he had been mustered out of the army, he was available if Lou would have him. Professor Clark assured her that his son was capable of building the house as she wanted it. In April 1919 Lou hired Birge Clark and work on the house began in earnest.

Lou designed the house herself. She consulted with Birge Clark almost daily to make sure it would be built to her specifications. "The lady is occupied these days correcting Mr. Clark's plans of the new house every time he draws them," Dare Stark wrote to Laurine Anderson Small. "It is going to be unique—pueblo Mexican Spanish with flat roofs and oriel windows and a wall and every corner of it habitable. A Hooverish place."[2] Overlooking the campus at 623 Mirada Drive, the house was built on three main levels, with stucco walls. In his *Memoirs,* Bert describes the decor as Hopi in its inspiration, while others thought it looked Moroccan. It took two years to complete, and cost $137,000.

Bert liked to call it a simple, "seven-room house"—blithely ignoring the spacious quarters for four servants and the many guest rooms on the lower level. Including bathrooms, hallways and large closets, the actual number of rooms was closer to fifty-seven. The interior featured a good deal of dark oak paneling, reminiscent of the Red House, and a spiral oak staircase. Some of the panels had cupboards built into them with doors that could only be opened with a hairpin. These "secret" cupboards were intended not to conceal things, but rather to keep from marring the appearance of the paneling with unsightly knobs. All of the windows were glazed with leaded glass, except those in Bert's study; he preferred the clearer view of plate glass. Lou, who loved fireplaces, made sure that there was one in every main room, as well as on the terrace outside. In March 1919 Lou sent for her Washington gardener, Alfred Butler, to landscape the one-acre lot, which included a swimming pool and a fountain designed by her artist friend Carrie Goodhue.

At the top of a winding stairway leading up from Lou's dressing room was her "secret room"—a private study where she could be alone. If anyone called while she was in this room, the staff had instructions to say that she was "out." The room had three windows above the desk overlooking the front drive, so that she could see people arriving. If she wanted to see them, she could come down from her hideaway in time to greet them.

Bert wasn't above teasing his wife about her architectural experiments. When she put an 'antique' finish on the ceiling over the stairway, Bert observed, "Well, I saw some basements in Belgium that looked worse than that." The living room had recessed lighting that gave off a soft general light without any visible source. Lou proudly pointed it out to her husband, who smiled and said, "Well, it looks kind of like early Pullman to me." Irritated now, Lou said, "Bert, it does not." Later, she called Birge Clark, who had been present during this exchange, and assured him that "Mr. Hoover was merely making a little joke to tease me, and he really thought the living room was just fine."[3]

While the house was being built, the Hoovers lived nearby in the small house on Cabrillo Road that Lou had bought in 1918 from Albert C. Whittaker for $10,000. The household, in Dare Stark's words, consisted of Lou, Allan, Herbert Jr., Carrie Goodhue, "two Chinamen, a student and a cow."[4] The "student" was George Harrison, a graduate engineering student whom Lou had hired to keep an eye on the house while she was away. Dare herself lived with her mother in Palo Alto, going "up the hill" each day to work as Lou's secretary.

That summer, Lou purchased another house across the street from the Whittaker house from J. E. McDowell, the university's assistant registrar. She intended to use the McDowell house for her parents when they came to visit, or for guests who might prefer more privacy than would be available in one of the guest rooms of the Hoover home.

In July 1919 Lou sent young Herbert to Theodore's ranch for the summer to continue recuperating from his health problems of the previous winter, which had left him with impaired hearing in one ear. Meanwhile, she and Allan set off to join Bert in Europe. They spent some weeks in Paris, during which Allan became friends with General John Pershing's son Warren. The two twelve-year-olds spent many happy hours exploring the city, escorted by an American sergeant. Lou and Allan toured some of the former battlefields, bringing home several trophies to add to the family's collection. One of Allan's prizes was an aerial torpedo. His escort had disarmed it, but when one of Bert's military colleagues heard about it, he was appalled. The general ordered the torpedo dropped into the Seine before it could explode and injure someone. "No explanation that we could give," Bert reported in his *Memoirs*, "satisfied Allan as to the General's character as a gentleman or his competence as a military man."[5]

George Harrison, whom Lou had hired to watch over the house, was charged with keeping an eye on young Herbert while she was away. Harrison dutifully wrote her long letters about her sixteen-year-old son's activities, including the car he was building from scratch in the basement. When the car was finished, a window had to be removed to get it out of the house. It had a motor, a strapped-on hood, a steering wheel, two seats made out of boards, and a gas tank; there was no body and no windshield. It had only two speeds, Lou told a friend: standing still and thirty-five miles per hour. Because it was difficult to crank, he had to lift one wheel on a jack and spin it until the engine turned over to get it started. When his mother returned from Paris, Herbert proudly took her for a ride.

The Hoovers returned to America in September. They had been home only a few weeks when a frantic call came from Washington: the King and Queen of Belgium were coming for a formal visit, and President Wilson was too ill to receive them. Could the Hoovers entertain them in California? Their house was still unfinished, but Bert, undaunted, called his friends to locate appropriate housing for the royal party. He then contacted the mayor of San Francisco to arrange a formal reception for the King and Queen. When the day arrived, Lou had to send her apologies. Allan had fallen from a tree and broken his arm that morning, and she couldn't leave him.

A few days later, Lou herself took a bad fall. She had to remain in California when Bert went back to New York in late October to deal with issues surrounding the transformation of the CRB into the CRB Educational Foundation, and the transfer of its parallel organization, the American Relief Administration (ARA), from public to private control. As the immediate need for food and clothing in Europe died away, the CRB and the ARA were shifting their focus to provide scholarships for French and Belgian students who wanted to study in America, and to fund selected philanthropic projects in the United States. Bert remained chairman of the two organizations, with Edgar Rickard as managing director.

Lou had no sooner recovered from her fall when another family crisis arose: her beloved mother, now seventy years old, was seriously ill. Lou sent a frantic wire to

Edgar Rickard: "Urgent please have Wilbur wire me soonest possible what doctor at Lane Hospital to put in charge of examination of Mother immediately regarding threatened malignant trouble in colon."[6] Florence Henry was operated on in early November. Her recovery, though slow, was satisfactory. In December Lou was able at last to rejoin her husband, who had gone back to Washington.

Expecting that the family would remain in California, Lou had given up the leases on their Washington homes. But Bert was not ready to abandon the East Coast. From his CRB office in New York he made speeches, wrote articles, gave press releases and received honors from various organizations. He traveled so much that he claimed he felt as if he had "adopted the Pullman berth as my eternal home."[7] His experiences in molding public opinion, first on behalf of Belgian relief and then as food administrator, led him to consider purchasing the Washington *Herald* from the Hearst corporation as a means of setting his ideas before the public. There was even talk of his running for president when Woodrow Wilson's term expired in 1920.

"A lot of [Bert's] friends and admirers, as probably you heard, tried to make him President last autumn, much against his own advice and desire," Lou wrote to a friend in February 1921. "Consequently, we were personally quite pleased when their efforts were beaten by the regular old politicians."[8] Lou was undoubtedly pleased, and relieved, that nothing had come of this proposal, but the experience seems to have kindled a spark of presidential ambition in her husband. Lou detested politics. Bert, though he was never completely at home in the political arena, was attracted by the possibility of applying his highly praised management skills to the machinery of government. For the moment, however, he intended to focus on journalism. This intention evaporated when the new president-elect, Warren G. Harding, asked Bert to be secretary of commerce in his cabinet.

Lou thus found herself back in Washington in December 1920, where she leased an apartment for the family on 17th Street NW. She had left Herbert Jr. behind in California, with George Harrison to keep an eye on him while he completed his studies at Palo Alto High. Allan came east with her and returned to the Sidwell Friends' School.

In February the furniture from London's Red House finally arrived in California—three years after the Hoovers had left it behind. Lou was not able to go out immediately to check it over, as Allan had come down with mumps. In April she had to be in New York on Girl Scout business (she had been on the organization's national executive board since October 1917). Not until June, when Allan's classes ended, could Lou go back to California. She had sold the Whittaker house to her old friend, history professor E. D. Adams, and the McDowell house had been rented. Although Herbert and George Harrison were living in the new house, it was still under construction and not really ready for occupancy, so Lou leased another house on Cabrillo Road to be her family's home for the summer. Now, at last, she had time to examine the London furniture and to decide what pieces to keep and what to discard. A lovely Oriental rug had been stained, and Lou decided to dye it brown, so that the stain wouldn't show. When an Oriental rug specialist saw it some years later, he was devastated. It could have been cleaned, he moaned; instead, it had been damaged beyond repair. Lou, however, was satisfied. She had never really liked its original color.

By fall the new house was habitable. When Lou returned to Washington in September, she left both boys behind in George Harrison's care. Dare Stark also remained behind to oversee the interior decorating. To help with her correspondence, Lou hired Philippi Harding, a competent stenographer who had just graduated from Stanford and was working in the office of the dean of men when Lou came in looking for someone "to help her when she was on campus."[9] Phil Harding would be Lou's strong right hand for the next four years.

Herbert Jr. was in his senior year at Palo Alto High, and Allan was now fourteen. Two young college men, sons of friends of the Hoovers, lived with them and George Harrison in the new house. Kosta Boris, the valet Bert had acquired at the Paris peace conference, temporarily took charge of running the household. Alfred Butler, the gardener, and Henry, the Chinese cook, remained on the staff. Butler's wife and his sixteen-year-old daughter Carrie came to California to join him in 1921. Carrie had worked after school for the Hoovers in Washington during the war years. While she lived in Palo Alto, she attended Palo Alto High, but unlike Herbert, she didn't enjoy her time there. Being the only black student in her class made her uncomfortable. She also felt that her preparation in Washington's public schools was inadequate for the work now demanded of her. Although Lou offered to pay her way through Stanford if she would stay in school, Carrie dropped out. She worked at the Hoover house with her father for two years, while her mother worked for another family. Determined to see that Carrie received some sort of education, Lou arranged for her to have lessons in shorthand and typing.

Since it looked as if they would be staying in Washington for some time, a permanent headquarters seemed necessary. The apartment on 17th Street was too cramped for the Hoovers' taste. Lou wanted something with larger rooms, where Bert could pace the floors in comfort, and where she could entertain as she was accustomed. Lou found the house she wanted at 2300 S Street, near the wooded area of Rock Creek Park. The first house that the Hoovers had actually owned in Washington, it was a three-story structure with a broad veranda in the back opening onto a large garden. Its twenty-two rooms allowed plenty of space for the kind of casual, open-handed entertaining the Hoovers excelled at: friends in every night for dinner, out-of-town guests who stayed days or weeks at a time. The house was filled with odds and ends that the Hoovers had brought back from their travels abroad: boxes, figurines, carved quartz. There were no carpets on the stairs. One of Lou's secretaries believed that this was Lou's idea of a security system to protect her husband and family from unwanted intruders, since the footsteps of anyone coming upstairs could be clearly heard.

Lou's "roustabouts"—Dare Stark and Phil Harding—had rooms of their own, as did Bert's valet, Boris. Several servants from the old house on Rhode Island Avenue returned to work for them, including Mary Rattley, the cook, and Ellis Sampson, the butler. Others were added as needed; at one time, the staff numbered eleven.

The Hoovers brought their elderly Irish Terrier, Rags, to Washington with them. He was soon joined by a Belgian Shepherd named Tut. Cats and birds also shared the Hoover household. In the garden was a pond where Allan kept his pet turtles and the two alligators given him by one of Bert's colleagues. The first winter, Allan moved his alligators into the bathtub, until his parents talked him into letting them winter at the Washington Zoo. There were also two ducks, which Allan trained to sit on the front porch.

Among the Hoovers' neighbors on S Street were the journalist Mark Sullivan and his family, who became good friends, and former President Woodrow Wilson, who lived in seclusion until his death in February 1924. One year, while the Hoovers were living there, several neighbors passed around a petition to establish a restrictive covenant that would prevent homeowners from selling or leasing their property to blacks or Jews. The Hoovers and Sullivans were among those who refused to sign. Whether or not they would have sold the house to a black family is a matter of conjecture. But they had several Jewish friends, including Lewis Strauss, a New York banker who had been Bert's personal secretary in the Food Administration. And, philosophically, the notion of restrictive covenants clashed with the Hoovers' dedication to economic freedom of action.

As she set about making the Washington home livable during the winter of 1920–21, Lou kept in close touch with her family in California. She was still worried about her mother's health. When Lou went to see her mother in May 1921, however, she found Florence Henry cheerfully busy making rugs. Although she was still weak from her operation a year earlier, Florence assured Lou that she was feeling much better. She was more concerned by the imminent collapse of her younger daughter Jean's marriage.

Jean's husband, Guthrie Large, had served overseas during the war, returning home in early 1919. The charming boy Jean had married in 1911 had turned out to be a petty tyrant with a distressing lack of business acumen. Guthrie's ideas of discipline for the children seemed to Lou to approach downright cruelty. The ranch under his direction was not doing well, and he and Jean frequently disagreed about crops and other financial issues. He had spent or invested badly all the money Jean had brought to the marriage, including "some thousands" loaned him by her father, in the hope that "the boy might amount to something."[10] Her mother, afraid that Guthrie might lay claim to a share in her property after her death, had gone so far as to deed the family's Monterey home, Henry Croft (which had been registered originally in Florence's name), over to Lou.

Early in 1921 Jean and Guthrie separated. Jean took her children to her parents' home in Monterey. It is typical of the Henrys that Guthrie Large is almost never mentioned in their correspondence after this time. Only in two letters, one to her Uncle Will and another to her sons, does Lou refer to the underlying causes of her sister's separation from her husband. Jean seems to have acquired title to the ranch, but her financial position as a single mother of three was precarious. While there is no record of what happened to Guthrie after he and Jean separated, Jean and Lou made sure that the children visited their Large grandparents in New York whenever possible. "His people acknowledge his worthlessness," Lou told her sons.[11] She assured Guthrie's parents that the children "hear nothing but the best of their father from any source, and [Jean] trusts time to erase the unhappy memories before they are old enough to make such memories iniradicable [*sic*]."[12]

Life for the Hoovers continued its hectic pace through 1921. While Bert took on the challenge of making the Commerce portfolio into something more than the two-hour-a-day job his predecessor had assured him it would be, Lou attended a Girl Scout convention in Cincinnati in January. In February she went to New York City to host the annual dinner of the Women's Auxiliary of the American Institute of Mining & Metallurgical Engineers. Boris brought Allan back to Washington in March to have his tonsils removed. When he recovered, the boy was sent back to California to recuperate. Because his mother felt he was not strong enough to return immediately to school, he was tutored privately for the remainder of the school year.

In March Aunt Jennie's husband George Mager died. Lou was especially fond of her Aunt Jennie, an independent-minded woman whose first husband had died within a few years of their marriage, and who had preferred to support herself rather than to return to her parents' home as a dependent. In the 1890s she had worked as a matron at the Women's Penitentiary in Anamosa, Iowa. Now she was a well-to-do widow. Lou took Jennie to Iowa in April to visit her sister Jessie in Waterloo. From there Lou went on to California to check on her mother and her sons. In May as she was returning to Washington, she invited British economist Francis Hirst, who was to lecture at Stanford in the fall, to stay at the new house at 623 Mirada while he was in Palo Alto. Although she would not be there, she assured him that he would be well looked after by George Harrison and the Butlers. She was back in Palo Alto again for six weeks in June and July. While there she attended Dare Stark's wedding to John Hays McMullin (a young man whom Lou described as "a perfect young rascal").

This was the beginning of the "Roaring Twenties," a period of unparalleled change in American attitudes and behavior. Electricity was becoming more widely available, changing America's working habits both by lighting up the night hours and by fueling an ever-increasing variety of machines and appliances to make labor—in the home as well as in the factory—more efficient. Henry Ford's inexpensive Model T and its imitators brought automobiles to small towns and rural areas, stimulating a demand for better roads and paved streets. Radio brought the latest news instantly to a wide audience. New fashions, publicized by movie stars, had become available to everyone through mail order catalogs. Skirts rose steadily throughout the decade. Women cut their hair short and used dyes and permanent wave solutions to overcome its natural defects. Life expectancy was increasing.

Birth control was more readily available, and more acceptable in society. Divorce rates were also climbing. More and more women were entering business, sports and (after the passage of the 19th Amendment giving women the right to vote) politics, all previously male preserves. Consumerism was the order of the day. The Hoover boys, like their contemporaries across the nation, learned to play the saxophone and dance the Charleston.

Lou leased tennis courts from the Holton Arms School for the summer for her boys and their friends to use. Herbert Jr. had graduated from Palo Alto High and was spending the summer working in a radio lab in Washington. Radios had replaced automobiles as his current enthusiasm, and he had built his own short-wave radio set. On their way east, he and George Harrison toured the Grand Canyon. Harrison was also working in Washington for the summer, at the Bureau of Standards. He had agreed to continue to look after the Hoover house when he resumed his graduate studies at Stanford in the fall. Young Herbert, who was to enter Stanford, expected to live in one of the dormitories, but Harrison would continue to keep a friendly eye on him on behalf of his parents.

A series of letters between Lou and her secretary, Philippi Harding, give a picture of life at 2300 S Street during the summer of 1921: Bert and the boys build a pond in the back yard for Allan's turtles and alligators; a second pond is proposed after the alligator eats the water lily; Allan is being tutored in music for the summer; the three Hoover men establish a fine of fifty cents per meal for being late to breakfast; Allan's fifty-cents-a-week "salary" is raised to one dollar, but he must still submit weekly accounts to his parents; Herbert Jr. wins a hundred-dollar bond from Edgar Rickard for having grown taller than Edgar, even though he is not yet eighteen; Allan sets up a workshop in the basement, where "even Daddy buries himself" at times.[13]

Lou's mother, Florence Henry, died on August 18, 1921. Lou was in Boston when word of her mother's sudden deterioration reached her. She took the first available train west, arriving on the nineteenth—a day too late. Lou refused to go into formal mourning, since her mother "disapproved of it herself," and it would be "inconsiderate of her wishes to do so."[14] But there would not be quite so much formal entertaining in Washington that fall.

Suppressing her own grief, Lou briskly took charge of her family's affairs. She arranged for her father and his Filipino houseboy, Matias Estella, to drive back with her to Washington in the Hoovers' Cadillac, camping along the way. Her father had always enjoyed travel, and she thought this trip would distract him and help him to deal with his grief. He could then stay with her at 2300 S Street for several weeks, where she could comfort him—and perhaps be comforted by him, though she would not admit to such a need—before returning to Monterey by train.

Jean's older son, Delano Large, accompanied them on the trip to Washington. Having lost both his father and his grandmother in the past the year, seven-year-old Del had apparently become difficult for Jean to handle. "Of course we have always to remember," Lou would write to her son Allan a few years later, "that their father was *terribly* strict with them. . . . So their mother would naturally go to the other extreme."[15] Lou proposed to keep Del with her in Washington for the school year. She enrolled him in the Montessori School, and arranged to keep him busy and entertained, with the help of her staff and Allan, who was now attending Washington's Western High School. The high school was in Georgetown, about three quarters of an hour away by roller skates—Allan's preferred means of travel.

"As I have often said," Lou wrote to Phil Harding in July 1921, "Washington ought to be in California."[16] Keeping up homes on both coasts wasn't easy. Commercial air travel was still in its infancy, and trains took several days to cross the continent. Once again she was separated from her oldest son for months at a time, and while she could rely on her father and sister to look after one another in Monterey, each of them caused her concern in their separate ways. She didn't waste time complaining, however. It was not Lou Henry Hoover's habit. As she had done for years, she took the situation as she found it and made the most of it.

As if her life were not complicated enough, Lou was about to become more deeply involved in two major projects of her own: the Girl Scouts and the National Amateur Athletic Federation. Her administrative talents would be challenged as never before. Yet she embraced these challenges with the enthusiasm and unbounded energy that was the touchstone of her character.

Chapter 9

Girl Scouts and Women's Athletics

Thus far, all of Lou's projects had, to some extent, been extensions of her husband's work. When a troop of Girl Scouts asked permission in 1917 to plant a War Garden at "In The Woods," she embarked on a field of endeavor entirely her own.

Lou had met the founder of the Girl Scouts of the USA, Juliette "Daisy" Low, in London during the early years of the war. Daisy Low was the Georgia-born widow of an Englishman who had been a part of British high society and a confidant of Edward VII when the latter was the rakish Prince of Wales. She still had many friends in court circles. During the early part of the war, Daisy had been involved in the various philanthropic efforts sponsored by American-born women like the Duchess of Marlborough and Jennie Churchill. It was then that she met Lou Hoover. Daisy's primary interest, however, was the Girl Scout movement. She was a close friend of Lord Robert Baden-Powell, founder of the Boy Scouts, who had encouraged her to set up a Girl Guide troop on her husband's property in Scotland. When she returned to her native Savannah in March of 1912, Daisy organized the first American Girl Scout troop at a school run by an old friend.

Inspired by Daisy's contagious enthusiasm, the program expanded rapidly. By 1913 it had established a national headquarters in Washington. In 1915 the organization was officially incorporated, a constitution and by-laws established, and a national board of directors elected under the presidency of Juliette Low. By 1917 membership had reached over seven thousand girls and adults. When war broke out, the Girl Scouts—in accordance with the part of their oath requiring service to their country—supported the war effort by planting War Gardens and selling bonds.

In the summer of 1917 Daisy Low asked Lou to help her with a problem that had arisen in the Washington area. The Girl Scouts had moved their national headquarters to New York City in October of 1916. With the departure of many of the national leaders, local leadership was faltering. Lou, who never made a commitment to any organization without first investigating it thoroughly, read the handbook, which Daisy had recently rewritten, and talked with Daisy and her associates about the group's goals. She was pleased with what she discovered. The Girl Scouts' stress on personal integrity, self-sufficiency, and service to the community, and its belief in the out-of-doors as a training ground for life, meshed perfectly with her own philosophy. She agreed to become acting Girl Scout commissioner for the District of Columbia. To assist her with the job of making the Washington area leadership viable, Lou hired Ruth Sampson, a young Stanford graduate who was a friend of Dare Stark. Ruth spent three months in Washington at Lou's expense, helping her to recruit competent women to serve as troop captains and on the local board of directors.

At the third national council session, held in New York in October 1917, Lou was elected second vice president of the organization. Mrs. Woodrow Wilson, wife of the president of the United States, agreed to serve as honorary president of the Girl Scouts, beginning a tradition that has continued ever since. Mrs. Wilson, Mrs. Calvin Coolidge, and Lou Henry Hoover (whose husband's name had become a national by-word as food administrator) were photographed together in Girl Scout uniforms for the national press. In 1918 Lou wrote an article on food conservation for the Girl Scout magazine, *The Rally.*

During these early years, a dispute arose with the Boy Scouts, whose leadership objected to the girls' use of the word "scout" in its name, rather than the word "guide" used by the British girls' organization. Some Boy Scout leaders feared that boys might be reluctant to join an organization if they thought girls were associated with it; it might make the organization sound "sissy." The Girl Scout leadership responded that there was no sign of any such reluctance by boys, and in any case, they would always use the full name, Girl Scouts, to describe their groups. The word "scout," they said, had a particular relevance to American folklore, invoking the frontier scouts who guided the wagon trains West and were famous for their self-reliance and their outdoor skills. Such a model was as inspiring to girls as it was to boys, and the Girl Scouts saw no reason to change their name. Despite the assertion by some men that "the Girl Scout program is another form of open defiance that woman is prepared to take her place in open competition and 'do things better' than the men . . . the program, the name, the uniform and the general attitude of the leadership is such as to finally cause the development of bold, aggressive, dominating women for future generations—the home a shattered symbol,"[1] the Girl Scouts held firm, and the furor eventually died down.

The Girl Scout organization grew rapidly, reaching 12,812 in 1917 and 34,081 in 1918. By that time, troops had been founded in forty-seven of America's forty-eight states, as well as Hawaii. Miss Windsor's School in Boston offered the first training course for Girl Scout captains in 1917. Within a short time, Girl Scout leader training was also offered at Columbia University in New York and Johns Hopkins University in Maryland. Pine Tree Camp in Massachusetts offered less formal programs sponsored by Helen Storrow, a Boston socialite and member of the national board of directors.

In January 1919 two women joined the movement who would have a significant influence on its future development. Edith Carpenter Macy, wife of millionaire industrialist V. Everit Macy, became chairman of the board of directors. And Jane Deeter Rippin, a prominent social service worker who had been active in combating delinquency among women and young girls, was hired as national director, becoming the national organization's chief executive.

Edith Macy, like Juliette Low, was born to a wealthy family and received her education in private girls' schools in New York City. She had met her husband during a year-long tour of Europe. One of the characteristics the couple shared was a deep commitment to charitable work. Mrs. Macy was particularly interested in the health and welfare of children. She was also active in the League of Women Voters, believing that the nation would benefit greatly by admitting women to full citizenship. Like the Hoovers, the Macys were Quakers whose simple faith encouraged a life of service to others. Edith Macy was an early supporter of the Girl Scout program, both with her time and her fortune; she donated $1,000 annually to the organization from 1916 until her death in 1925.

Jane Deeter Rippin came from a more modest background, but her ideas on how to help girls grow into young women who would be an asset to society matched those of Edith Macy, whom she met in Washington during the First World War. Trained as a teacher, Jane had gone into social work in 1908 as assistant director of an orphanage. In 1910 she became a caseworker for the Philadelphia Society for the Prevention of Cruelty to Children. She organized a cooperative boarding house with five other women; two men soon joined the co-op, one of whom, James Yardley Rippin, would become her husband in 1913. It was an egalitarian marriage, in which each partner supported the other's career. Jane had worked as a probation officer and director of a women's prison in Philadelphia before coming to Washington in 1917 to take charge of a program to keep alcohol and prostitution away from army bases. As part of a study on the causes of delinquency among women, she studied girls' organizations in the United States, and was impressed by the potential that the Girl Scouts offered to keep adolescent girls involved in wholesome pursuits.

Jane Rippin and Edith Macy teamed up to transform the Girl Scouts from the informal organization set up by Juliette Low into a well-run, self-supporting nationwide organization, one of the largest for girls in the country. In January 1922 Lou Henry Hoover joined this team when she was elected president of the Girl Scouts at a national council meeting held in Savannah.

Lou recalled her investiture ceremony, held in Juliette Low's drawing room: "I seem to remember Mrs. Storrow conducted the ceremony . . . Mrs. Low managed it . . . Mrs. Munday had earlier given me my first class tests upstairs in the bed-room." There had been a " 'freeze' storm in Savannah . . . beautiful . . . stopped all traffic." She remembered Daisy Low as "a lovely lady who had never really grown up. . . . In many ways she stayed fourteen. . . . At a staid grownup party she might slip out and play with the other children in the back garden."[2]

Juliette Low had resigned the presidency in 1920 to assume the honorary posi-tion of founder. Not a highly organized person herself—she once gave a ball that she forgot to attend—she was much better at inspiring and recruiting people than at administering what was now an organization of over fifty thousand members. According to Lou, Daisy would "descend suddenly—work feverishly for a few days or weeks—disappear for months."[3] She used her deafness as a tool: she would "put down her ear trumpet when annoyed—or when presiding."[4] Another volunteer observed that Daisy was never so deaf as when you tried to tell her you could not do what she wanted of you. Her advancing age—she was sixty years old in 1920—and her deafness also made it difficult for her to keep up with the pace of the move-ment's rapid growth. She "did not see the vision of a great organization in the coun-try—she thought it would be wonderful to have 5,000 [members]."[5] After stepping down from the presidency, Daisy became the United States' representa-tive to the International Council of Girl Guides and Girl Scouts, founded in Feb-ruary 1919 in London with representatives from a number of European countries and the United States.

Daisy's successor as president was Anne Hyde Choate, whose mother had been one of Daisy's schoolmates. While Anne was devoted to the movement, she found the president's job too time-consuming, and was more than willing to step down when her two-year term ended in January 1922. She remained on the board, one of several women whose support Lou was glad to have.

Many things happened in the Girl Scout movement that first year of Lou's presidency. A five-year grant from the Laura Spelman Rockefeller Memorial Foun-dation made it possible to increase the number of colleges offering Girl Scout lead-ership courses as part of their curriculum. The Brownie program for girls aged seven to ten was officially organized, with a new book for leaders published in March and a conference held in Maryland in November to present the new program to repre-sentatives of the various states. A monthly newsletter for leaders, *Field News*, was introduced in April. Eight training sessions for leaders were held during the sum-mer around the country, and national training schools were established at Camp Juliette Low in Georgia and Camp Chaparral in California. National dues were raised from twenty-five cents to fifty cents per year. The national organization now employed seven field organizers, including Dare Stark's sister, Vaal, who taught one of the Girl Scout courses at Stanford. Lou spent her summer on a tour of in-spection of Girl Scout camps around the country, finishing up with a conference on camps held in New York in September.

With Girl Scouting now solidly established all over the country (membership for 1922 was 73,018), the practice of holding national council meetings in January came under review. Winter weather conditions often made it difficult for representatives of distant states to attend. Consequently, the board decided to move the date of the national council meetings to the spring. The ninth national council meeting was therefore held in April 1923 in Washington, D.C. At this meeting, the council adopted the first statement of national standards for Girl Scout troops.

The organization also in 1923 set up a system of logging membership demographics. For the first time, the national leadership was able to determine accurately not only how many girls were registered as Girl Scouts, but also what their ages were, whether they lived in cities or rural areas, how long the average girl remained in the program, and various other facts. This system made it possible to develop program materials with a greater degree of assurance.

Involved as she was with the administration of the Girl Scout program at the national level, Lou nevertheless felt the need to interact with some of the girls themselves. When the captain of Troop 8 in her Washington, D.C. neighborhood resigned in 1923, Lou took over her job. She held this post for the next ten years, although she often delegated the actual running of the troop to her lieutenants (generally one of her secretaries). The troop met in her home at 2300 S Street, and later in the White House itself. Lou also enjoyed playing hostess to visiting scout troops. One leader recalled with pleasure her troop's visit to 2300 S Street in 1927: "You sat on the floor beside the piano and told a story." Lou later signed autographs for all twenty girls.[6]

The more deeply she became involved with Girl Scouting, the more Lou was impressed with its potential for helping girls to develop their full range of talents. "Girl Scouts are girls who have gathered together in a group, quite of their own volition," she said at the 1925 convention, held in Boston from May 19 to 23, "as one of the happiest means for the expression of their unbounded good spirits and good will. Together they explore many trails which lead out of the pleasant fields of childhood toward the broad and teeming highways of adult life. . . . a frequent result of the voluntary cooperation and comradeship in Girl Scout activities is the development of thought and helpfulness for other people. This makes our girls better home-makers, better citizens, better friends. Individually, it tends toward a keener mind, a finer character, and a happier self."[7] More freedom for girls, she insisted in a later talk in Washington, D.C., provided not a "license to be boisterous . . . but opportunity for self-expression."[8] The Girl Scout movement "aims to conserve and direct wisely [the] energies of girls."[9]

In 1922 Herbert Hoover, as secretary of commerce, became chairman of the Better Homes for America campaign. Ably championed by *The Delineator*'s editor, Marie Mattingley Meloney, the Better Homes campaign promoted the design of modern, efficient, inexpensive homes for middle-class Americans. Architects were challenged to prepare designs, which were then published in the nation's magazines. In 1923 a sample house was built in Washington on park land provided for the purpose by the District of Columbia. Don Barber, the architect, used the exterior of the East Hampton, Long Island, home of John Howard Payne, composer of the ballad *Home Sweet Home*, as his model, but updated the interior to contemporary standards. The General Federation of Women's Clubs paid for its construction. Some three thousand persons a day passed through the house in the two weeks it was on display.

When the demonstration ended, the Federation of Women's Clubs offered the house to the Girl Scouts to use as an educational homemaking center. It would have to be moved from its original site, and the cost of this move, plus the maintenance of the building, would be borne by the Girl Scouts. It promised to be an expensive undertaking, but Lou and her board felt that it would be worth the investment. Lou personally raised $12,000 toward the cost of moving the house to a site loaned to the Girl Scouts by Mr. and Mrs. Duncan Phillips, directors of the Phillips Gallery in Washington. Mrs. Calvin Coolidge laid the cornerstone on the new site on March 25, 1924. During the next three years, a basement, heating plant, and landscaping were provided, and the house was furnished by donations from national manufacturers and other interested persons. In 1927 Lou Henry Hoover officially presented the Little House, as she called it, to the Girl Scouts.

Gertrude Bowman, who had been closely associated with Lou in forming the Food Administration Club, was hired as the Little House's official hostess. Mrs. Bowman worked closely with the national public relations division of the Girl Scouts, planning programs and demonstrations for visiting Girl Scout troops that emphasized cooking, cleaning, and homemaking skills. The Little House opened a tea room, whose income helped to offset the expenses of the whole operation. Non–Girl Scout visitors were welcome to attend the demonstrations, and presidential wives were persuaded to appear for the openings of special programs. Soon other states began imitating this successful project. By 1930 there were seventy Little Houses scattered around the country.

Louisette Aubert Losh, a chemistry graduate from Stanford whose journalist husband was working in Washington, was Mrs. Bowman's assistant. A classmate of Dare Stark's, Louisette sometimes acted as Lou's back-up secretary at 2300 S Street, but she could not work full time because she had an infant son. In 1924 Louisette called to Lou's attention a typographic error in a recipe that Lou had submitted to *The American Girl.* The article, as printed, suggested serving a camp snack of hard tack with tobacco juice (instead of tomato juice)!

Lou was re-elected at the April 1924 national council meeting in Chicago, although a severe attack of laryngitis kept her from attending. Under a new constitution approved at this meeting, the United States was divided into twelve regions, each of which was to be represented on the national board of directors. Membership had now reached a total of 91,994. In October 1924 the national headquarters was moved to 670 Lexington Avenue in New York City, in a building purchased by the Girl Scouts and specially renovated for their purposes.

On February 1, 1925, the Girl Scouts suffered a major loss when Edith Macy died of a heart attack at the age of fifty-four. Lou had intended to skip the national council meeting planned for Boston in May so that she could be with her family, but she felt compelled to change her mind when she heard the news. "I have always been the one to take on her work when she went abroad or when it needed assistance," Lou wrote to her sons, "and in this special convention there is great need of one who knows all the ins and outs of it, for it is the time of a change from one type of constitutional government to another. So it really seems that my duty was certainly there."[10]

Lou resigned the presidency and took over Edith Macy's position as chairman of the executive board. Sarah L. Arnold, retired dean of Simmons College, was elected president in her place. Because her acceptance of this unpaid position would cause Dean Arnold a severe financial loss, Lou wrote to a number of the dean's friends and former students, asking them to contribute to a fund that would pay for her living expenses while she served as Girl Scout president.

The changes Lou referred to in her letter had to do with the implementation of the constitutional changes made at the 1924 convention. The expanded board of directors now had twenty-four members, two from each of the twelve regions. To facilitate operations, a ten- member executive committee would be empowered to make most of the day-to-day decisions, consulting the rest of the board as needed on matters of policy.

During the early 1920s the Girl Scout leadership set a goal of establishing Girl Scout councils in every city in the country with a population of 20,000 or more. These local councils would be responsible for recruiting and training leaders, running local camps for girls, securing publicity and handling registration of members. As Lou explained, "headquarters is primarily a mouthpiece and executive arm of mind and desires embodied in the field."[11]

Among the issues facing the organization's leadership in 1925 were a revision of the merit badge program, the further improvement of the Brownie program, and the financing of the Girl Scout magazine, retitled *The American Girl* in 1920. To solve the latter problem, Lou approached her old friend Edgar Rickard, who among his many responsibilities was vice chairman (and effective director) of Bert's American Relief Association. The ARA now raised funds for charitable causes both at home and abroad. In Europe it administered a scholarship program at the University of Louvain in Belgium and supported a group of private children's libraries in Paris and Brussels that had been established by Mrs. John Griffiths, widow of the former American consul-general to Great Britain. Now the ARA agreed to give a two-year grant to the Girl Scouts to underwrite *The American Girl*.

Lou herself wrote an article for the magazine, profiling her good friend Grace Coolidge, wife of the president, whose childhood she described as bearing a remarkable similarity to the kind of life Girl Scouting now offered. The article was very well received, but the magazine was reprimanded by Mrs. Coolidge, a quiet woman with no taste for publicity, for releasing it to the newspapers for reprinting without her permission. The permission to reprint was hurriedly withdrawn, where it was still possible to do so, and the editors apologized profusely to the first lady. (Some years later, when Lou was first lady, she tried to interest Grace Coolidge in becoming active in the Girl Scouts, but Grace declined. "Perhaps," Grace wrote, "I can write a story of your little girlhood for the magazine. But I guess we both learned our lesson there.")[12]

Following the April national council meeting in St. Louis in April 1926, Lou spent a happy four days at a national Girl Scout training convention held at a Boy Scout camp near Irondale, Missouri. The delegates slept outdoors in tents and ate meals cooked over campfires. A close comradeship developed among these women who came from all parts of the country. Among the delegates from California was Lou's sister, Jean Large, who had recently become Girl Scout commissioner for Palo Alto.

The biggest event for the Girl Scouts in 1926, however, was the international conference held at Camp Edith Macy in Briarcliff Manor, New York, from May 11 through 17. This was the fourth international conference of Girl Guides and Girl Scouts, and the first to be held outside Great Britain. Twenty-nine countries sent delegates to the camp, donated in 1925 by V. Everit Macy in memory of his wife as a national training center for Girl Scout leaders. Juliette Low, who was dying of cancer (although she kept her condition secret), was responsible for the choice of the United States as host to the meeting. The camp, designed by Jane Deeter Rippin's architect husband, James, was barely ready in time. Board member Mrs. Lyman Delano, a cousin of Franklin D. Roosevelt, took charge of the arrangements. The encampment was a great success, with the appearance of Lord and Lady Baden-Powell, founders of the scouting movement, as a highlight for many American participants.

Juliette Low died in January 1927. Membership in the organization she had founded fifteen years earlier with eighteen girls in Savannah, Georgia, now numbered 167,925, spread throughout the entire United States. Its connection with the international Girl Scouting movement was firmly established; in August 1927 a delegation of girls attended an international camp in Switzerland, beginning a new tradition of international cooperation.

At the 1926 national council meeting, it was decided to move the date of the annual convention to October. The 1927 meeting was held in New York City, and 289 delegates attended. New York Governor Franklin D. Roosevelt was asked to give the keynote speech, but time pressures forced him to decline. At this meeting, two major decisions were made: to change the color of the uniform (which since 1913 had been khaki, like that of the Boy Scouts) to dark green, and to establish a memorial fund in the name of the Founder, Juliette Low, that would support projects and events promoting international understanding. Juliette Low's birthday, October 31, was made an official Girl Scout holiday. A major handbook revision was authorized, and the word "Girl" was inserted into the promise before the phrase "Scout Laws," to emphasize the difference between the Girl Scout and the Boy Scout Laws.

This was Lou's last full year on the board of directors for some time. In 1928 her husband decided to run for president of the United States. Lou had to miss the October national council meeting, held in Colorado Springs, because she was too busy campaigning with Bert. A new Girl Scout president, Mira Hoffman, succeeded Sarah Arnold. Lou was elected first vice president, the post whose holder was generally responsible for supervision of field work. Lou had talked Abbie Rickard into joining the board in 1927, and Abbie would serve as the organization's treasurer from 1929 to 1937. Following Bert's election to the presidency in November 1928, Lou resigned as the Girl Scouts' first vice president, believing she would not have time to do the job properly. In March 1929, after her husband was sworn into office, she agreed to serve as honorary president, as her predecessors since Mrs. Wilson had done.

She continued to take a close interest in the organization's affairs. She could count as her closest friends many of its most influential figures. A young woman who worked with them in those years would later describe them as "dynamic women," economically privileged, but so absorbed in living that they weren't conscious of their privileged state. They were less concerned about women's rights than about encouraging young women to take advantage of the opportunities opening up around them. Well educated, energetic, and committed to charitable works, they were "a brilliant group of women of all religions and political affiliations, all extremely active," who took Juliette Low's vision and gave it form and substance.[13]

In the next decade, Girl Scout membership would surpass 500,000; by 1944, when Lou Henry Hoover died, it would reach one million. Today, nearly three million girls are served by Girl Scouting. Much of the organization's success is due to the inspired leadership of Lou Henry Hoover and her colleagues in those important formative years.

Her connection with the Girl Scouts involved Lou in another nationwide movement aimed at improving the well-being of women and girls. World War I had brought to light several disturbing facts about the general health of America's youth. Large numbers of young men had been rejected by the military for physical defects, and the standard of health of the nation's rural population was reported to have fallen below that of urban areas. This was true not only of young men, but of young women as well.

Organized sports, such as baseball, basketball and football, were becoming increasingly popular, but they were spectator sports, involving fewer athletes than observers. The spread of radio broadcasting, with its live coverage of sports events, increased the passive aspect of athletic competition. New heroes appeared, promoted by the press and radio. American participation in the Olympic Games, begun in 1896, led to intensified training programs for prospective competitors.

This growing popularity of spectator sports, professional athletes, and commercial exploitation of sporting events disturbed many physicians, educators, and sports enthusiasts who were committed to promoting physical fitness and sport for the sake of sport. In the fall of 1921 a group of concerned men (ex-President Theodore Roosevelt among them) contacted Secretary of War John W. Weeks and Secretary of the Navy Edwin Denby to propose the formation of an association that would encourage healthy sports for both men and women. The two secretaries were supportive of the idea. They asked Lou Hoover to help them bring interested women into the proposed association. They chose her because she was President of the Girl Scouts—an organization they hoped to involve in their association—and had earned a reputation as a talented organizer through her war work in London and Washington. Also, she was the wife of Herbert Hoover, whose name had become synonymous with humanitarianism and nutrition.

Lou shared the men's concerns. She had always enjoyed sports herself. She had served on the basketball committee as a student at Stanford and was president of the Stanford Women's Athletic Association in her senior year. One of the things that drew her to the Girl Scout movement was its emphasis on outdoor living as a means of developing character for girls. Keen minds in healthy bodies was one of her goals for young people.

A group of gentlemen called at Lou's home one day in February 1922 to discuss their plan. Although Lou applauded their goals, she objected to the idea of having identical standards, regulations, and programs for both men and women, boys and girls. "Although I did believe in men and women having the same membership and activities in nearly all organizations, I felt that there were such fundamentally differing factors in their athletics that it would be advisable to have them grouped under separate sub-divisions," she said.[14]

Unable herself to attend the May 1922 meeting at which the groundwork for the National Amateur Athletic Federation (NAAF) was laid, Lou sent Ruth C. White to represent the Girl Scouts and report back to her on the decisions made. More meetings were held, many of them at the Hoover home. When the NAAF held its first annual meeting in December 1922, Lou was chosen as one of its vice presidents—the only woman on the governing board. The following year, when the NAAF's new constitution was written, Lou was reelected as vice president, and six other women were named to the extended board of directors, giving the organization equal representation from both sexes.

The new federation defined its purpose as raising the overall health level of the nation and training its youth for citizenship through the medium of amateur sports. All existing athletic organizations were invited to join the federation and to find ways of working together. Local federations would be established in the various states. The national organization would encourage "wholesome" athletic competitions and create a series of progressive tests of physical fitness that could be used to rank contestants. Former assistant Secretary of War Henry Breckinridge was elected president of the organization, but the real force behind its efforts came from its executive secretary, Elwood Brown.

Accepting Lou's view that women's athletics faced different challenges from men's, the federation proposed separate divisions for men and women. Lou organized a second conference, held in Washington on April 6 and 7, 1923, to discuss the issues facing women in athletics. The delegates included physical education professors from a large number of colleges around the nation, as well as health professionals and representatives of such organizations as the Girl Scouts, the Red Cross, and the YWCA. Among the issues to be discussed were the need for rules appropriate to girls' sports, the scarcity of space, facilities, equipment and qualified women coaches for girls' athletic programs, as well as the lack of understanding and support from community leaders for women's athletics. A major debate arose over the kinds and amounts of activity suitable for girls, from a medical as well as social standpoint, and the degree of intensity of training and competition that ought to be permitted. Even the definition of what constituted "serviceable, modest" clothing for participants came under discussion. A major issue for many of the delegates was women's—and men's—participation in the Olympics. Their objection was based on their belief that the degree of intensely focused training required was not healthy. This issue became a serious bone of contention between the NAAF and the American Athletic Union, which sponsored Olympic athletes and promoted team sports from a competitive rather than a participatory perspective.

Lou personally absorbed the costs of the women's conference (estimated at around $1000), with the assurance that the NAAF would develop funding for the division's continuance. Financing proved to be one of the federation's most frustrating issues. Elwood Brown, whose competence and enthusiasm did much to put the NAAF on a solid footing in its early stages, died suddenly in 1924, of blood clots caused by a tooth infection. It was 1925 before the federation found a permanent successor. John L. Griffith, the new NAAF executive officer, then moved the Men's Division headquarters to Chicago. Despite his efforts, however, the men's organization soon began to founder.

The Women's Division remained in New York, where it soldiered on, hampered by the weakness of its parent organization and by the fact that the majority of its most active members were academics, with little skill at fund-raising. Lou, whose fund-raising skills had been honed under the CRB, proved an invaluable resource. She recruited her Girl Scout friends, Edith Macy and Ruth Pratt (whose husband Herbert was the NAAF treasurer), to serve on the Women's Division board. She hired one of her Stanford classmates, Susan Bristol, to undertake the massive job of preparing the minutes of the 1923 organizational conference for publication. In 1924, Lou brought philanthropist Hattie M. Strong, widow of Eastman Kodak President Henry A. Strong, onto the board of the Women's Division, and talked her into donating $500 a year (the same amount Lou herself had pledged) to the group's budget.

Lou served as chairman of the executive committee from 1923 to 1927. Recognizing, however, that the Women's Division needed a full-time administrator, the committee hired Lillian Schroedler in September 1923 as executive secretary. Over the next few years, the organization struggled to write standards for women's sports, held regional conferences to expound their views on women's athletics, and published a newsletter to keep member organizations informed on current issues.

When the NAAF appealed in 1924 to the Laura Spelman Rockefeller Memorial Foundation for funding, the result was a challenge fund drive. If the NAAF could raise $20,000 by the end of the year, the foundation would match the amount; these funds were to be divided equally between the Men's and the Women's Divisions. By late December, the Women's Division had raised $9,416.90 of their $10,000 goal; the remainder was raised at the last moment, with $1.90 to spare. Lou had sent an emergency check for $1,500, to be used in the event that the fund drive fell short; it was returned to her with thanks in January 1925.

The Rockefeller grant took some of the financial pressure off the women's organization for the time being—in 1926, its budget actually showed a surplus—and Lou was able to tap her husband's American Relief Agency (ARA) for additional funds to enable the Women's Division to hire a field secretary who would take on a public relations outreach function, relieving the executive secretary of one of the more stressful parts of her job.

The field secretary post could not be filled immediately, however, because Lillian Schroedler resigned as executive secretary in June 1926, complaining of what today would be called burn-out. The stress of trying to handle the organization's extensive correspondence, deal with fund-raising problems (especially the Rockefeller challenge drive), and do the necessary outreach work—speaking, writing, conducting conferences around the country—single-handed was exhausting her. She had tried to resign in 1925, but had been persuaded to stay on. In December, the NAAF had hired Mary Wallace Weir to help Miss Schroedler with the office work, but this was not sufficient to prevent the latter's resignation. Mary Weir then took over as executive secretary, but stayed only a year. In September 1928, Mary Van Horn assumed the position, which was retitled office executive to give its holder more prestige. A stenographer handled much of the correspondence. In 1930 the first field secretary, Anne Hodgkins, was finally hired. When Jane Deeter Rippin, former executive officer of the Girl Scouts, took over as chairman of the Women's Division in 1931 (her title was then changed to president), the organization at last had a strong, effective leadership team in place.

Lou had stepped down as chairman of the Women's Division in April 1927, feeling that she did not have the time the job required. She remained on the board, however, as vice chairman. Hattie Strong took over as chairman, but resigned in 1930 because of ill health, and was replaced some months later by Jane Deeter Rippin. Lou left the board in November 1928, following her husband's election to the Presidency. The organization offered her the title of honorary chairman, which she gladly accepted. She continued to take an interest in the group's activities, and to provide financial assistance as needed.

Despite the administrative and financial challenges it had to overcome, the NAAF Women's Division was successful in achieving many of its goals. Play days, where women of varying ages and abilities participated in a wide range of sports and games, became popular at the nation's schools and colleges. The lack of spectators and of pressure to win at all costs allowed the girls to enjoy playing for the fun of it. Intramural and interclass sports became more widespread. Many women's organizations developed educational programs stressing the advantages of an active lifestyle for women. Lou herself gave a number of talks to groups such as the Girl Scouts and Republican women's clubs in which she promoted the ideas of the NAAF.

In one of her speeches, Lou tackled the issue of appropriate clothing for women in sports. This was the era of the flapper, whose bobbed hair and short skirts were scandalizing the older generation. Lou saw nothing wrong with comfortable clothing, which allowed more freedom of movement for physical activity. Though she disapproved of trousers for everyday wear, she had often worn them when hiking, riding horseback, or visiting mines in Australia or China. The middy blouses and bloomers that were coming into fashion in schools for physical education classes seemed quite sensible to her. She was more ambivalent about the tank tops and shorts affected by female track and field athletes. She objected to sports uniforms that stressed sexual appeal rather than convenience. Comfort and function should be the criteria, she felt. Her conservative views reflect her age—she turned fifty in March 1924—and the discomfort her generation felt when confronted by the flapper phenomenon.

In its early years, the Women's Division enjoyed widespread support among physical education professionals and recreation leaders. Its opposition to women's participation in the 1932 Olympics held in Los Angeles, however, was not successful. During the 1930s other groups with competing agendas began to make inroads on the group's clientele. At the same time, the Depression was making funding even more difficult to find. In 1933 a lack of funds forced the Women's Division to eliminate the field secretary's position. Jane Rippin, whose health was beginning to fail, resigned as president in May of that year. To save money, the offices of the organization were closed for three months during the summer. Lou resigned from the position of honorary president, which she felt was intended only for presidential wives. To her surprise and pleasure, the executive committee refused to accept her resignation. They begged her to stay on with the title of honorary president and founder.

From this low point, the Women's Division fought its way back. Its efforts in establishing ideals and standards for women's athletics were widely recognized. In 1937 the American Physical Education Association praised the NAAF Women's Division's "concise platform," which it asserted "has been placed in the hands of teachers and organizers of women's athletics in every part of the world."[15] New leadership emerged on an expanded executive board, and money was found to keep the office running all year again by 1938. The 1939 financial statement showed that the organization had run a deficit for nine of its fifteen years of existence, with only two of those years (1925 and 1927) being serious deficits. However, its most consistent source of funds, the ARA, was closing down. A proposal to merge the Women's Division with the American Association for Health, Physical

Education and Recreation won approval at the final annual meeting, held in San Francisco in April 1939. The merger took place on June 15, 1940.

Although the Women's Division no longer exists as a separate entity, it continues to function as a major component—the National Association for Girls and Women in Sport—of the American Alliance for Health, Physical Education, Recreation and Dance. It has had to modify its position on competitive sports, in line with the obvious wishes of the nation's women and girls, but it continues to publicize the need for sports opportunities to be open to everyone. In the mid-1970s, the group worked to secure the passage of Title IX of the Educational Amendments Act requiring equity in sports for males and females.

Many of the issues that Lou Henry Hoover and her colleagues faced in the 1920s remain areas of concern today. Despite Title IX, men's varsity sports still receive more funding and support than women's sports. Americans still prefer watching sports events from the comfort of their homes to participating, and the inflated salaries of professional athletes have become a matter of controversy. Teenagers spend long hours preparing for Olympic events, risking both their health and their mental stability. The alliance between professional sporting events and the media is stronger than ever.

The NAAF Women's Division's crusade was not entirely in vain, however. A national standard for physical fitness was developed, and is still used by physical education teachers in the public schools as a goal for student achievement. Physical education participation for all students, male and female, is required at all levels through high school, and in many colleges and universities as well. Although American fitness is said to be at an all-time low, a large percentage of Americans work out in fitness centers or include running or jogging in their daily routine. Hiking and camping are so popular that many national parks have become overcrowded. Most communities have public swimming pools with regular programs of lessons and aquatic exercise.

Lou's contribution to this movement, both as master fund-raiser and as "professional parliamentarian," able to preside over meetings in such a way that everyone was heard and no one felt slighted, was substantial. Her tact and competence, her calm in the face of emergencies, helped the Women's Division succeed in achieving many of its goals.

Lou and Jean Henry, 1883.

Wedding day, February 10, 1899, at Henry home in Monterey, California. In front, Lou and Bert. In back, Charles Henry, Jean Henry and Florence Henry.

The 1903 Panhard automobile that "ran some of the time." Lou Hoover smiles at the camera while Herbert and the chauffeur work on the engine.

Henry family portrait, 1910. Back row: Charles Henry, Allan Hoover, Lou Henry Hoover. Front row: William Henry, Mary Ann Dwire Henry, Herbert Hoover Jr.

On vacation in Piazza San Marco, Venice, 1912. Herbert and Lou Hoover, Abigail and Edgar Rickard.

Executive Committee of The American Women's War Relief Committee, October 1914.

Campaign train leaving Cedar Rapids, Iowa, 1928. Left to right: Herbert Hoover Jr., Lou Henry Hoover, Herbert Hoover, George Akerson (aide) and Allan Hoover.

President and Mrs. Hoover on the porch of their cabin at the Rapidan Camp, August 1930.

President and Mrs. Hoover attending services at the National Friends' Meeting House in Washington, D.C., April 1931.

Gravesite at the Herbert Hoover National Historic Site in West Branch, Iowa. Author's collection.

Chapter 10

A Working Wife
and Mother

Busy as she was with the Girl Scouts and the Women's Division of the NAAF, Lou always put her family's affairs first. Herbert Jr. had entered Stanford in the fall of 1921. Though he lived in a dormitory, he was still supervised (at a distance) by George Harrison, who hoped to complete his Ph.D. by the end of the spring term. Lou was never completely happy when she was separated from her sons for extended periods of time. She felt it was important that they have someone responsible nearby to advise them and, if necessary, inform her of any serious problems. George Harrison was a particularly good choice for this role—young enough for Herbert to be able to relate to him, sufficiently mature to provide a good example, and sensible enough not to interfere unnecessarily in Herbert's affairs.

Harrison was also responsible for looking after the new house. While Lou had hired her longtime servant Alfred Butler and his daughter Carrie to do the day-to-day house and garden work, she was reluctant to give them the added responsibility of paying bills and making decisions about upkeep. Harrison supervised their work and looked after the house, sending Lou regular reports, in return for his room and board and a small stipend.

In early 1922 Lou accompanied her husband to Colorado for a meeting of the Colorado River Commission. When it ended, Bert and Lou went to Palo Alto, where their old friend and former professor John Casper Branner had recently died. For both Hoovers, this was a significant loss. It was Branner who had inspired both of them as young students in his geology classes. The former university president had been writing his memoirs, and Lou undertook to help his heirs find a publisher for them.

While at Stanford Bert attended the trustees' meeting where he proposed an alumni fund drive (the university's first), which he called the "First Million Campaign." Among the beneficiaries of the campaign was the new Stanford Union, which opened in the fall. Bert had personally donated $100,000 toward the building. He also, through the CRB, donated $200,000 to the Stanford Library, to be used to preserve the CRB files. This donation, and the papers associated with it, were the foundation of the Hoover Institution on War, Revolution and Peace.

Lou's father and sister came up from Monterey to visit, bringing along Jean's children Janet, aged ten, and Walter, aged five. (Eight-year-old Del was still in Washington.) They had not been there long when one of the servants rushed into the house. He had found young Walter floating unconscious in the swimming pool. The Hoovers rushed to the scene, sending an urgent message to Ray Lyman Wilbur, who was a physician as well as Stanford's president and Bert's closest friend. They were too late. The boy was dead.

As usual, Lou reacted to this newest crisis by plunging into action. She sent a hasty message to her secretary, Philippi Harding, in Washington, asking her to break the news of his brother's death carefully to Del, and to report back immediately about his response. She explained that she and Jean both felt that because Del was so young, it would be better for him to remain in Washington rather than to rush home for his brother's funeral. Lou later wrote to Del's paternal grandmother, "It is . . . likely that the fact of having their father and their greatly beloved grandmother both leave them recently, with such full explanation of their going both times, and the assurance that we are all to meet again under even happier conditions sometime in the future, is what makes Del accept Walter's loss so philosophically. He always speaks of him in the present time, and seems to feel that he is only a little farther away than Janet."[1]

Jean returned to her ranch near Monterey, where she was surrounded by friends and family, who collaborated in distracting her from her grief. Del joined them when school ended in 1922. Since Guthrie's departure Jean had been living with her father in Monterey, although she still kept the ranch, spending a portion of each summer there with her children. She had a Filipino foreman who ran things in her absence. Jean had grown into a competent woman with considerable strength of character, but she was more easy-going than her older sister. Her niece Hulda later described her as "friendly and relaxed . . . not nearly as vital or strong-minded as Lou."[2] It was easy for Lou, who felt very protective towards her younger sister, to persuade Jean to do things that Lou felt she should be doing, whether it was sending her son to school in Washington or becoming involved with the Girl Scout movement in California.

Bert and Lou went back to Washington in April, where they both had much work waiting for them. Lou's increasing involvement with Girl Scout affairs led her to hire a second secretary, Mary Stevick. She also rented an apartment in New York so that she and Bert would have a place to stay whenever their activities required them to spend more than a night there. Feeling that Washington's custom of making formal social calls and leaving cards was a waste of time, she refused to take part in it, and talked several other cabinet wives into discontinuing the practice as well.

Lou spent the summer of 1922 visiting Girl Scout camps. She returned to Palo Alto in September, where she dealt with a changeover in domestic staff. The fall and winter were devoted to working on Girl Scout matters and becoming involved in the early stages of organizing the NAAF.

Her husband's busy schedule also kept her on the run. "We have the usual casually running household," she wrote Evelyn Allan in December 1922, "people coming and going . . . Bert making three engagements for the same night—which I have to untangle to everyone's discomfort."[3] One evening, shortly after the Hoovers and their guests sat down to dinner, the doorbell rang. Ellis the butler, appearing upset, hurried in to tell Lou that two senators and their wives had just arrived. They had been invited to dinner by Bert, who had forgotten to mention it to his wife. Lou told Ellis to put the newcomers in the parlor, while the maids quickly cleared the table and set it afresh. In a few minutes the dinner started over again, with a larger contingent of guests than before.

Bert wasn't the only one to impose on Lou's generosity. When the Daughters of the American Revolution (DAR) planned to hold a reception at the White House, Grace Coolidge became ill and was unable to serve as hostess. Lou's friend Gertrude Bowman, who was an active member of the DAR, asked Lou if they could hold the reception at her house instead. Lou agreed, and so one spring afternoon some 1,500 women passed through the house on S Street. They entered through the front door, where they were received by Lou and the DAR officers, shown some of the Hoovers' more interesting mementos, and directed onto the back porch for cookies and punch before leaving by the garden gate. When the last guest had left, Lou and the committee gathered in the living room for refreshments and a discussion of the afternoon. Showing no sign of fatigue, Lou remarked complacently that she thought everything had gone extremely well.

During the spring of 1923 Lou orchestrated the foundation of the Women's Division of the NAAF, received an honorary master of the arts degree from Mills College, and addressed a gathering of Republican women in Philadelphia. It was only three years since the passage of the 19th Amendment, and Lou was asked what she thought women's role in politics should be. She replied that "women should put into their new duties of citizenship the same amount of serious application and study they give to their work in the schools, colleges and business of the country."[4] On another occasion, she told the League of Women Voters, "We need women as well as men in politics."[5] Whether they were wanted or not, women were "here to stay."[6] Politics, civic affairs, public service, and public policy were natural fields of interest to women, she believed. Though she had not taken an active part in the suffrage movement, she now said that it was as important for women to vote as it was for men, since by failing to vote, they could easily "elect" bad public servants.

That summer Lou and her husband were invited to accompany President Harding and his entourage on his official cruise to Alaska from July 1 to August 1,

1923. It was a very pleasant trip, with beautiful scenery, and Lou, who loved water journeys, thoroughly enjoyed herself. Her husband observed that Harding, whose administration was coming under fire for a wide range of fiscal irregularities, seemed under considerable stress. When the ship reached Vancouver on the return leg of the voyage, Harding fell ill. Within twenty-four hours of their landing in San Francisco, the president was dead.

A telegraph message was sent to Vice President Calvin Coolidge, himself vacationing at his home in Vermont, where he was sworn in as president by his father, a local judge, on the evening of August 2. The Hoovers, with the rest of the presidential party, returned to Washington on Harding's funeral train. It was an experience the Hoovers would never forget, charged as it was with gloom and uncertainty concerning the future.

Coolidge announced his cabinet a few weeks later. There were a number of changes, some of them a result of the Teapot Dome scandal, in which Harding's attorney general and secretary of the interior were both implicated. No discredit attached to the secretary of commerce, however, and Coolidge asked Bert to continue in that post. Although he disliked Bert personally, referring to him sarcastically as "the wonder boy," Coolidge nevertheless recognized his ability and his popularity with the public. Hoover's energetic management of his office—implementing a national standard for construction materials, promoting the Better Homes for America movement, and working with the Colorado River Commission to develop a power and water use scheme for the Colorado River—had met with national approval. In October 1923 he sponsored a law-enforcement conference in Washington, which addressed among other things the rise in crime resulting from Prohibition.

Lou was very fond of the new president's wife, Grace. The two women became good friends. One Easter Lou sent Grace Coolidge a lily, and received a bleeding heart plant in exchange. The following year, the exchange was repeated, until it became a tradition between the two women, continuing long after both of them left Washington. Lou enrolled Grace as the third honorary president of the Girl Scouts, and talked her into appearing publicly in the official Girl Scout uniform. When the Coolidge's son Calvin Jr. died in July 1924 of a staphylococcus infection following a minor injury to his toe, Lou sent the bereaved mother her deepest sympathy. No doubt she recalled her own panic when Herbert Jr. was so ill in the flu epidemic of 1918. In those days before the discovery of antibiotics, a child's life was always at risk.

Lou had taken Allan back to Palo Alto in the fall of 1923 to spend his last year of high school at Palo Alto High. She was concerned about the quality of education he was receiving, and felt that Palo Alto would prepare him more adequately to enter Stanford the following year. George Harrison had left California for Harvard, but Lou found another graduate student to take his place, looking after her sons' welfare in return for room and board and a small stipend. Jean would also be spending the winter at the Stanford house, so that her children could attend the Palo Alto schools.

There was a different staff now at the Palo Alto house. Alfred Butler and his family had returned to Washington in 1922, and Lou had sent another black couple, Clarence and Bessie Doleman, to take their places. Lou was quite fond of Bessie, whom she described as "a brick," but Clarence had a weakness for liquor that caused some concern. Nevertheless, she kept the Dolemans on until 1927, when they resigned to return to Washington.

Herbert Jr., now in his third year at Stanford, was still fascinated by radio. In 1923 he contacted Switzerland by short wave, setting a long-distance radio reception record that was duly reported in the press. Of more interest to his mother was the fact that he was seriously dating Margaret (Peggy) Watson, a charming young woman whom he had met at Palo Alto High.

Severe laryngitis in April 1924 forced Lou to miss both the Girl Scout and the NAAF conventions, both held in Chicago. In May she returned to Palo Alto for the summer. Bert joined her for a few weeks. Claiming that it was important for husbands and wives to take vacations from one another occasionally, he joined San Francisco's Bohemian Club, an exclusive men's club headquartered in San Francisco, with a camp (the Bohemian Grove) located in the mountains north of the city. It's not clear why he should feel it necessary to "take a vacation" from a wife from whom his frenetic lifestyle frequently separated him for extended periods of time. The club membership probably had a more practical purpose. Many of Bert's close friends in the engineering community and in the Republican Party were also Bohemian Club members, and these informal gatherings were a useful means of cementing alliances as well as fishing and socializing in an all-male atmosphere. Lou herself belonged to a number of women's clubs in Washington, New York, and California. They provided her with access to the women she needed for her many projects, and their clubhouses offered meeting space and occasional overnight facilities.

Lou was deeply concerned about her sister's welfare during this period. The sharp contrast between her own situation—happily married to a wealthy, highly respected man who acknowledged her abilities—and Jean's made her uncomfortable. Lou had written a will in 1924 leaving her property to be divided among her husband and sons. But she began to have second thoughts. In a letter to her sons in April 1924, she wrote, "Now a trust which I think we all agree we have, is Auntie Jean and her children. There was no way by which she could well know that the man she married was going to turn out such a scoundrel as he did. His people acknowledge. . . . an obligation to take care of her and their children,—but they have only enough to get along on very quietly themselves, and . . . they are very old, too. . . . So I feel that . . . since you are each very comfortably off . . . that my next duty should be to make assurance that Auntie Jean has ample comfort for herself and to educate her children. . . . If any least little thing should go wrong with Auntie Jean's ranch, she would have nothing at all, practically, to fall back on. . . . Therefore, I think that . . . if I should die as things are now, I should leave enough in some way that will assure comfort to her and her children. . . . So if you should discover that I have left no money at all to you, you will know that it was only because there was not enough to do that and take care of her too,—and besides . . . I was quite assured that you had as much as you could need for yourselves anyway."[7]

Lou's assets at that time included the trust fund her husband had established for her during the war, the Henry home in Monterey, $10,000 she had received from the sale of the Bank of Monterey stock her father had once given her, plus some other money that was in her name, but in her mind still belonged to her father. Her sons each had trust funds of their own. "At present," she confessed, "the family has a great deal more than it needs to do with in the world as far as taking care of its members materially. There is no great fortunes [sic] that we could perform great missions with,—but there is more than enough to what is known as 'live on.' "[8]

Bert and Lou were still providing financial assistance to a number of relatives, primarily in the form of educational "loans." Though he was an orphan, Bert had a large number of cousins scattered around the country, and the Hoovers helped many of them and their children with college expenses. As the Midwest farm depression deepened, he also became concerned about his aunts and uncles in rural Iowa. Lou's Uncle Will was also facing financial difficulties in North Dakota. When Lou discovered that the farm depression was threatening some small banks in which Uncle Will held a major interest, she sent him a "loan" of $1,200, and asked Bert to put in a good word with the Agricultural Credit Corporation on Will's behalf. Bert did so, and the banks survived this temporary crisis, although they would eventually be liquidated as the farm credit situation continued to worsen.

Stanford had grown significantly in the years since Lou's graduation, and housing—especially for the lower ranks of professors—had become extremely tight. Bert had been working with the administration to increase professors' pay—he was particularly upset that some of them could not afford to hire servants, making it necessary for their wives to do their own housework! Lou proposed to Jean that the two sisters join in a partnership to build several small cottages on the campus, suitable for young faculty members. These would be rented, or sold on time at low rates. Using the money her father had realized through the sale of his bank stock, Lou acquired the needed property leases. With Birge Clark again serving as her architect, she had five small houses constructed. George Harrison, who returned to teach at Stanford in the fall of 1925, purchased one of them.

In November 1924 Lou lost her valued secretary, Philippi Harding. Phil had met Lt. Frederick Butler in Washington, while he was stationed at Camp Humphrey. Now he was in China, as aide to General William D. Connor in Tianjin. Phil was to travel there to marry him. Lou gave the couple $500 (Bert added another $250), and an abundance of advice about life in China. On being a foreigner in populous Tianjin, she said, "it will seem funny when you get home, not to be tagged about by twenty people watching your minutest move!"[9] Chinese porcelain (which Lou loved and collected assiduously) she said was "so lovely and the affection of both sender and recipient get so wrapped up in the things——and then they break! I learned even while in China not to let my affections get entangled in bits of china and glass!"[10]

Replacing Phil Harding, who had been her right hand since 1920, was not easy. Dare Stark had been married in 1922, and Mary Stevick had also left her employ by this time. Another young Stanford grad, Virginia Burks, lasted only a year as Lou's secretary before she also left to be married. Virginia was followed by Anna Fitzhugh, who stayed for two years, and Martha Noyes, who served as Lou's secretary in Washington for a year while working on an M.A. in psychology at George Washington University. Not until Martha left to take a position with the Girl Scouts in New York did a worthy successor to Phil Harding appear in Mildred Hall, who would be Lou's chief "roustabout" for the next seven years. Mildred was the first of Lou's secretaries who was not a Stanford graduate. Born in Maryland, she had attended secretarial school in Washington, D.C. Hazel Grant Edgar, a newswoman, had introduced her to Lou, who arranged for Mildred to work as a secretary for the Girl Scout's Little House. In June 1927 Lou hired twenty-three-year-old Mildred to replace Martha Noyes.

In addition to handling Lou's correspondence—now much increased because of her involvement in the Girl Scouts and the NAAF Women's Division—these young women took charge of her Girl Scout troop in her absence and assisted with social events. They might be asked to serve as Lou's deputy in California when she was in Washington, or in Washington when she was in California. During the eighteen months that Anna Fitzhugh lived with the Hoovers in Washington, she was paid $50 per month, plus room and board. When she went to Palo Alto in September 1926, she received $125 per month to look after things there.

Young Herbert spent the summer of 1924 in Maine working at the Pejobscot Paper Mill (one of Edgar Rickard's companies). In June 1925 his father delivered the commencement address at his graduation. A few days later, on June 28, Herbert Jr. and Peggy Watson were married in the Stanford chapel, with a reception at the Hoover home. It was a small wedding, with only twenty guests, including family members, the Rickards and Dare Stark McMullin. Lou took home movies of the wedding, which Edgar Rickard pronounced "remarkably good." Lou was fond of taking motion pictures, but her niece Hulda remarked in an oral history interview many years later that the results were often compromised by Lou's failure to understand that it was the people, and not the camera, who were supposed to move!

The newlyweds set out by auto—not the homemade Ford, which had now become Allan's, but the family's "Dodgie"—for a cross-country honeymoon, ending at Cambridge, Massachusetts, where Herbert was to enter Harvard Business School in the fall. The young Hoovers would sublet the apartment formerly occupied by the George Harrisons. Once again, however, New England proved unhealthy for Herbert. In October he developed ear trouble again. His parents insisted he consult a specialist at Johns Hopkins in Baltimore, Maryland. He and Peggy, who was pregnant with their first child, remained in Maryland until the

New Year, then returned to Harvard for the spring term. Their daughter Margaret (called Peggy Ann) was born two months prematurely on March 17, 1926.

Allan Hoover graduated from Palo Alto High in 1925. Caught up in the Girl Scout crisis following Edith Macy's unexpected death a few months earlier, Lou was unable to attend. It was a disappointment both to her and to Allan, but she felt she simply could not get away. In the fall Allan entered Stanford. He lived in a dormitory his freshman year, but didn't enjoy it. The following year, he and some friends, including a graduate student named Allen Campbell, son of the former governor of Arizona, set up housekeeping at the Hoover home. The Hoovers had met Allen Campbell in 1923, when Bert went to Arizona to discuss the proposed Boulder Dam project with Governor Campbell and other Arizona officials. Observing that he also had a son named Allan, Bert said he hoped the boys would meet sometime.

Seated next to Lou at dinner that night, Allen Campbell confided that he was thinking of transfering from the University of Arizona, where he was a freshman, to Stanford. Lou insisted that he stay in their home until he could find housing. He did so, spending his first semester in Herbert Jr.'s unused room and becoming good friends with the younger Allan, who was then a junior at Palo Alto High. With some other Stanford friends, the boys formed a club called the Psychical Research Society. Allen Campbell joined the Beta Theta Pi fraternity, but after a year he decided that it was too noisy in the fraternity house, and happily accepted Allan Hoover's invitation to move back to the Hoover home.

The two boys came down with flu in the spring of 1926. They went to Arizona when they recovered to recuperate with Allen Campbell's family. While they were there, Allan Hoover received a telephone call from his father, proposing that he and Allen Campbell spend the summer exploring Europe. Delighted, the boys agreed. They spent the next three months touring France, Belgium, Germany, Switzerland, Italy, and Great Britain. The Hoovers wrote to their many friends abroad, asking them to look out for the boys as they traveled. Hugh Gibson, a former CRB colleague now serving in Geneva as chairman of the U.S. delegation to the preparatory committee for the disarmament conference, accompanied the boys on the first lap of their journey. Charlotte Kellogg, who had rented a villa in Florence for the summer, entertained them there. Allen Campbell, the senior by three years, sent Lou a series of diary-style letters, describing their adventures, including attendance at the King's Garden Party in London. By the time they reached England, their funds were running low and they were tired of traveling, so they settled down for the last several weeks at an inn in Sunningdale, Surrey, where they took lessons in golf.

Although Allen Campbell and many of Allan's other friends were members of a fraternity, Allan Hoover followed his father's example and remained a "barbarian." He often ate at the Beta house, however. Again following his father's lead, Allan started out as a mining major, but his Uncle Theodore felt that he wasn't working up to his potential in the field. "He used to make me study in his office," Allan recalled.[11] After a year or so, Allan switched his major to economics.

Bert's brother Theodore had become dean of Stanford's new engineering school in 1925. He and Mildred had acquired a good-sized house on the campus when he began teaching there in 1919, although they still considered the Rancho del Oso their home. In 1922 their oldest daughter, Mindy, had married Cornelius Willis, son of the dean of the geology department, and now she had two sons. Their youngest daughter, Louise—named for her Auntie Lou (with whom she shared a birthday)—had been seventeen when she married Ernest Dunbar just a week before her cousin Herbert's wedding in 1925. When their middle daughter, Hulda, married Charles "Chuck" McLean while still attending college in 1926, the family was dismayed. It was bad enough that Louise had foregone a college education for marriage. Now Hulda, who had spent three years at Stanford, was endangering her own college degree. Chuck flunked out of Stanford following the marriage, but a relative managed to get him accepted at McGill University in Montreal.

Theodore may have been experiencing financial difficulties, and did not offer to pay his daughter and son-in-law's expenses. He and Mildred had sold their large home in Palo Alto shortly after Hulda's wedding, and moved into a smaller duplex on the campus. Lou paid Chuck and Hulda's college bills at McGill, and provided them with a small allowance. As always, she called her financial assistance a "loan," but when the young couple later tried to repay her, she returned their check, telling them to use the money to help someone else. Hulda sent her regular reports from McGill on her budgeting, and on Chuck's academic progress. Later, Theodore repaid part of the "loan."

Bert's sister May was another source of concern to the family. May was a tiny woman, quiet but strong-minded. Her husband, Cornelieus Van Ness Leavitt, was a plumber, a charming man but not too bright, with a fondness for alcohol. Neither Bert nor Theodore liked him, although they accepted him on May's behalf.[12] Every Christmas, Bert sent May a check for $250, to make sure that the family remained solvent. During the 1920s, the Leavitts moved from California to Clarksdale, Arizona. Their son, Van Ness, was a year younger than his cousin Allan. Like most of the Hoover men, he had a strong mechanical bent, but he refused to go to college to study engineering, which disappointed his mother and uncles.

Lou's sister Jean was adjusting to her life as a single mother. Lou had recruited her for the Girl Scout movement, and with Lou's encouragement, Jean wrote a book for girls entitled *Nancy Goes Girl Scouting*. With the help of one of Lou's friends who was an editor at Doubleday Page, it was published and sold well enough to inspire Jean to write two further books along the same lines.

Jean's daughter Janet was now fifteen, ready to enter high school. Lou and Jean were worried about her friends, and the large number of college boys she would encounter if she attended high school in Palo Alto. Lou suggested that Jean send Janet to Washington, where she could live at 2300 S Street and attend the Holton Arms School. She did so, but at the end of the year, Lou declared herself dissatisfied with the results. She wrote to her friend Katherine Everts, who was now running an arts academy in Vermont, and arranged for Janet to attend there from 1928 to 1929. Meanwhile, Lou had convinced Jean to send Del east, too, and enroll him at Mercersburg Academy in Pennsylvania, a prep school that had been recommended to her by one of her friends, White House doctor Joel T. Boone.

As young Herbert became a father and Allan settled into college life, the older Hoovers moved relentlessly forward across the invisible line dividing one generation from another. 1924 saw both Hoovers attain their fiftieth birthdays. Within the next four years, their sons and most of their nieces and nephews would leave home to make lives for themselves, many of them marrying and having children of their own. At the same time, the members of Lou's parents' generation were becoming fewer in number. Her mother was dead, as was her father's youngest brother, Addison Henry. Her father celebrated his eightieth birthday in 1925, a significant milestone for the times. In June 1927 her mother's sister Jennie Mager died in California, where she was visiting her sister Jessie (who had moved to Los Angeles with her husband, Ed Jones, in 1924) and her niece Jean. Jennie's will named Lou as one of the trustees of her estate. Half her money went to her sister Jessie, the other half (in trust) to her brother Wallace, who had been in ill health for several years. Lou arranged for Wallace and his wife, Lillian, to receive regular payments out of the interest from the trust, advancing the first payment from her own funds until the will was probated.

These signs of the passage of time do not seem to have affected Lou's zest for life. She was working at full tilt, for the Girl Scouts, the NAAF Women's Division, and numerous lesser endeavors. She was, in fact, at the peak of her powers. She surrounded herself with young people, but old friends were not neglected. Her social life was as frenetic as ever. In a November 1926 letter, Lou informs her secretary Martha Noyes that forty women (the members of the Girl Scout national board of directors) will be coming to dinner at 2300 S Street, and three of them will stay overnight. However, because Mr. Hoover has invited their old friends the Kelloggs to stay also, the house will be crowded. As Lou cannot return until the last minute, she asks Martha to oversee the preparations, with the assistance of Ellis Sampson, the butler, and Mary Rattley, the cook—to whom she also wrote letters with explicit instructions for the meal.

In 1925 Leon and Agnes Thompson joined the Hoover's staff. Leon had first met the Hoovers when he was working as a steward on the Navigation Bureau's yacht, the *Kilkenny*, which the secretary of commerce and his family often used for weekend cruises. Teenaged Allan especially enjoyed these outings. Now Leon became assistant butler, and Agnes became Lou's personal maid, replacing Carrie Butler, who had left the Hoover household when she married in 1924.

Lou sent Agnes to a hairdressing school in New York, and she became especially skilled at dressing Lou's hair, now a silvery white and worn in a coil on the back of her head, with side combs at the temples to keep stray locks in place. Lou was philosophical about her prematurely gray hair. She once remarked that people often told her she resembled her grandmother, Mary Ann Henry. That might be so, she said, but Mary Ann had kept her black hair well into her seventies, while her own had started to fade as early as 1917. Though she had worn her hair short as a child, Lou was not tempted to "bob" it in the new fashion. And while she shortened her skirts gradually in accordance with the styles of the times, she objected to women wearing trousers except when hiking or riding horseback. She wore shoes that were fashionable but "sensible," comfortable enough to be able to stand in for hours at parties or to walk several blocks down the street in good weather.

With the Dolemans' return to Washington in 1927, Lou was again in need of servants for the Palo Alto house. Carrie Butler and her new husband, Bland Massenberg, agreed to take the job. Lou wrote to Allan, now a twenty-year-old college student and living in the Palo Alto house, with instructions on how to supervise them. "You will have to see that Carrie and Bland keep the whole place clean, cook the way you want, serve and answer the door nicely, and dress more or less correctly," she told him. He must not be "too criticial of the way they do it,— but explain either that *you* happen to like the other way *better*,—or that you think I would."[13] Carrie, who had grown up in the Hoover house, knew how Lou liked things done, but Bland and his new employers did not get along, and after a year the Massenbergs quit. In their place Lou hired a Belgian couple, Frank and Marie Franquet, who took care of the house from 1928 to 1933.

In 1927 a group of congressmen's wives put together a cookbook. They asked Lou to write the foreword. She was the only contributor who credited her cook, Mary Rattley, with the recipes she submitted for mushroom soup, spoon bread, and sweet potatoes with marshmallows.

Young Herbert's health improved, enabling him to complete his course at Harvard's business school. On November 11, 1927, Herbert Hoover III (commonly known as Pete) was born in Boston. Lou enjoyed having her grandchildren relatively close by. It was a pleasure to have them come to Washington for the holidays, or to run up to Boston to see them after a Girl Scout meeting in New York. She missed Allan intensely. He received a steady stream of chatty, loving letters written by his mother in the mornings as Agnes brushed and arranged her hair. She was particularly concerned about his expressed interest in learning to fly an airplane. Although Charles Lindbergh was a good friend of the Hoovers, who had known his father, and was a frequent visitor at 2300 S Street, Lou believed airplanes were dangerous. She reminded Allan that one of Bert's young aides had died recently when his small plane crashed. When Allan decided not to become a pilot, his mother was deeply relieved.

Except for a wistful desire to live in California rather than Washington, Lou seemed to have her life well under control as the end of the decade came into view. But events were conspiring to offer her a still greater challenge.

On August 2, 1927, Calvin Coolidge issued a formal statement declaring that he did "not choose to run for President in 1928." These cryptic words turned Lou Henry Hoover's life upside-down.

Chapter 11

The White House Beckons

For the past eight years, Bert's friends had been urging him to run for president. Gradually, he had come to accept the idea. As secretary of commerce, he had worked hard to streamline his agencies and to promote a more efficient lifestyle for Americans. As a progressive Republican in the old Theodore Roosevelt tradition, he was dismayed by Calvin Coolidge's conservative approach to politics. Although he had little support among the party's leadership, he was not concerned. He had been a fighter all his life, and so far had managed to succeed—often against the odds—at everything he had set his mind to do. When Coolidge announced, from his Rapid City, South Dakota, summer home in 1927, that he did "not choose to run," Herbert Hoover was ready to step forward as his successor.

Lou was less pleased at this development. Edgar Rickard would recall that Bert only discussed his political plans in those early days when Lou was not in the room. In January she wrote her sons, "affairs are going with uncanny rapidity towards making your Daddy President. Even he is perfectly amazed at it, and sometimes says it just does not seem possible that it can all be happening on its own impetus, and practically without any effort on his part."[1] This is undoubtedly naive, since Bert was certainly working very hard toward that goal, though he may not have admitted as much to his wife.

The whole concept of deliberately seeking election to the highest elective position in the land bothered Lou. Some years later, she chided a would-be biographer for encouraging "each little boy to think it is a wonderful thing to *be* the President, —and that he may *succeed* to that position himself! . . . We want our Presidents to be chosen for that post because they have succeeded in doing worthwhile things elsewhere,—in doing things successfully that are a preparation for what we think we need of them from the White House. (And which we trust we will empower them to do when we have elected them there!) Isn't it better to encourage them to do things together for their country from many simple positions, rather than be striving each to attain the one post considered highest? Isn't it better, in other words, to encourage our young people in *fellowship*, in achieving for the country's good by all pulling together, shoulder to shoulder, rather than to strive for '*leadership*,'—as seems to have become the too frequent watchword to this last generation!"[2]

Nevertheless—as always—Lou gave her husband her unconditional support. She wrote to her son Allan, describing "this *game* of Daddy's. . . . It is very important, and we are all helping whenever and where-ever we can, sometimes at tremendous cost to us."[3] She warned him that there might be "whispered accusations" against his father, but he was not to worry about them. "Just deny them calmly and humorously to your friends, and don't under any circumstances be lured into anything more than flat denials to anything that might savor of publicity."[4]

Lou threw herself into Bert's presidential campaign with the same energy she had applied to every other task he had asked of her through the years. The Hoover name, which during the war years had been synonymous with efficiency and relief for the poor, had been burnished again in 1927 when Bert was put in charge of directing relief efforts following a massive flood in the Mississippi River basin. The newspapers had been full of reports of the tent cities the government had set up to shelter the homeless. Herbert Hoover was everywhere, it seemed. Calvin Coolidge soon began to regret having appointed him to the job.

Lou accompanied her husband on campaign trips, listening approvingly to his speeches, awkwardly presented as they were—for Bert had never been a good public speaker. He read his speeches with his head down, right hand jingling the coins in his pocket, speaking clearly but not passionately. "I always feel," Lou wrote Bert's cousin Edna Heald McCoy, "that people are working *not for* Bert—but for the principles for which he and they stand, and for what they consider his ability to carry out such principles in our country, with their cooperation."[5]

In 1928 it didn't matter whether he was a charismatic speaker or not. The people loved him. They knew, thanks to the fulsome biographies by his friends Vernon Kellogg and Will Irwin, that Hoover was a "Master of Emergencies"—the title of a film Will Irwin produced—and were assured by Madison Avenue maven Bruce Barton and newsman Henry Sell that no one could run the country more effectively than Herbert Hoover. They believed him when he said that "we shall soon with the help of God be in sight of the day when poverty will be banished from this nation."

It was traditional at that time for the nominee-to-be not to attend the party convention, held in June of that year in Kansas City. Allan managed to wangle an invitation from one of his father's colleagues to watch the proceedings, abandoning his studies (and suffering a drop in his grades) to do so. After the party had made its choice, seventy thousand people jammed into the Stanford football stadium on August 11, 1928, to hear Herbert Hoover accept the Republican nomination for president of the United States.

In the midst of all this excitement, Lou heard from her sister that Charles Henry had become ill while on a trip with her into the mountains in early July. Back in Monterey, he had rallied, sitting up and smoking. But at 5:30 A.M. on July 18, just three days short of his eighty-third birthday, he suffered a fatal stroke. Jean and Allan were with him. Lou and Bert hurried to Palo Alto for the funeral, held in Stanford's University Chapel, where young Herbert had been married only three years before.

Lou had little time to grieve for the man who had meant more to her than anyone except her husband. Once Bert's nomination was official, the campaigning went into high gear. Lou traveled around the country with her husband, adding her gracious image to his. In August, she received an honorary doctorate of literature from Whittier College in Whittier, California. In September she arranged for Uncle Will to have a radio installed in his home in Wahpeton on his birthday, so that he could listen to the campaign news. On October 24 she reported that "Madison Square Garden was a wonderful sight," the night of her husband's New York speech, "with each of the 20,000 persons waving a flag, and the enthusiastic applause and cheering and singing being such as only New York can give!"[6]

Ten thousand people met the train bringing the Hoovers to Palo Alto on November 5, 1928, where they would cast their votes at the Women's Club house of the Stanford Union. As the votes rolled in on November 6, the family gathered together—Allan and Herbert Jr. and his family were there, as well as a large group of friends—to listen as the returns came in on the radio. Jean Henry Large, who had returned to Washington in September to put her children back in school, played hostess at 2300 S Street to the Hoovers' Washington friends.

Dorothy Bowen, a graduate student at Stanford that year, wrote of that evening: "It was so close all afternoon that by six o'clock we were standing on our ears. Then we dashed to dinner, dashed back to the radio, dashed to our rooms . . . and to the basketball pavilion to hear [John Philip] Sousa's band. . . . It was Sousa's seventy-fourth birthday. . . . When the concert was over, a youth stepped up on the platform and read us Smith's telegram to Hoover. Then there was a general stampede for automobiles. Sousa and his band led the way. . . . Faculty members and other privileged souls stood along the various levels of roof and looked down into the courtyard. We Stanford roughs and other of the proletariate [*sic*] banked the hillside opposite the house. The band stood in the courtyard and played. . . . Presently Hoover, looking very mild and very solemn and very neat, but all-in-all extremely dependable and pleasant and dignified, came through the front door, and then the elements—in the form of the Stanford roughs and others—broke loose. And it was all, so much of it, a Stanford thing. . . . So after our yell leaders had led a yell for 'President Hoover,' we gave a Stanford skyrocket and 'Six for Mrs. Hoover.' Presently the Hoovers went inside and appeared again amidst the crowd on the roof, so that we could see them better. Sousa struck up the Stars and Stripes Forever and then the Star Spangled Banner; and it was the first time that that worthy song ever really thrilled me. . . . And after that there was Auld Lang Syne. Then everything was very quiet and the band went away, and from the hillside and the courtyard and the roofs came our own song, 'Where the Rolling Foothills Rise, Up Toward Mountains Higher.' We all sang. . . . Then Mrs. Hoover said, 'I thank you all for coming here,' and we went away."[7]

Herbert Hoover had been elected by 58 percent of the popular vote, a stunning victory for the orphan boy from West Branch, Iowa. Resigned to giving up the next four years of her life to a busy round of social commitments and public appearances, his wife smiled proudly and cheered with the rest.

Not wanting to embarrass his predecessor by his presence in Washington between the election in November and the inauguration in March, Hoover undertook a six-week goodwill tour of South America, leaving from California a few weeks after his victory at the polls. Lou and Allan went with him. Former Undersecretary of State Henry P. Fletcher and prominent California lawyer John Mott were members of the official party. Twenty members of the press were aboard, including the Hoovers' friends Will Irwin and Mark Sullivan. Lou's new secretary Ruth Fesler also joined them.

Sailing down the west coast of Central America on the battleship *Maryland*, they made brief stops in El Salvador, Honduras, Nicaragua, Costa Rica, Ecuador, and Peru. When they reached Chile, they disembarked to cross the Andes by train. Ruth Fesler remarked on how surprised and delighted the children in the crowds were when Lou smiled and waved back at them as the American entourage passed. They were apparently unaccustomed to having visiting dignitaries notice them.

There were a few awkward moments. Some of the Central American ports were so small that the big American battleship could not reach the dock. When this happened, a launch was lowered from the ship to ferry the passengers ashore. To get from the launch to the dock, the passengers sometimes had to jump. In Ecuador the party could not get ashore at all, so the Ecuadoran president came out to the ship to see them. At the border between Chile and Argentina, they had to change trains because the trains in the two countries were built to different gauges. The most unnerving episode occurred as they reached the train station in Buenos Aires. An unruly crowd surged around the party, tearing the coat of Argentina's President Irigoyen. Surrounded by naval aides, the Hoovers were distressed but unharmed, and the remainder of their visit passed without further incident. From Argentina, they went on to Uruguay and Brazil before boarding the battleship *Utah* to return to the United States.

Despite these occasional contretemps, the party had a wonderful time. Politicians and press mingled in happy camaraderie. Lou wrote to her nephew Del about the "menagerie" on the USS *Maryland*: a baby wildcat, a monkey, parakeets and parrots belonging to various members of the crew. As they crossed the equator, Allan had his face painted black and was thrown into a tank of water in the navy's traditional King Neptune ceremony. Later, as they crossed the Andes, Lou the geologist pointed out unusual rock formations to her fellow passengers.

The Hoovers reached the United States at the end of January, and proceeded to Florida for a few weeks' fishing at the J. C. Penney estate on Long Key. The Rickards and the Charles Lindberghs were fellow guests. Lou brought her movie camera and Kodak along, taking pictures of her family and friends as they enjoyed these last days of private life. In mid-February they boarded the train for Washington.

In later years Herbert Jr. would confide to his cousin Hulda McLean that his father's election to the presidency was the worst thing that ever happened to the family. Certainly no challenge Lou Henry Hoover had yet faced could equal the ordeal she would endure during the four years of her husband's term in office. The extensive entertaining, the severe illness of her older son, the lack of privacy and the steadily increasing criticism of her husband's economic policies by the press would test her strength and courage as never before.

Herbert Hoover was elected president at the height of the most economically progressive era in the nation's history. Except for a persistent farm depression, Americans had never known such physical well-being. Business was booming, churning out increasing volumes of merchandise to be enthusiastically purchased by consumers with more spending money in their pockets than ever before. Automobiles, airplanes, washing machines, refrigerators, vacuum cleaners, even air conditioners and televisions (in their earliest forms) were transforming the lives of ordinary Americans into something their grandparents could not have imagined. Herbert Hoover had managed to identify himself with this prosperity to such an extent that when it ended abruptly, eight months into his term of office, the nation felt that it must be his fault, as if he had offered a child a piece of candy and then inexplicably taken it away.

It would have taken a crystal ball to see this in the wake of the 1928 election, however. Immediately after returning to Washington in February 1929, Lou set about preparing for the inauguration festivities. She arranged housing with her neighbors on S Street for the many out-of-town friends and relatives who planned to attend. Others, like her sister Jean, Bert's sister May, and Uncle Will Henry and his Native American ward Mary Paul, would stay in the White House itself. There were receptions and teas to arrange and to attend. The Rickards came down from New York early, and Abbie met with Alida Henriques to discuss staffing needs for the White House. It was Abbie who recommended Ava Long, who had previously worked for a wealthy family on Long Island, as housekeeper for the White House.

At last Inauguration Day dawned, a cold and rainy day such as only March can produce. By the time the outdoor ceremony at the Capitol was over, both Bert and Lou were soaked to the skin. They went on to the White House, where they hosted a buffet luncheon for 1,800 guests in the State Dining Room. They then went back out into the cold drizzle to the reviewing stand, where they stood for over an hour watching the official inaugural parade pass by. Once the parade was over, tea was held for the governors of all the states and their staffs—another 1,500 people, all eager to shake the new President's hand. The Hoovers did not, however, attend that evening's Inaugural Day Charity Ball. Vice President Charles Curtis presided over it in their place.

It did not take the Hoovers long to settle into their new surroundings. They kept on most of the previous White House staff, including Chief Usher Irwin "Ike" Hoover (no relation to the president), who had overseen the behind-the-scenes operations of the White House for nearly forty years. They also kept the Irish head cook, Katherine Bruckner. Their longtime cook at 2300 S Street, Mary Rattley, who was elderly and not in the best of health, felt that the White House job would be too much for her to handle. But others from 2300 S Street did come with the Hoovers to the White House, including Ellis Sampson, the butler, his assistant Leon Thompson, Leon's wife, Agnes, and Bert's valet, Kosta Boris. Agnes Thompson, who was pregnant during the winter of 1928–29, had assumed Lou would not want her in the White House in her condition. Lou, however, saw no problem. She allowed Agnes to use the elevator, and even let her work shorter hours so that she could spend time with her other children at home.

Lou had a clear vision of how the White House, as the residence of the nation's highest executive, should be run. The service should be impeccable, the food of the highest quality, the entertainment first class and representative of the nation's best talents. The decor should combine comfort with elegance, and at the same time reflect the historical significance of the building itself. She informed the staff of her expectations, and made it clear that her wishes were to be obeyed to the letter. "Each detail had to be as precise as a ritual," recalled Alonzo Fields, one of the White House butlers.[8]

There were some difficult moments as the staff adjusted to its new employers, but on the whole the household ran smoothly—much more so than popular belief (based on ghost-written memoirs by staff members, many of them published during the intensely anti-Hoover years of the early Roosevelt administration) would suggest. The Thompsons were not the only servants whom Lou treated with special consideration. When one of the butlers developed tuberculosis, Lou contacted the director of the asylum where he was staying and told him that if he couldn't take proper care of her employee, she would have him replaced by someone who could. She also hired the man's wife as a maid. Another butler, who suffered from ulcers, had milk and cream delivered to his home at Mrs. Hoover's expense.

Lillian Rogers Parks, a young polio victim whose mother, Maggie Rogers, had worked as a White House maid since 1909, was hired to do sewing. Lillian was allowed to ride in the presidential elevator and often given special treats, including cookies from the White House Christmas tree. Asked in an interview in 1971 why her book, *Thirty Years Backstairs at the White House*, was so critical of the Hoovers, Lillian denied that it was: "I liked Mrs. Hoover for her ways, her kindness, thoughtfulness, and the way she would run the house."[9] Lou Hoover "set the best table" of any first lady she had known, she added, pointing out that the Hoovers themselves paid for much of the food served in the White House. She seemed unaware that her book gave an overall impression that the Hoovers were so preoccupied with their own affairs—Bert with government, Lou with entertaining—that they were oblivious to the feelings of their servants.

Perhaps the most devastating criticism, from Lou's viewpoint, came from the posthumously published book, *Forty-Two Years in the White House*, by Ike Hoover, the chief usher. Ike Hoover, who died six months after the Hoovers left the White House in 1933, had only completed his manuscript through the Taft administration. The remainder was assembled by a ghost-writer from notes the chief usher had made. Although Ike Hoover occasionally resisted Lou's efforts to change the way things were done—"The Hoovers came in and upset the whole private part of the house"[10]–he had always gotten along well with his employers. A note from him to the Hoovers dated May 8, 1933, says, "The situation here is as different as day from night. We miss you all every hour. . . . Personally, I am not very happy."[11]

His book described the Hoovers as "dictatorial" and hard to work for. It claimed that Bert surrounded himself with "Yes-Men," preferring to talk only with people who agreed with his point of view. Lou objected vigorously to these comments. "I do not feel that such an agglomeration of utterly petty and uninteresting detail was arranged for publication by our old friend," she wrote to Grace Coolidge.[12] The general opinion among the Hoovers and their friends was that the chief usher's wife, needing the money, had allowed the ghost writer to twist things from her husband's notes into something that would make the book more lucrative. The Hoovers were not the only ones to suffer from his pen. His description of Calvin Coolidge sulking in his bedroom at the White House on the night that the Republican Party nominated Herbert Hoover for President hardly shows Silent Cal at his best.

According to Agnes Thompson, neither of the Hoovers ever made a sharp or critical comment to anyone. They always said "please" and "thank you"; if they didn't like the way you were doing something, they would quietly suggest you do it differently. Ruth Fesler agreed. "At times I could sense their displeasure,"[13] she said, but they never expressed it openly. Several servants—Alfred Butler, Ellis Sampson, and the Thompsons among them—remained in the Hoovers' employ for decades, evidently not finding them at all autocratic or unfeeling.

There was, certainly, a degree of arrogance in Lou's nature, the kind of self-assurance often present in strong personalities who have never had reason to doubt that what they want done is the correct thing to do. Edgar Rickard once complained that Lou didn't like for his wife to have other plans when Lou was in town, and her niece Hulda observed that when Lou tapped her foot, you knew something was wrong, and "someone had better change course."[14] The White House staff resented being asked to stay out of sight when guests were passing through the halls, or having to respond to silent signals from Lou while serving meals. But though Lou was sure of her own convictions, she was also tolerant of others' opinions, never self-righteous, and always able to put others at ease. It was her habitual reticence and reluctance to share her inner thoughts and feelings with others that made some observers consider her aloof.

Lou brought two secretaries with her to the White House. Mildred Hall had been working for her since the fall of 1927, but as the presidential campaign got under way in 1928, Lou realized that she would need a second secretary. Ruth Fesler had formerly worked for Vernon Kellogg in the Food Administration. She had taken graduate courses at George Washington University and hoped to enter the Foreign Service, which was just beginning to hire women on a professional level. When Ruth did not receive the Foreign Service appointment, Lou asked if she would come and help with her growing correspondence. Ruth agreed. Mildred Hall dealt primarily with Lou's personal correspondence, while Ruth Fesler handled organizational matters.

At first Lou also used Mary Randolph, who had been Grace Coolidge's social secretary, to deal with social correspondence and planning. However, Mary preferred a more formal routine than Lou was accustomed to. The Hoover habit of changing plans at the last minute irritated her, and after a few months, she resigned. After Mary's departure Lou took over the planning function of the social secretary's job herself. She hired another young woman, Doris Goss, to deal with the White House social correspondence. Lou paid the salaries of all three secretaries herself.

"You know," Lou once said, "I've never yet seen a room I didn't want to do something *to*."[15] The White House was filled with such rooms. Lillian Parks recalled that "Mrs. Hoover was always moving furniture around,"[16] as she and Bert worked out which of the private rooms they wanted to use for what purpose. Bedrooms became drawing rooms or studies, and former studies became bedrooms. Bert had the bookcases removed in the former presidential study, only to find that the walls had not been painted behind them. While the walls were being painted, he changed his mind about using the room as a study, and it became a drawing room instead.

The room Bert finally chose for his study had been a presidential study for presidents from Adams through McKinley, but since Theodore Roosevelt's time it had been used as a bedroom. Lou had found a painting that showed Lincoln signing the Emancipation Proclamation in this room. Bert was delighted; he liked the idea of using Lincoln's study as his own. While poking around in the storage rooms in the attic, Lou located many of the furnishings from Lincoln's day which appeared in the painting. She returned them to the study, and hung the painting there as well.

Although Lou was the lady of the house, she was not entirely free to decorate the White House to her own taste. During the Coolidge administration, a committee had been formed to redecorate the state rooms, then looking somewhat seedy. With Mrs. Coolidge's cooperation, the committee had suggested an American Colonial decor, inspired by the American Wing of the Metropolitan Museum of Art. Coolidge himself—possibly concerned about the potential cost of such an overhauling of the decor—sent the committee packing, but it had not disbanded, nor given up hope of someday being able to implement its plans. One of the committee's leading members was Mrs. Harold I. (Harriet) Pratt, whose husband, a prominent capitalist and trustee of the Pratt Institute, had established a fund to purchase furnishings for the White House. Harriet Pratt had served on the national board of the Girl Scouts when Lou first became involved with that organization. This provided the two women with common ground.

Lou met with the committee to discuss its proposals. Although she allowed it to go ahead with its plans for the Green Room—one of the state reception rooms located on the first floor—she did not sympathize with the committee's vision for the White House. The furnishings it purchased (or donated from its members' own personal collections) were reproduction eighteenth and nineteenth century pieces. None of them had ever been used in the White House, nor did they resemble furnishings that were in style in the building's earlier days. A large cut-glass chandelier, bought in England, was hung over a custom-made rug patterned with the presidential seal. The walls were covered with silk damask, and matching draperies hung in the windows.

While the committee was busy in the Green Room, Lou took the full-length portrait of George Washington by Gilbert Stuart and hung it in the East Room, balancing it with the equally large painting of Martha Washington that had been painted for President Hayes. The Washington portrait was the same one saved by Dolley Madison in 1814 when the White House was set afire by British troops. The two portraits still hang together in the East Room, the largest reception room in the White House.

One day, while visiting Fredericksburg, Virginia, Lou stopped in at the recently established James Monroe Law Office Museum. Among the items in the museum's collection was a suite of French furniture purchased by Monroe in Paris when he was minister there during the Washington administration. Determining that these chairs, tables, and the desk on which Monroe was said to have penned his Monroe Doctrine were actually used in the White House, Lou had them reproduced at her own expense. The reproductions were placed in the upstairs room known as the Rose Parlor. Monroe's descendants donated a small tea table and a terra cotta vase that Monroe had used in the White House, and Lou had the portrait of Mrs. Monroe dressed in black velvet, which hung in the Smithsonian, copied to hang on the parlor's wall.

Lou had always had a strong interest in history. She was thrilled to be living in such an historical building. Her success with the Lincoln and Monroe rooms inspired her to do further research into the old house's historic furnishings, which had never before been catalogued. In 1930 Lou enlisted Dare Stark McMullin (recently divorced from her "young rascal" of a husband) to help her identify and catalogue all the antiques in the White House. For the next three years, Dare rummaged through the pantries and attics of the White House, and searched the records of the officer in charge of public buildings (then a branch of the Army Corps of Engineers). With the assistance of the Corps of Engineers, she had each object photographed and listed in her inventory. When she was finished, Dare wrote a book about the White House furnishings, but it was not finished when the Hoovers left the White House in 1933, and was never published.

Lou Hoover was an inveterate collector. In addition to the Chinese pottery and the guns she had brought back from China and Europe's World War I battlefields, she had an extensive pewter collection. Now she began to collect prints of the White House and the Capitol building. Friends and aides, knowing of her interest, frequently sent her such prints that they had found in antique stores or stationery shops. Lou framed several of them to hang on the wall at the east end of the long corridor on the second floor of the White House.

Another innovation was the installation of moving picture projection equipment in the Oval Parlor. One of the major motion picture studios donated the equipment and paid to have it installed. The Hoovers loved movies, and Lou frequently carried a home movie camera to record family events. Guests who stayed at the White House were often entertained with first-run films as well as Lou's own productions.

The Hoover White House had a number of resident pets. There were caged birds in the Oval Parlor, a couple of cats and several dogs who lived on the grounds. The Hoovers' beloved Belgian shepherd, Tut, who had been left at 2300 S Street, died in October 1929. But now they had Pat, a German shepherd, and in 1931 they would acquire Weegie, a Norwegian elkhound. The dogs liked to wait for the president each morning at the entrance to the west wing. They would sit quietly, side by side, watching the door intently until he appeared, knowing that when he emerged, he would throw a ball for them for several minutes before going on to the executive office building. The chief usher claimed, however, that the dogs belonged more to Lou than to Bert, who had very little time for them. Weegie won a particularly warm place in her heart.

Having by now spent nearly ten years in Washington, the Hoovers were familiar with the capital's social and political routines, and with its often oppressive climate. They decided to invest in a weekend hideaway, close enough to Washington that the president could return quickly in an emergency, but far enough away to achieve the rustic simplicity they both enjoyed. The site they chose was on the upper Rapidan River in Virginia's Blue Ridge Mountains. Twenty-five hundred feet above sea level, the 164 acres of pristine woodland was eminently suitable for hiking, camping, and fishing.

With the help of James Rippin, architect husband of the Girl Scouts' national director, who had designed camps for the Girl Scouts in New York, Lou created Camp Rapidan. The cluster of log cabins, each with its deep porch and large stone fireplace, was built at the Hoovers' personal expense. Its Filipino mess staff was seconded from the presidential yacht, the *Mayflower*. A company of marines provided security. A road was built so that the president (who, unlike his wife, disliked riding horses or mules) could reach it by car. Hoover also built a series of dams along the river to make trout pools, where he could indulge in his favorite form of relaxation. He firmly believed that "all men are equal before fish."[17]

The Hoovers escaped to Camp Rapidan nearly every weekend, enjoying the quiet woods and the evenings around a roaring campfire, where Lou regaled visitors with ghost stories and tales of pioneer days. "Mrs. Hoover herself quite obviously enjoys the process of the tale's unfolding," wrote her friend Charlotte Kellogg in the *Saturday Evening Post*, "elaborating her background with an artist's love for each detail of color or pattern, uncovering essentials in character and situation, winding on from point to point of humor or surprise with relish. Her characteristic stories are merry ones, for her outlook on life is joyous."[18] Lou usually had her knitting with her, or one of her cameras. She didn't care for games, except perhaps solitaire, and never observed conventions at bridge, then a highly popular party activity.

Although the camp was intended as a retreat, the Hoovers rarely went there alone. Friends, aides, visiting dignitaries were regular guests. And rustic though it was, Lou made sure that the cabins were provided with the necessary comforts: indoor plumbing, hot water, electricity. "It is just as complete as the White House is as a place of residence," reported Chief Usher Ike Hoover, following his first (and only) visit to the place in 1931. "There is not a detail lacking."[19] Meals were prepared by the *Mayflower*'s Filipino cook. A typical weekend's menu included bread brought from Washington, flapjacks and dumplings, ham, bacon, fresh fish and game. Hardtack, tinned meat, and jerky were also kept on hand.

The drive from Washington took three hours (Lou usually made it in two and a half) along a good, but winding, two-lane highway that went as far as Criglersville, the nearest town. From there, another eight miles of unpaved mountain road led to the camp. Lou liked to drive her Cadillac the whole way, but confessed that most guests preferred to leave their cars in Criglersville and ride the rest of the way in the camp's Ford.

As the pressures of state built up, the Hoovers came to prize this hideaway more and more. "I have almost had to make a rule not to make engagements for Sundays and leave that time for being with my husband, and whenever we can manage it to get him into the country," Lou wrote a friend in April 1930.[20] A direct telephone line connected the camp with the White House, permitting the workaholic president to enjoy his weekends without guilt. These were perhaps the only times he was able to relax.

Though Lou accepted her own Secret Service escort only grudgingly, she had no doubt about her husband's need for protection. White House security had developed over the years and was now well established. Guards stationed at the main entrance to the White House checked the credentials of everyone who entered, and Secret Service agents accompanied the president and his wife when they left the building and patrolled the halls when they were at home. It was therefore a shock when one evening, shortly after the Hoovers moved into the White House, a strange man walked into the dining room where the president was entertaining several guests. As he approached the table, the president looked up and asked, "What do you want?"

"I want to see you," the man replied.

"I have no appointment with you," said the president.

"You better have an appointment with me!" said the man, coming nearer. He stretched out his hand as if to shake the president's.

At this point, one of the butlers (who had been out of the room) entered. Lou told him to call a Secret Service man. Another butler took hold of the man and pushed him toward the door. There he was taken into custody by the guards, who had heard the commotion in the dining room and rushed in to find out what was happening.

The man proved to be a harmless sightseer, who had been walking along Pennsylvania Avenue, found himself in front of the White House, and simply strolled in through a door that had been left open because it was a warm evening. As he was well dressed and wore neither hat nor overcoat, the guards at the door had assumed he was a Secret Service man and let him pass unchallenged. He was released with a warning. The two policemen who had been on duty at the door that night were transferred, and the incident was not repeated.

Hoover later remarked that such a situation had never occurred in all his years at 2300 S Street. Now, when he was supposedly guarded on all sides, a stranger had found his way into the White House with no difficulty.[21]

By the end of her first summer in the White House, Lou had her domestic arrangements fairly well in hand. Now she was able to give her full attention to the job she felt the First Lady was primarily called upon to perform: entertaining guests and visitors on the President's behalf.

Chapter 12

A First Lady's Duty
Is to Entertain

Although Lou had been entertaining on a regular basis for many years, the White House social schedule presented new challenges. In addition to the friends and associates the Hoovers were accustomed to entertaining, there was a regular program of official dinners and receptions, with guest lists of between fifty and one hundred people, and still more attended the musicales that often followed. Diplomatic receptions ran into the hundreds. Distant relatives and vague acquaintances—sometimes even total strangers—wrote to solicit invitations to White House events. Although there was now a government subsidy for official dinners, passed by President Taft (who did not, however, get to enjoy the benefit of it), Lou frequently supplemented it from her own funds. "Mrs. Hoover just reveled in elaborate menus, both for their private table and for company," reported the chief usher.[1]

Washington's official social season ran from the first Tuesday in December until the beginning of Lent, but White House entertaining continued through most of the year. As first lady, Lou was expected to serve as hostess for official dinners and teas, represent the president at formal events that he could not attend (such as the launching of a ship), supervise the White House staff, entertain a steady stream of house guests, and during the social season, host or attend the nine to ten large annual receptions and numerous weekly dinners that tradition prescribed. When Bert, who detested mass gatherings, suggested that they might consider cutting down on the number of official receptions, Lou refused. It was part of their job, she maintained, and she did not want to appear snobbish by limiting the number of people allowed to shake the hands of the president and his wife, even though her hand often became swollen by the end of the evening. In order to talk more intimately with the wives of the diplomatic corps, she instituted a series of small teas as an alternative to the huge diplomatic reception, an innovation that was much appreciated.

Although she had been one of Washington's more popular hostesses in her own sphere, Lou was not a "society woman." She was not interested in fashion or society gossip. Perle Mesta, for years Washington's society maven, found Lou "scholarly and austere," more interested in geology and Girl Scouts than social affairs, at least until she reached the White House. Even then, Ms. Mesta felt that Lou's parties remained disappointingly low-key, although she admitted that the times might have contributed as much to the atmosphere as the hostess.[2] The loss of Mary Randolph as social secretary was more serious than Lou seems to have realized. Mary had been familiar with Washington's accepted social practices, and had diligently cultivated society editors on behalf of the White House. Lou's other secretaries were all young and inexperienced in the ways of Washington society. Despite her energetic efforts to carry out her responsibilities as first lady so as to reflect highly on her husband's administration, Lou never quite succeeded in behaving as Washington expected her to do. As public opinion became increasingly critical of Herbert Hoover, Washington society refused to rally behind his lady. Like the Old Guard of the Republican Party, which hastened to distance itself from the president, society seemed to shrug its collective shoulders and say, "What else can you expect from such people?"

Despite her exalted social position, Lou remained the same informal, unpretentious woman she had always been. She continued to drive her own car, and occasionally did her own shopping. According to Bert, Lou took her role as first lady very seriously, believing that she "must be the symbol of everything wholesome in American life."[3] She had not previously taken a serious interest in clothes, but now she made a special point of being tastefully, if conservatively, dressed. And she took great pains to make sure that White House social affairs ran as smoothly as possible.

Lou also maintained her unflappable attitude toward last-minute changes in plans, and expected her staff to do the same. Ava Long, the housekeeper, told the *Ladies' Home Journal* in 1933, "I thanked heaven that my husband had been the sort of man who felt he could bring home to dinner an unexpected guest or two without precipitating a domestic tragedy!" With this personal experience to draw on, Long was able to deal with a White House in which "we had guests for breakfast, luncheon, tea, dinner and for weekends . . . and . . . we seldom knew how many covers to lay until the last minute."[4] If a dinner suddenly outgrew the intended menu, Lou assumed the cook would be able to come up with alternatives. Once, when a dinner for four suddenly became a party of forty, Ava Long and Katherine Bruckner, the cook, created a dish consisting of croquettes of ham, beef, lamb, and whatever else happened to be in the refrigerator, topped with mushroom sauce and chopped parsley and served on rice. "A distinguished foreign guest asked for the recipe," Ava Long recalled. "Katherine and I went into a huddle, tried to remember what had been in the ice box, and christened the new dish White House Surprise Supreme."[5]

On another occasion, in 1929, 485 people showed up for a tea to which only two hundred had been invited. The Hoovers had planned to leave afterwards for their camp in Virginia, and a picnic supper had been packed in the car. As the guests continued to arrive, the car was unloaded and servants were sent out to the nearby shops for additional supplies. When it was over, Mary Randolph, then still Lou's social secretary, turned to the chief usher and asked him, "Is the housekeeper still alive?"[6]

These frequent, unexpected alterations in plans distressed the staff, and undoubtedly contributed to their later ambivalence about the Hoovers as employers. On the whole, however, they coped with very few complaints. Lou was aware of their feelings, though not especially sympathetic. "It is a funny house downstairs here," she wrote to her sister, "not like 2300, where old Butler or Lucille or almost anyone could stay on and concoct small meals for us in the kitchen! It seems to necessitate three or four cooks here if they can get some soup and a steak and dessert."[7]

One of the first social challenges Lou faced came early in the 1929 season. Dolly Gann, half-sister of the widowed Vice President Charles Curtis, believed that as her brother's official hostess, she was entitled to the same rank as his wife would have held in social gatherings. Alice Roosevelt Longworth, wife of the speaker of the house and daughter of former President Theodore Roosevelt, was the outspoken leader of the faction that challenged Mrs. Gann's claim. Washington gossip was full of the alleged feud between the two women. If they were both to be invited to dinner at the White House at the same time, who would be given the higher ranking, the speaker's wife or the vice president's sister? Lou solved the problem by adding a fifth dinner to the schedule, in honor of the vice president. At this dinner, Mrs. Gann would be the honored female guest. At the speaker's dinner, it would be Mrs. Longworth.

When questioned about her decision, Lou claimed that the Gann-Longworth feud was a media invention. She insisted that it was the prominence of the men involved that had inspired her to make the change. It would have been awkward, she said, to have both the vice president and the speaker of the house at the same dinner. As there were already official dinners for the chief justice, the speaker of the house, the cabinet, and the diplomatic corps, it was clear that the vice president deserved his own dinner as well. The press, firmly convinced of the feud's existence, regarded Lou's solution as a convenient face-saving device. Even Lou's friend Susan Dyer observed that Lou preferred to have the women come at different times "to avoid ill feeling."[8]

A more serious dilemma concerned the series of teas that Lou was expected to give during the spring of 1929 for the wives of congressmen. Among the freshmen representatives that year was Oscar DePriest of Chicago, the first African-American to be elected to Congress in nearly thirty years. The Hoovers were aware that to invite a black woman to the White House for a social event would invite criticism, especially from the Deep South, which had abandoned its traditional Democratic voting pattern to help elect Bert president. Nevertheless, both Bert and Lou always preferred to do what they believed was right, no matter what the consequences. DePriest had been properly elected to Congress. He had every right to be there—and his wife had every right to be invited to the White House with the other congressional wives.

That said, it was nonetheless clear that the tea would have to be very carefully planned. Lou divided her list of guests into five sessions. The first four, held on May 27, May 29, June 4 and June 6, included the majority of congressional wives. The fifth, held on June 12, included only women whom Lou knew she could count on to behave appropriately in this highly sensitive situation. The guest list included three other congressmen's wives—Mrs. Free, Mrs. Clyde Kelly, and Mrs. Bacon—as well as the wife of Attorney General William D. Mitchell. Also invited were James C. Dunn, the state department's chief of protocol, and his wife; Miss Grace Burton, niece of the Ohio senator; Lou's sister, Jean Large; Lou's long-time friend, Gertrude Bowman; and her secretaries, Mary Randolph and Ruth Fesler. Mrs. James W. Good, wife of the secretary of war, poured. The tea was not announced to the press. Lou had the security staff warned not to challenge a black woman who arrived claiming to have been invited to the White House.

At the appointed time, Mrs. DePriest appeared, dressed in a blue georgette dress and wearing a small hat. Dignified, reserved, apparently at ease, she made her way into the Green Room with the others to meet Mrs. Hoover. The Marine Band played under the magnolias outside. After chatting and drinking their tea in the adjoining Red Room, the women left. Several of them, including Mrs. Hoover, shook Mrs. DePriest's hand.

"I remember the butler, Ellis," Ruth Fesler later recalled, "his eyes just popping."[9]

The reaction was swift and very nasty. Newspapers throughout the South headlined their fury at this "degradation" of the White House. On June 18, Senator Thaddeus H. Caraway of Arkansas read into the Congressional record an article from the Washington *Daily News* describing the tea party. Newspapers quoted members of Congress as saying they felt forced to "bow our heads in shame and regret." The Georgia, Texas, and Florida legislatures passed resolutions condemning the first lady's action.

Masses of angry letters and telegrams poured in, addressed to Lou. "It was unfortunate for Mrs. Hoover," Ruth Fesler observed, "that she opened and read them."[10] Although many other letters approved Lou's decision, the criticism "wounded her deeply," according to Bert. He observed that she was "over-sensitive" to the "stabs of political life."[11] To be accused of having "defiled" the White House by supporting the notion of "social equality" between the races was very painful to her.

Lou Hoover's attitude toward African-Americans was fairly advanced for her generation, although she rarely made an effort to reach across the color barrier in her personal relationships. She had grown up in a society that assumed the superiority of white Anglo-Saxons to any other race, and of American Anglo-Saxons to the British variety. Until she moved to Washington, she had not encountered many African-Americans. The one black family she had known in Whittier, California, during her youth had been respectable, but on a different social level from the banker's daughter. Most of her experience with people of other races had been as an employer, except in China, where cultural differences and strict rules of behavior prevented her from making close friendships. She did, however, maintain a lifelong friendship with a Ceylonese woman, Mrs. Tiru-Navuk-Arasu, who was the daughter of a prominent lawyer in Colombo, and a member of that country's ruling class. Lou seems to have been torn between a conscious desire to treat every human being equally, and a subconscious discomfort when dealing with people of another race in social situations. She was always gracious, but her close friendships were always with women of her own background.

Lou's letters sometimes contain condescending comments about the Chinese, Filipinos, Mexicans, and blacks in her employ, and often reflect the stereotyping prevalent in America during the first quarter of the century. Nevertheless, she always treated individuals courteously. Agnes Thompson insisted that there was no racism in the Hoover White House. She felt, however, that Lou's understanding of the condition of blacks in American society was somewhat naive. When the Thompsons went to Florida with the Hoover entourage in early 1929, Lou suggested they go sightseeing. She did not realize, Agnes said later, that there were places where blacks simply could not go. Agnes didn't enlighten her. She was afraid that if she had explained the situation, Lou would have found a way for them to go anyway. This, Agnes feared, could have had unfortunate political repercussions.[12]

Lou Hoover's dilemma was not uncommon for many liberal-minded Americans in her day, when the most virulent forms of racism were openly practiced—and widely accepted—throughout the country. The 1920s saw race riots in northern cities and a revival of the Ku Klux Klan in the Midwest as well as the South. Anti-Semitism was also widespread, and crude jokes about minorities were popular everywhere. Though Lou deplored such behavior, and made a conscious effort to avoid it, she was unable to escape its effects completely.

After a few weeks, the storm roused by the DePriest tea party blew over. Washington emptied for the summer, and those—like the Hoovers—who remained behind resumed their normal lives.

One of the things Lou enjoyed about being first lady was the freedom it gave her to indulge her passion for music. Although she was not musically gifted like her sister Jean—Lou played no instrument and sang only reluctantly, and not altogether tunefully—she loved to listen to good music. She once confided to Allan that the thing she had missed most during her years of traveling early in the century was the opportunity to hear good music. There were no phonographs then, and live concerts were only available when they were in Europe or America. Once settled in Washington, Lou became a member of the Washington Fine Arts Society. She had helped to arrange concerts for the Pro Arte Quartet of Brussels, one of the world's finest ensembles, in 1926, and was a guarantor for the Washington Opera Company during its early years.

With the assistance of Henry Junge, an agent for Steinway & Sons, who had been arranging musicales in the White House since the days of Theodore Roosevelt, Lou brought many of the world's eminent musicians to Washington to play for her guests. A typical musicale, following a state dinner, included thirty minutes of performance by two artists before an audience of between 150 and 200 in the spacious East Room. Among those featured at the White House between 1929 and 1933 were Vladimir Horowitz, Jascha Heifetz, Rosa Ponselle, Gregor Piatigorsky, Carlos Salzedo, and the Gordon String Quartet.

When Vladimir Horowitz appeared at the White House on January 8, 1931, the immensely talented young Russian pianist was worried about his poor command of the English language. Henry Junge advised him, "Just say, 'I am delighted,' and nothing more when you pass through the receiving line." The grateful Horowitz tried to follow Junge's advice. As he greeted the waiting dignitaries, he dutifully exclaimed, "I am delightful! I am delightful!" The amused dignitaries presumably agreed.[13]

Lou especially enjoyed furthering the careers of young American artists, such as baritone Lawrence Tibbett (from Bakersfield, California), harpist Mildred Dilling (from Marion, Indiana), and harpsichordist Lewis Richards (from St. Johns, Michigan). In 1930 she invited Chief Yowlache of the Yakima tribe of Washington state to sing for her guests. The chief, who had a magnificent voice, sang not only Indian chants but also Italian operatic arias, to the enchantment of his audience. Although they had to pass Henry Junge's strict auditions, many aspiring unknowns were also granted their moment of fame in the East Room. One of these was Frank Bishop, a pianist from Detroit, whose wife, Claire Huchet Bishop, was one of Lou's protégées from the war years. Born in France, Claire had studied at Stanford after the war on a CRB scholarship, and later worked with Lou's friend Mrs. John Griffiths in establishing children's libraries in Brussels and Paris. Although not a world-class talent, Frank Bishop was able to use the connections he made with Henry Junge to eke out a living during the Depression years as a musician in New York.

Two all-black choruses, the Hampton and Tuskegee Institute choirs, were also invited to sing at the White House—the first black groups to do so since 1882. Unlike the DePriest tea incident, which aroused such a storm of protest, the appearance of these black entertainers at the executive mansion seems to have been publicly accepted. The Hampton Choir sang on the south lawn in 1930 and the Tuskegee Institute Choir in a semi-formal indoor setting in 1932.

During that first strenuous year in the White House, 1929, Lou struggled to find time for her family and friends amid the crush of public duties. On April 19, during the dedication of Constitution Hall, the new DAR headquarters in Washington, she became the first president's wife to speak over the radio. A flying visit to friends in New England and Philadelphia punctuated the congressional wives' teas in early June. She accepted honorary degrees from Radcliffe and Swarthmore. Much of July was spent in fixing up the camp on the Rapidan.

Lou was disappointed that her busy schedule made it impossible for her to attend Allan's graduation from Stanford in June. She had found it hard to endure the four years of separation from her beloved younger son. "You can't *guess* how *terribly* pleased—overjoyed—rejoiced—I am that your old college is done," she wrote him. "I have just hated it all. And I am so relieved that it is over that my heart just goes around singing all day."[14] Her pride in Allan's accomplishments radiates in her letters to him. Her husband shared that pride. Although Bert seldom wrote letters any more (preferring the brevity of the telegram), he sent Allan a congratulatory wire that said, "May you commence today a life as satisfying to yourself as your past one has been to your parents."[15] In August Allan entered Johns Hopkins Hospital in Baltimore for treatment of what his mother called his "little attacks," possibly a recurring bladder infection. In the fall, following his brother Herbert's example, he enrolled in the Harvard Business School.

In North Dakota Uncle Will (now eighty-two years old) had his right eye removed. He then took his ward, Mary Paul, on a lengthy tour of the Southwest. Mary had been thrilled by her invitation to the inauguration, and on her return had enjoyed a brief period of fame among her fellow students at the University of North Dakota. She had graduated in June 1929, and was considering going on to earn a teaching certificate. In a letter to Sue Dyer in September 1929, Lou attempted to describe Mary's position in the family: "I don't know whether to call her his nurse or companion or daughter or what, because she has lived with him so many years and is a very petted member of the family, but on the other hand has a perfectly good mother and father of her own!"[16] But Lou was grateful for Mary's devotion to Will, who had no other family living nearby to look after him.

Lou's sister Jean spent the summer looking for yet another boarding school for her daughter Janet. Although Janet had been happy at Elm Lea, Jean wanted to have her closer to Mercersburg, Pennsylvania, where Del was enrolled, so that she could keep an eye on both her children. She transferred Janet to Highland Hall, which was only a few miles away from Mercersburg. Lou was still subsidizing the schooling of both her sister's children, and occasionally invited Janet to Washington for parties at the White House.

In September 1929 Lou went to New York City to open a special exhibit of Early American furniture, a benefit for the Girl Scouts. She stayed several days with her friends the Rickards in their uptown apartment. Then she had to hurry back to Washington to prepare for the visit of British Prime Minister Ramsay McDonald and his daughter Ishbel in early October. The Hoovers took the McDonalds to the camp in the mountains, where Bert and the prime minister discussed international political problems while sitting on a log by a trout stream. After the McDonalds left, the Hoovers were off to Detroit for a celebration of the fiftieth anniversary of Thomas Edison's invention of the electric light, and then to Cincinnati and Louisville, where Bert took part in discussions on flood control.

On October 29, 1929, the Stock Market crashed. Like most of the rest of America, Lou Hoover found the sudden upheaval hard to understand. As the economy staggered and came near to collapse, the Hoover administration's honeymoon with the American people came to an abrupt end. A stunned first lady was shocked to find her husband—whom she considered the most public-spirited man in the nation—accused of betraying the American people.

Chapter 13

Shadows Begin to Fall

Like many thoughtful observers of the American economic situation in 1929, Herbert Hoover had anticipated some sort of slump in the overheated stock market, and a corresponding slowdown in the nation's economy. Such things had happened before; in fact, most economists regarded such periodic "corrections" of the system as inevitable. What no one foresaw was how long it would take for this particular economic crisis to end, or how widespread its effects would be.

Black Thursday, when the stock market fell abruptly, dropping the value of securities by a total of $26 billion, set off a descending spiral of wages, prices and production that affected not only the working classes, but many seemingly wealthy people as well. While there were only two actual suicides on Wall Street as a result of the stock market crash, thousands of people saw their life savings evaporate. Many of the Hoovers' friends were among them.

Edgar Rickard, like Hoover, had anticipated the market's downturn and moved his money out of speculative stocks. He was able to keep the Hoovers' money relatively secure, too, although the overall value of their investments, like everyone else's, decreased sharply. Rickard's son-in-law, Rex Mohun, lost $2,500, not all of it his own. The stress of this loss, coupled with the birth of his first child, drove the young man into a nervous breakdown. Rickard was forced to assume fiscal responsibility for his daughter's family, as well as his own.

Sarah L. Arnold, the seventy-year-old retired dean of Simmons College who had succeeded Lou as president of the Girl Scouts in 1925, had invested her meager savings in a company that went under in the wake of the crash. She spent her last years leading a very restricted existence on a farm in New Hampshire, supported by the generosity of her friends. Another Girl Scout volunteer, naturalist Dr. Bertha Chapman Cady, also fell on hard times. When she became ill in September 1930, Lou arranged for the Girl Scouts to send money to help tide her over.

Lou was distressed by the news of her friends' troubles, but like most Americans in the early days of the Depression, she did not expect the hard times to last. The leading economists of the time believed that the market would recover in another year at most. People harked back to the financial crises of the 1870s and 1890s, and confidently asserted that with a little belt-tightening, they would come safely through. Bert spent long hours in his office, working to counteract the effects of the Depression with the kind of voluntary-action programs that he had used successfully to deal with previous crises. He and Lou tried to help those who were in serious trouble through the same private, often anonymous methods they had been using for years.

The 1929 holiday parties at the White House were as joyous as the season demanded. Not even a fire during the traditional Christmas Eve party for the children of the staff could shake Lou's equanimity. When word of the fire reached the party, the men immediately got up and left. Lou calmly informed the children that this was "a most unusual dinner party," and so the men would leave the room first. Once the men had left, rushing out to the West Wing, where the executive offices were ablaze, she gathered the children together and led them to the West Sitting Room on the second floor. Leading the children to the window, Lou told them, "Here is something that will excite you. Look at all those fire engines!"[1] They watched, entranced, as the firemen worked to bring the fire under control. When the excitement was over, the children returned to the first floor for gifts and Christmas cookies around the tree. Later, Lou salvaged the damaged beams from the affected area and sent them to a veterans' hospital, where the patients carved them into bowls and bookends. She gave some of them to friends the following year as Christmas souvenir gifts.

Among the new projects commanding Lou's attention was the proposal to establish a national Quaker meeting house in Washington. Soon after Bert's election as president, members of Washington's Quaker meetings approached him to discuss this idea. The Hoovers had seldom attended meeting before Bert was elected to the presidency. Even then, if it was not too cold or wet to drive up to Rapidan, or if political matters were "too demanding," they often skipped services. Sundays were their days of rest, when they left the cares of the week behind to picnic in the country and spend time with close friends. Nevertheless, their religious beliefs were sincere and firmly held.

Lou called herself a Quaker "by adoption."[2] She found the reflective silences of the formal meetings inspiring. But although she admired the Quakers, she also retained a fondness for the Episcopalian traditions of her childhood. Her ancestors had come from a variety of Christian religious affiliations, she would tell people, and she believed each to contain an element of truth. She was a deeply religious woman whose faith was associated not with sectarian practices, but with life choices. "Moral standards were infinitely more important [to her] than intellectual qualifications," her husband later said.[3]

Bert was much taken with the notion of a national Quaker center, built on the traditional Friends' design, that would embody the faith's fundamental principles. He agreed to sponsor the project, and he and Lou cooperated closely with the committee in charge, providing both financial and moral support. Fund-raising began in April 1930, and in January 1931 the new meeting house opened on Florida Avenue. Mr. and Mrs. Herbert Hoover were enrolled on the list of founding members.

One of the instigators of the meeting house project was Mary Vaux Walcott, widow of the former head of the Smithsonian and a prominent scientist in her own right. A geologist who specialized in glaciation, a talented artist who published a definitive five-volume book on native American wild flowers, and an advocate of the welfare of Native Americans who spent her vacations visiting Indian reservations, Mrs. Walcott was the type of woman Lou Hoover could not help but admire. As treasurer of the project, Mrs. Walcott corresponded regularly with Lou, working with her to place the meeting on a sound financial basis. The two women developed a profound friendship that would continue for many years.

To provide spiritual guidance for the new community, the Washington Quakers invited Dr. Augustus Murray, professor of classics at Stanford, to come to Washington as their leader. Professor Murray received a two-year leave of absence from the university for this purpose. It is quite possible that the Hoovers, with their many contacts at Stanford, played a role in this choice, although Murray had a sound reputation among his fellow Quakers. Lou enjoyed his thoughtful meditations on those Sunday mornings when she attended services at the new meeting house. She also donated freely to the fund that paid his expenses during his time in Washington.

Another charitable project that the Hoovers undertook during the first year of Bert's administration was the President's School, established in the mountains near the Rapidan camp. The Hoovers were celebrating Bert's fifty-fifth birthday at Rapidan in August 1929 when a boy named Ray Buraker presented the president with an opossum he had killed in the woods nearby. Ray told the president that he was eleven years old, had seven brothers and sisters, and had never attended school, because there was no school where he lived in the mountains near the camp.

By the end of the year the Hoovers had purchased a site, constructed a school building and living quarters for a teacher, and recruited a teacher. Christine Vest had been teaching at Berea College in Berea, Kentucky, when she was recommended for the job. "The week after Thanksgiving, I was on my way to the White House for an interview with President and Mrs. Hoover," she remembered. "Meeting the Hoovers and the other wonderful people was well worth the trip even if I had not been selected as teacher."[4]

The school opened on February 24, 1930. Located on the side of the mountain, it was "surrounded by rough mountain pasture land, a few oak trees, and an abundance of wild flowers with Columbine predominating."[5] Seventeen pupils were enrolled; a year later enrollment reached thirty-two, although daily attendance was usually about half that. The Hoovers paid all the expenses of the school, although they accepted some donations from outside sources as news of the project reached the public. Lou took a personal interest in all of the children and their families, knitting sweaters for them, visiting their homes when she was out riding. She soon knew them all by name. Most of the families were tenant farmers. When the father of some of the students told Lou that he couldn't find the liniment he needed for his rheumatism at the nearby town of Syria, Lou brought him some the next time she came up to the camp from Washington. She purchased clothing for all the children at Christmas. She also paid to send them to the County Fair, including a little spending money for each child to use as he or she wished.

The school continued until 1936. Christine Vest left in 1933 when she married a marine from the Rapidan camp. After the Hoovers left office, they gave the land on which the camp and the school stood to the state of Virginia. In 1935 it became part of the newly created Shenandoah National Park. By 1938, all the families had moved out of the area. The school, like the cabins where its students had lived, was abandoned. The Hoovers' camp was used for a time by the Boy Scouts, and later as a conference center, but eventually it too was vacated.

Although she was no longer directly involved in the day-to-day work of the Girl Scouts, Lou still took a close interest in the affairs of her favorite organization. She attended its yearly conventions, in New Orleans (1929), Indianapolis (1930), Buffalo (1931), and Virginia Beach (1932). She continued her role as captain of Troop 8, although her secretary Mildred Hall ran most of its meetings at the White House. The girls of Troop 8 "were members of other troops but worked with Mrs. Hoover as a group to be called upon for participation in civic demonstrations, parades, international conferences, and so forth," a former member recalled.[6] "We served at international Scout luncheons, demonstrated Scouting to the public and perhaps were the first Senior Service troop." Lou sent wedding gifts to the girls as they married, and became godmother to some of their offspring.

Abbie Rickard, who had become the Girl Scouts' National Treasurer in 1929, kept Lou up-to-date on Girl Scout proceedings. In 1929 Bert's colleague Julius Barnes of the ARA (whose wife Harriet was the board's corresponding secretary) suggested that the Girl Scout executive board hire Mark Jones, a business consultant, to prepare a five-year development plan for the organization. This plan aimed to increase membership from 200,000 to 500,000 and to raise $3 million to make the national organization self-supporting. Twelve regional offices would be set up to better serve the far-flung membership.

Lou was concerned at first that such centralized planning might endanger the democratic nature of the administration, a subject that "has always been a perfect obsession of mine."[7] While she realized the need for a national policy—indeed, she had done much herself to promote standardization of the Girl Scout program through leader-training courses and the publication of books on outdoor activities, nature study, homemaking, and the like, to supplement the regular handbooks—she was adamant in her belief that policies and standards must reflect the needs of local troops, and not be imposed arbitrarily from above. She did not want the Girl Scouts to become as rigidly centralized as some other youth organizations—including, in her opinion, the Boy Scouts. At the same time, she recognized the necessity of establishing a solid financial base for the organization. The days when Juliette Low could pay all its expenses from her housekeeping money, hocking her pearls to cover urgent debts, were long past. With Abbie Rickard as the national treasurer, Lou knew that the Girl Scouts' finances would be in good hands. She consented to announce the plan formally at a press conference in September 1929.

The discussions surrounding the acceptance of the five-year plan caused some dissention in the upper ranks of the Girl Scouts. Mark Jones, the author of the plan, had the support of the Barneses and of Executive Board Chair Genevieve (Mrs. Nicholas) Brady. He was opposed by President Mira Hoffman and National Director Jane Deeter Rippin. Lou herself considered his ethics questionable. She had learned that one of his proposals, to combine the Girl Scout magazine *The American Girl* with *Parents Magazine*, would have netted him a $2,500 commission.[8] She was quite relieved when he gave up his consultant's position in May 1930.

The five-year plan, however, survived, although the discord it had aroused continued. Jane Rippin, who had been the Girl Scouts' National Director for twelve years, announced at that same May 1930 meeting that she would be resigning as of September 1. To cushion the effect of Mrs. Rippin's departure on the staff, the board announced that she was taking a year's leave of absence for reasons of health. Meanwhile, the search for a successor began. Lou deeply regretted her long-time friend's decision. In her private correspondence, she complained that "the bickering of two people and the lack of assurance and independent judgment of a third" had deprived the Girl Scouts of one of their most valuable leaders.[9]

To replace Mrs. Rippin, Lou suggested that the Girl Scouts hire Dr. Lillian Gilbreth, a prominent engineer noted for her work in time and motion studies, whose life story would later be dramatized in the movie *Cheaper By the Dozen*. Dr. Gilbreth was then doing an organizational study of the central office. "She has done a great deal of work remodeling old and setting up new engineering organizations and industrial plants," Lou wrote to Genevieve Brady, "so that she has a very good idea of the co-ordination of departments and the work of such a plant as ours when it is devoted to industrial products instead of girls. . . . She is very interested in the children's and young people's development and has studied modern tendencies very carefully. She is raising a family of eleven children herself most satisfactorily."[10] Although the Girl Scouts did not hire Dr. Gilbreth as National Director, they did offer her a seat on their executive board, which she accepted.

Meanwhile, unwilling to allow Jane Rippin's talents to go unexploited, Lou persuaded her in March 1931 to become director of the NAAF Women's Division. Mrs. Rippin held that position until 1934, when her health forced her to resign. She also served as director of research for women's news for the Westchester

County Publishers, owned by the Macy family, and continued to take an interest in the Girl Scout movement, serving in a volunteer capacity on its national advisory council until her death in 1953.

Despite the controversy surrounding its adoption, the five-year plan was successful, although the Depression prevented it from meeting all of its goals. By 1935 membership had risen to 382,971, an 85 percent increase over the five-year interval. The Five-Year Development Fund remained solvent, in the capable hands of a three-person committee headed by Edgar Rickard. In spite of the economic stresses of the time, the Girl Scout program continued its steady growth.

Much of the credit for this success goes to the continuing high quality of adult leadership that the organization attracted. Birdsall (Mrs. Frederick) Edey, elected President in 1930, had been vice president in charge of field activities for several years. Two of her vice presidents, Mira Hoffman and Anne Choate, were former presidents, and Genevieve Brady, the chairman of the board of directors, had served on the executive board since 1919. They and their newer colleagues all invested much time, energy, and money in the organization, and were personally dedicated to its principles.

In September 1931 Lou invited the executive board to hold its annual pre-convention meeting at Camp Rapidan. The field staff were treated to tea at the White House before the meeting. During this conference, any lingering remnants of ill feeling from the previous year were dispelled, and the camaraderie that had previously marked the organization's leadership was restored. The participants credited Lou with this happy result.

Lou Hoover was becoming more comfortable with her role as first lady. There was solid organization underlying the clutter of her study, where papers covered every surface. She described her calendar system to a friend: lead pencil meant a tentative engagement; black ink meant a definite engagement in town; red ink meant a definite commitment out-of-town. In December 1929, when protocol required her to send a wedding gift to Belgium's princess, she wrote to a friend, "I am not accustomed to sending princesses wedding gifts from the White House, and I hesitate at the wording. But for a moment only! Promptly I say, oh well—you can do that too!"[11] She sent the princess a sealskin coat, with America's best wishes.

1930 proved to be another stressful year for Lou Henry Hoover. Beginning with the New Year's Day reception, when over 6,000 people passed through the White House, each eager to shake the hand of the president and his wife, the pace was intense. Charlotte Kellogg estimated that in the first year of the Hoover administration "there have been more than three thousand guests at meals and an average of nearly thirty house guests a month. Teas seem continuous."[12] The New Year's reception was followed by a reception for the members of the Judiciary. Then came the dinners for the vice president (with thirty-six guests) and the Chief Justice (with thirty-eight guests), each followed by a musicale for up to ninety. In February there was the dinner and musicale for the speaker of the house, and the annual dinner for the members of the diplomatic community, always a huge affair.

When the social season closed down in mid-February, the Hoovers left for Florida, to spend a few days fishing off Long Key with their friends the Jeremiah Milbanks on Milbank's yacht, the *Saunterer*. Several other friends were in the party, and a group of secretaries and aides were accommodated on the government yacht, the *Kilkenny*. Almost everyone caught a big sailfish. Lou's fish was just under seven feet, while Bert's was seven feet six inches long.

On her return to Washington, Lou helped dedicate a women's war memorial, then drove up to Philadelphia at the end of March to attend the Philadelphia Quakers' Yearly Meeting. Back in Washington she presided over the annual Easter egg roll on the White House lawn. Lou was the first first lady to think of providing portable latrines for the convenience of the participants at that event. On April 12 she welcomed the birth of her third grandchild, Joan Ledlie Hoover, in Los Angeles, where Herbert Jr. was now working as a communications engineer for Western Aircraft Express. The Stanford Class of '98 asked if they might hold their reunion in her Stanford home, and she agreed, arranging with her cousin Dorothy Matthews and Uncle Will Henry to act as hosts. And she wrote Edgar Rickard, asking him to hire her nephew Del Large to work during the summer at the Pejobscot paper mill in Maine, where Herbert Jr. had worked a few years earlier.

In mid-April, Lou slipped and fell against a piece of furniture in the White House, severely spraining her back. For the next several weeks, she spent most of her time upstairs on a sofa in her workroom, using a wheelchair when she needed to go downstairs. Such a check on her mobility was annoying, although she accepted it with her usual good humor. The wheelchair, she wrote her niece Janet, was great fun, rolling up and down the halls and riding up and down in the elevator. She could not, however, propel the wheelchair herself, because using her arms put stress on her injured back muscles. It was July before she was back to normal, able to go horseback riding again in the city parks.

The most distressing event of the year, however, occurred in September, when Herbert Jr. reported for duty as a reserve lieutenant in the army air corps. During a routine physical, the doctors discovered that he had tuberculosis. This was still a very serious disease, the fourth leading cause of death in America, after heart disease, pneumonia/influenza, and cancer. His worried parents rushed him to Washington, where he was examined by the White House doctor, Captain Joel T. Boone, U.S.N. Boone confirmed the diagnosis.

Treatment of tuberculosis at that time consisted primarily of fresh air, a diet heavy on dairy products, and complete rest. Herbert was sent to the Rapidan camp, where he was kept isolated and quiet. He was not allowed to do anything stressful, including anything that "would make him think."[13]

As the autumn weather grew cooler, it was clear that Herbert could not remain at the Virginia camp. The dry climate of the Southwest—Arizona and New Mexico—made it one of the most popular places for recovering tuberculosis patients, but Bert refused to allow his son to be sent so far away. Dr. Boone recommended a sanitarium in Asheville, North Carolina, and in October Herbert was sent there.

He spent most of his time listening to the radio, especially transatlantic conversations, and trained his Belgian police dog to bring him his cod liver oil.

Peggy Hoover had come to Washington with her husband, leaving the children behind in Pasadena in the care of servants. When it became clear that Herbert would be hospitalized for several months, Lou invited her and the children to stay at the White House until he recovered. For the next year, the three grandchildren—Peggy Ann, five, Herbert III (Pete), four, and baby Joan—would add their lively exuberance to the White House ambience. Every morning after breakfast, they would escort their granddaddy to the executive office wing, and every afternoon they would wait to escort him "home" again.

There were the inevitable minor disasters. One day Peggy Ann got into the ink, spilling it all over herself and the floor, but fortunately not on the rugs. Another time, she was found in a guest's bedroom, happily applying the guest's best face powder to her face. The housekeeper, Ava Long, enjoyed the children, whose antics reminded her of her own granddaughter. She showed them a picture of her granddaughter, whereupon young Pete demanded to see a picture "of your little boy!" He was bitterly disappointed when he learned that she had no grandson.[14]

Bert's political advisers, wanting to improve their president's image, suggested publicizing the children's activities. The suggestion was not well received. The Hoovers remained adamant in maintaining their family's privacy. Peggy even refused to send Peggy Ann to school, fearing she might contract one of the prevalent childhood illnesses. With her father so ill, her mother wanted no risk of further infection in the family.

Preoccupied with his efforts to stabilize the steadily declining economy, Bert managed only once to visit his son in Asheville. Lou, however, went down as often as she could. Gradually this oldest son, whose frequent illnesses had been a long-standing concern, fought his way back to health. After ten months in Asheville Herbert Jr. was able to return to California, where he resumed his career in aviation as a communications engineer with Transcontinental Western Airlines (TWA). Oddly enough, this battle with serious illness seems to have strengthened him. His hearing, damaged by recurrent ear infections following influenza in 1918, improved, and his health in later years remained satisfactory.

The Hoovers celebrated their second Christmas at the White House with a party for fifty guests. A small table was set for the children in the middle of the room and larger tables arranged in a horseshoe around it for the adults. This time there was no fire to disrupt the festivities. After dinner the guests formed a procession and paraded through the house, ringing bells, up to the second floor where they watched a movie in the Oval Parlor. Lillian Rogers Parks recalled in her memoir that her mother, one of the senior maids, brought home some of the table decorations, as well as some of the cookies from the tree as a treat for her invalid daughter.

The festivities this year, however, were overshadowed by the continuing spread of the Depression. It was no longer possible to carry on as usual in the blind faith that things would soon be better.

Chapter 14

The Depression Deepens

As the months passed, the nation's financial situation grew steadily worse. Nothing that Hoover's government did to try to contain the damage seemed to work for any length of time. To complicate the situation, the president faced opposition to his programs not only from the Democrats who had become the majority party in the 1930 elections, but from his Republican "allies" as well. The obstructionists in Congress frustrated the president and outraged his wife.

"She was oversensitive," Bert wrote in his *Memoirs*, "and the stabs of political life which, no doubt, were deserved by me hurt her greatly. . . . Her only departures from sweet urbanity were in outrage at some unfairness in our opponents—and that in private. . . . Loyalty to a cause, to a party, to a leader, were part of her moral standards."[1]

The Depression had become a worldwide problem. Europe was also in serious trouble, and foreign markets for American goods were drying up. Foreign debts, left over from the war, went unpaid. At home, a prolonged drought paralyzed the Midwest, where thousands faced starvation in the region now called the Dust Bowl. As Bert's cousin Harriette Miles Odell wrote from her home in Kansas, the wind blowing on the dry fields carried away seed and soil alike, so that "you don't know when you plant if you'll raise the wheat of your neighbor to the south, or the oats of your neighbor to the north."[2]

As the months passed with no improvement in sight, the number of those who needed Lou's help continued to grow. Lou's correspondence, already much increased, grew larger still as individual citizens appealed to the First Lady to help them out of their difficulties. Relatives, friends, even strangers wrote to ask for assistance in finding work or paying bills.

Uncle Will Henry had extricated himself from the collapse of two banks in which he had been a partner during the mid-1920s, but by 1930 he confessed to Lou that his income barely covered the taxes on his property. Lou had been helping him to pay the expenses of his Indian ward, Mary Paul. She promised to send him $75 a month, so that he would not have to sell his home at the prevailing low price, and suggested that he move to California, where Mary could do her graduate work at Stanford. Will and Mary spent the first half of 1930 in Palo Alto, but when Will's renters moved out of the house in Wahpeton in June, they returned to North Dakota.

In July 1931 eighty-four-year-old Will received a letter from an extortionist who demanded $75 under an unspecified threat. Will was to drive into the country and throw the money from the car when he received a signal. Although the police followed him, the thief managed to escape with the money. When the affair was over, Lou sent Will a dog for protection, and urged him again to move to California, where she had people on her staff who could look after him. In November he and Mary moved into the Henry home in Monterey. Concerned about her uncle's welfare, Lou promised Mary that if she would stay with Uncle Will through the next few years, Lou would see that she was able to resume her education after his death.

Her mother's aging relatives also caused her some concern. In Los Angeles Aunt Nannie Henry had trouble scraping together the money to pay her property taxes during the early 1930s. In 1929 Lou learned that her eighty-eight-year-old great-aunt Nettie Eastman had become destitute in Florida. She wrote to her Aunt Lill in Shell Rock, asking if Lill could find Aunt Nettie a place to stay. Aunt Lill and Uncle Wallace had been taking in boarders to supplement their income from Aunt Jennie's bequest. Lou promised that she and Aunt Jessie would pay Aunt Nettie's expenses. Lill reluctantly agreed, and Aunt Nettie went to live with the Wallace Weeds in Shell Rock. This temporary expedient proved more permanent than either Lou or Lill expected. In 1941 Aunt Nettie celebrated her 100th birthday in Shell Rock, Iowa.

There were also the numerous Hoover cousins, most of whom lived in modest circumstances. Every month, Bert and Lou sent "hundreds of dollars" to Minthorns and Hoovers who were too old to support themselves, or to younger ones unable to afford the college education the Hoovers regarded as so important to a young person's future. Ethel Heald Rensch, who by 1930 owed Lou some $1,300 in school fees for herself and her husband, wrote to ask for another $750 to build a house that she could share with her elderly mother. Before Lou could decide what to do, Aunt Ann Heald died, making the question of a home for her moot, but this did not end the Rensch family's pleas for help. Ethel's husband, Hero, who, after many years of study, had finally completed his M.A. in history in 1929, was having trouble finding work. Hero's problem, Lou confided to Theodore Hoover, was that he tended to prolong his research projects beyond all reason. She would like to have recommended him to the staff of the Hoover War Library, she said, but because of his dilatory habits, she felt she could not do so. "I just can't scrape together year after year more funds to give the able-bodied and well-educated ones a living," she wrote Ethel's sister, Bertha, who had added her own pleas to her sister's.[3]

Among the Hoovers' friends who were struggling financially was Dare Stark McMullin, now divorced and unable to support herself, who spent months living at the White House, helping Lou to research the White House furnishings. Alida Henriques, who had helped Lou so much with the Food Administration Club, had to give up her independence and become a paid companion when her rents and investments dropped. She asked Lou to take over one of her own charitable projects, providing an education for a young man from North Carolina. Vernon Kellogg, who had developed Parkinson's disease, faced an uncertain future when his retirement fund went bankrupt. Lou wrote to Edgar Rickard on his behalf, and was assured that both the CRB Educational Foundation and the National Research Council had arranged for Kellogg to receive a modest "salary" in recognition of his years of service to both organizations.

Even the Rickards were feeling the stress of the times. Although Edgar had managed to give his younger daughter, Peggy, a debutante ball in November 1930, he and Abbie gave up their New York apartment to live year-round in their summer home in New Canaan, Connecticut. He was still supporting his older daughter, Elizabeth, and her family, as her husband could not find work. Nevertheless, they were still far better off than most Americans.

Lou did her best to help as many of those who appealed to her as possible. To handle the growing volume of appeals she received, Lou decided she needed another secretary. Philippi Harding Butler had returned to Washington in the fall of 1930, when her husband, Fred, was assigned to the Bureau of Public Buildings and Parks. Although she had two children now, Phil agreed to come back to work part time to handle the requests for assistance. She later explained the process that Lou followed. When an appeal came in, it was reviewed to see whether it could be dealt with by one of the existing government departments. Phil had contacts in every department to whom the appeal could be referred. If an appeal did not fall into this category, it was turned over to someone in Lou's nationwide network of friends, to be evaluated and to have action recommended. Sometimes the friend would be able to assist the applicant personally; more often, Lou sent money to the friend to pass on, as from an anonymous donor who lived in the neighborhood.

This anonymity was essential, because if word got out that the president's wife was single-handedly running a relief program, the flood of requests would swell beyond her ability to control it. In October 1931 she wrote to Allan in California, "if you know any of our old retainers who are not doing comfortably this year, see if you can't think out something that can help them—with as little expenditure as possible! (For there are more we know who need help than we can help.)"[4]

Lou's charitable efforts had political implications, too. Somehow the word got out that she had helped an old classmate, Ludema Sayre, who happened to be post-mistress in Fairfax, Virginia. Although Lou's aid had been limited to the gift of some dresses she no longer needed, and a loan to cover a mortgage payment (sent through Phil Butler, who told Miss Sayre that the money was her own), the press spoke darkly of influence peddling. There were hints that Miss Sayre—who had been appointed in 1923 during the Harding administration—owed her position to her friendship with Lou.

In addition to her unpublicized personal relief network, Lou encouraged others to form similar networks of their own. At the 1931 Girl Scout leadership confer-ence at the Rapidan Camp, Lou proposed enlisting the 250,000 Girl Scouts throughout the country in voluntary relief work in their communities. An official plan was drawn up and presented at the subsequent national convention by Dr. Lillian Gilbreth. Lou expanded on this theme in a radio-broadcast speech to the nation's 4–H clubs a month later. Young people who were in "no actual want," she said, should "help plan that the excess in your community may be systematically gathered together and through the aid of the many channels for relief may be sent where it is needed."[5]

As time passed and the Depression persisted, the press became increasingly critical of Hoover's administration. In January 1931 a book appeared, entitled *The Strange Career of Herbert Hoover; or, Under Two Flags*, by John Hamill. This was the beginning of what the Hoover party came to call the Smear Campaign. Its chief ar-chitect was a man named Charles Michelson, a longtime Democratic Party activ-ist. Michelson's persistent claim that Hoover had somehow failed to prevent the Depression, and was not concerned about the needs of the millions of American working people struggling for existence, gradually acquired widespread accep-tance. Lou's granddaughter Peggy Ann still recalls an incident when she was speak-ing with a friend after school one day and the friend's mother came up and grabbed her daughter by the arm. "Don't talk to her!" the woman said angrily. "Her Grand-daddy put your father out of work!"[6]

The Democratic critics searched out every incident in Herbert Hoover's past that could possibly have a negative spin put on it. They cited the complex shenani-gans in China after the Boxer Rebellion, including the lawsuit brought against him by Chang Yen-Mao (failing to note that Bert had actually been acquitted of wrong-doing). His long years of residence in London were presented as indicating an elit-ist preference for British society over American. His close friendship with America's captains of industry (many of whose ships were now foundering on the economic rocks) became evidence of capitalist chauvinism. His efforts to counter the De-pression with persuasion and voluntary controls—tactics he had used successfully to provide food for war-torn Europe, control production to further the war effort in the United States, and bring relief to the flooded Mississippi River basin in his pre-presidential years—were derided as pandering to the wealthy at the expense of the workingman. In a cruel parody of the 1917 "Hooverisms," the press began attaching Hoover's name to signs of poverty, such as the shantytowns popping up on the edges of the big cities, which were labeled "Hoovervilles." To Hooverize had once meant doing without for the good of the country; now it simply meant doing without.

Lou was infuriated by the insinuations and outright falsehoods promulgated in the smear campaign. "The absolute injustice and downright lying of these statements infuriated" her, she wrote; "all that he has been doing so endlessly and so courageously has been for the small individual, the millions of them."[7] She told Democratic journalist Anne Hard, "So far, [Hoover] is the only man I know who has *never* 'forgotten' those other men, but who *works* for them, and accomplishes things for them, day and year in and out, instead of talking about them."[8] To Allan, she wrote sadly, "Those years of his [during World War I] . . . he gave up to the cause of the little man, millions of him. And . . . the kind of happiness, of pleasure, that had been his before. A certain definite, and very original kind of joy of life was stamped out of him by those war years. . . . Not that he became altogether solemn and serious, not that a quaint whimsicality does not persist and is highly entertaining,—but the old sparkling spontaneity is now only occasionally glimpsed far below the surface."[9]

Sitting down at her typewriter, Lou wrote down her impressions of all that her husband had done, from his earliest days with Bewick Moreing through the war years to his present efforts to combat the Depression. It was important, she felt, that someone "should begin to keep a real record for his grandchildren!"[10] Her writings were private, however, intended only for the eyes of her sons and their children. She did not go to the press herself; Bert had press aides for that, and she left the public refutation of the smears to them. Lou had never completely trusted the press. Although she talked freely with reporters, she gave no press conferences and steadfastly refused to be either interviewed or quoted. She had learned early on, she wrote to Marie Meloney, editor of the *New York Herald Tribune Sunday Magazine*, that "I can't write anything not full of dynamite."[11] She was no politician; she thought it was better for her husband that she hold her tongue. She made few speeches except on behalf of the Girl Scouts or other noncontroversial programs. Smiling, she told the members of the Women's National Press Club at a luncheon in February 1933 that one day she would write her own life story. It would appear in two columns: the fiction that they had printed over the years on one side, the truth on the other.

Somehow the year 1931 passed. Lou dedicated a memorial to the victims of the Titanic disaster, set the stone of the Women's Porch of the National Cathedral in Washington, received an honorary degree from Goucher College, and attended the Girl Scout convention in Buffalo, New York.

Ruth Fesler, who had been Lou's secretary since 1928, left in May to be married to a San Francisco lawyer, Robert L. Lipman. As organizational secretary, Ruth had dealt with such matters as the Quaker meeting house project, the NAAF Women's Division, the Girl Scouts, and the President's School near the Rapidan camp. An historian by training, she also researched the president's ancestry and located the burial place in North Carolina of the first Hoover (Andreas Huber) to arrive in America.

Ruth traced Lou's genealogy, too, and identified an ancestor who had fought in the Revolutionary War. This would have qualified Lou for membership in the Daughters of the American Revolution, had she wished to join. Her sister-in-law Mildred Hoover and her friend Gertrude Bowman were both active DAR members. Mildred was state regent for California. But Lou preferred not to join the organization herself. In 1930, when the national DAR convention took a formal stand against the World Court and arms reduction, a large number of its members (including about half of the Palo Alto chapter) resigned. Lou wrote to a friend, "I was very thankful that I never had time to join the organization, because I would have felt it imperative to have adopted the same course that you did . . . under the circumstances."[12] She was not one to brag about her ancestry. To Allan she wrote, "You *did* have ancestors on the Mayflower you know. But one is always ashamed to mention it."[13]

Despite the underlying gloom of the Depression, life in the White House had its lighter moments. At one of the first official dinners of the 1931 season, the naval aide responsible for announcing arrivals introduced the Hoovers as "President and Mrs. Coolidge." Hoover, who according to his chief usher "seldom laughed at anything," found this hilarious. As the laughter filled the room, Lou smiled and said to the aide, "I wish they *could* be here."[14]

One of the more enjoyable events of 1931 was the visit to the White House of thirteen-year-old Bryan Untiedt, a homesteader's son from Towner, Colorado. Young Bryan had achieved national fame by saving his schoolmates when their school bus was stranded in a snowstorm. After the bus driver went for help, Bryan had kept the children distracted and warm for two days until help arrived. Five people had died in the disaster, including the bus driver and Bryan's nine-year-old brother. Thanks in large part to Bryan, fifteen survived. Although Bryan arrived in Washington on the same day as the King and Queen of Siam, the Hoovers took time to chat with him personally. The boy's unpretentious and open manner charmed the whole White House community. His cheerful antics kept the staff amused. Bert was delighted when Bryan greeted him with a handshake. The President declared that the boy should be allowed to stay for several days in the White House as his guest. He was even allowed to visit the president informally in his office on several occasions. Lou instructed her secretaries to take him sightseeing and see to it that he was properly entertained. When he left for home four days later, she presented him with two suitcases full of new clothes.

Not even the Depression could prevent Cupid from casting his darts among the White House staff. The youngest of Lou's secretaries, Mildred Hall, had met Allan's old friend Allen Campbell when he came to Washington at Christmas in 1928. Allen's father, the former governor of Arizona, was Hoover's civil service commissioner. After graduating from Stanford, Allen had worked briefly for the *Los Ange-*

les Times before finally securing a teaching job. In 1931 he came to Washington to do graduate work at George Washington University. By the time he completed his M.A. in 1932, he and Mildred were engaged.

Cupid also struck Bert's valet, Kosta Boris, a stolid, middle-aged bachelor who had come to the United States from the Balkan region before the war. On an errand to buy stationery for the White House at Kann's Department Store, he met Essie, a young Irish immigrant working as a sales clerk. Boris returned to the store several times, always managing to exchange a few words with Essie. At length, he invited Essie to a reception at the White House. Her boss didn't believe her story at first, then insisted on helping her choose an appropriate gown to wear from the store's stock. When she arrived at the White House, Boris was on duty as usual at the front door, greeting the guests. One of the butlers relieved him so that he could escort Essie for the remainder of the evening.

Allan had graduated from Harvard Business School with no particular plans for the future. His mother vetoed a suggestion that he might join the Commerce Department. She explained that with so many unemployed, she did not think Allan should take a government salary away from someone more needy. Besides, it might look like nepotism to a highly critical public, already inflamed by the smear campaign. After a short vacation in Hawaii, Allan went back to California, where he took a job with a Los Angeles bank.

Jean and her children also returned to California that summer. Janet had graduated from Highland Hall and was to enter Mills College in the fall. Del wanted to attend Palo Alto High School for his last year. He spent the summer of 1931 working in the fish hatcheries in Alaska. He would enter Stanford in 1932, but transfer the following year to a junior college to study archaeology.

The political storm clouds darkened steadily as 1932 began. It was another election year. Bert would be standing for reelection, but his chances looked increasingly slim. At the White House, Lou continued to entertain at her usual pace, doing her best to distract her husband from the cares of the day and to maintain her vision of the dignity of the White House. In keeping with the more inward-turning spirit of the times, she arranged to showcase more home-grown American talent during the evening musicales. In April she wore a ball gown made of cotton to a reception to show support for the struggling cotton industry.

She also continued to work with those organizations closest to her heart. In February, she invited the NAAF Women's Division board to a reception at the White House. The members discussed means of publicizing the group's opposition to women's participation in the Olympic Games being held in Los Angeles that year. Funding was another major concern, since it was becoming increasingly difficult to find the money to run the organization. Lou frequently found it necessary to dip into her own funds to cover shortcomings in the group's finances.

Following the end of the 1931–32 social season in February, the Hoovers again spent a week in Florida, fishing with their friends the Milbanks. It gave them an opportunity to recuperate from the pressures of life in Washington, and for Bert to discuss campaign finance with Milbank, one of his loyal supporters. Lou went to Connecticut in early May 1932 to attend the wedding of Marguerite (Peggy) Rickard, Abbie and Edgar's younger daughter.

A few days later, the nation was shocked by the kidnaping and murder of the infant son of aviation hero Charles A. Lindbergh. Friends of the Hoovers, Lindbergh and his wife had visited the White House on several occasions. They sometimes accompanied the Hoovers on their fishing holidays in Florida. The tragedy therefore had a personal meaning for Lou and her husband.

It also caused the Hoovers to reconsider their own security arrangements. Until this time, the Secret Service had provided protection only to the president and his wife. While other members of his immediate family were also entitled to protection, Hoover had not thought it necessary to protect his grown sons. Even the press showed only a mild interest in the affairs of Allan or Herbert Jr. and his family. The Lindbergh kidnaping caused the President to change his mind, however. He immediately ordered the Secret Service to provide guards for his grandchildren in California. If a popular hero like Lindbergh could be attacked in this manner, an embattled president feared his own family might also be at risk.

Recovered now from his bout with tuberculosis, Herbert Jr. had begun lecturing at California Institute of Technology in the fall of 1931. He was also working for TWA. In June 1932 he moved his family from Pasadena into the hills at Sierra Madre. Not wanting him to have to sell securities from his trust fund at a loss to finance the new house, Lou offered to loan him the money she had realized from the sale of the Adams house at Stanford. She asked Allan to make the necessary arrangements for the loan through his bank.

Overriding every other consideration during the summer of 1932, however, was Bert's reelection campaign. To many members of the Republican Party, the major campaign issue was Prohibition, whose repeal the Roosevelt forces advocated. The Hoovers were not strong defenders of Prohibition, although they did believe firmly in obeying the law of the land. Lou rarely drank alcohol herself, although she didn't object to others doing so, within reason. In Europe, she had served wine with meals; in Prohibition America, she served ice water. She had even kept a case of wine in the Palo Alto house for her father, who had insisted that he needed a glass of port with each meal for his health, and champagne to treat his "spells."[15] Like most Americans, the Hoovers had associates who occasionally ran afoul of the nation's liquor laws. At the height of the smear campaign, Bert's alcoholic brother-in-law, Van Ness Leavitt, was arrested for possession of bootleg liquor. Though Leavitt was later exonerated, the incident caused the president considerable embarrassment and did not improve his opinion of his brother-in-law.

It was not Prohibition that would bring down the Hoover administration, however. Much more damaging was Hoover's response to the arrival in Washington in the summer of 1932 of twenty thousand impoverished World War I veterans, demanding the immediate payment of the bonus they had been promised in 1924, over Calvin Coolidge's veto. This bonus was to have been paid in 1945, but the marchers claimed that they needed the money now. Unable to afford hotel rooms, they pitched tents on the Mall while they lobbied Congress. They succeeded in convincing the House to support their cause, but the Senate refused to approve the measure. Hoover managed to get an appropriation to send some six thousand of the marchers home. The rest refused to leave, remaining in their tent city along the Anacostia River, where communists and demagogues of various stripes kept the situation simmering.

An attempt by the District police to clear the area led to rioting, whereupon Hoover—at the request of the District of Columbia commissioner—sent in the army, under General Douglas MacArthur, to restore order. Using bayonets and tear gas, MacArthur evicted the "Bonus Army" and burned its shanties to the ground. Several protesters were injured. The photographs that appeared in the press seemed to support the Democrats' contention that Hoover, seeing a threat to the government in what was essentially a peaceful demonstration, had overreacted.

Whether Hoover acted reasonably or not, the incident hammered one more nail into the coffin of his political career. Lou, typically, supported her husband's position. Not only did she believe that the government had acted in the only proper fashion, she also questioned the right of the bonus marchers to special consideration. "I . . . have seen so much of the war . . . that I . . . do not believe that beyond recompense for actual physical handicaps they received in the service, any man enlisted in the service of his country should have any advantage over the others," she wrote Mary Walcott in August 1932. "I do not think that an ablebodied man, unharmed by his service, now thirty-five years old, should have preferential treatment by reason of his enlistment, over a man twenty-eight years old, who was too young to have the opportunity of enlisting."[16]

Little as she enjoyed her own role as first lady, Lou was convinced that America needed four more years of Bert's leadership. Journalist Anne Hard wrote her, "If you want another four-year jail sentence—well, I suppose you do." Lou replied, "Well, I don't. But I think the American people need it. And I don't very often get to do what *I* want, in big things."[17]

This time, the boys made a point of staying away from the campaign. While Lou devoted all of her energy to maintaining a cheerful atmosphere, deliberately keeping from her husband any hint of rifts within the official family, she could not prevent an air of defeat from descending over the White House. Allan, home for a visit, observed that he would have to get away soon, before the place gave him the "willies."[18]

Lou loyally accompanied her husband on his campaign trip through the Midwest during October, taking time out to attend the Girl Scout convention in Virginia Beach, Virginia, from October 8–12. When she began to give her speech at the convention, it was discovered that someone had damaged the wires, preventing her words from being carried on the radio. She was appalled by the thought that partisan politics had penetrated even her beloved Girl Scout movement.

On November 3 the Hoovers headed west to cast their votes in Palo Alto. It was quite a different atmosphere from four years earlier. Once again crowds cheered them at the railroad station, though in fewer numbers than before. As the returns came in, disappointment spread. A crowd of Stanford students again waited outside the Hoover home. They cheered their president enthusiastically when he appeared on the second floor balcony, shortly after wiring his congratulations to his Democratic opponent. When the cheering died down, however, the evening collapsed into anticlimax. Instead of a speech, Hoover said only, "I thank you for your fine loyalty, and I deeply appreciate this very hearty greeting. Thank you."[19] And he went back inside.

By eleven o'clock the guests were gone and the Hoovers ready for bed. "Mrs. Hoover was so tired she put her head on my shoulder," recalled Mildred Hall.[20] Many of the guests had already departed, apparently unwilling to remain as guests in the home of a defeated president. Bert shook hands with each member of his staff, something he had never done before, and wished them all a good night.[21]

"Democracy," Herbert Hoover would later observe, "is not a polite employer."[22] It had been a wild ride, from the mines of the Rocky Mountains all the way to the White House, and now it was over. Lou, for one, was ready to go home.

Chapter 15

Civilians Once More

Herbert Hoover once remarked that the train ride back to Washington following the news of his defeat at the polls reminded him of Harding's funeral train. Much as she disliked the idea of four more years in the White House, Lou was deeply distressed by the American people's rejection of her husband at the polls. In her mind it was a betrayal, and she blamed it primarily on the Democratic Party's smear campaign.

"We have all the lugubriousness of farewell parties before graduation," she wrote to Allan in December 1932.[1] They had originally planned a trip to Honolulu after the election, but Bert now felt he must put everything in order for his successor. He agreed, however, to take a few days off in December, spending the holidays in Florida on the *Sequoia*. He had never cared for the traditional New Year's Day reception, with its endless handshaking, and this year Lou allowed him to cancel it, with the explanation that the president was out of town. It would never be held again.

On their return to Washington, the Hoovers received word of the death of Calvin Coolidge in Vermont. The resultant period of mourning delayed the resumption of the social season, forcing several planned parties to be rescheduled. Lou began packing up her family's belongings. She sent forty-two boxes to Herbert Jr. and Allan in early February. Sixty-nine further crates were loaded onto a steamship bound for San Francisco, where Sue Dyer waited to direct them to Palo Alto.

On January 28 Mrs. Roosevelt came for a tour of the White House, to see what she might need to bring with her when she moved in. Lou and Mildred Hall guided her through the main rooms on the first and second floors. Lou told her what furniture was her own, and what belonged to the White House. She explained about the Lincoln study, and how she had had the Monroe furnishings copied for the White House. She would leave one of the Monroe desks as a gift to the White House, she said. The chief usher thought Mrs. Roosevelt was not particularly interested. When Mrs. Roosevelt admired the curtains in the Oval Parlor, Lou offered to leave them behind for her. Then they went up to the servants' and secretaries' quarters on the third floor.

Afterward, as they entered the elevator, Lou observed that if Mrs. Roosevelt wanted to see the kitchens, she would ask the housekeeper to show them to her. She herself didn't know much about them, she said, since she had left the details of meal planning to Mrs. Long after the first week. Mildred went in search of Ava Long, who guided Mrs. Roosevelt through the kitchen, the storage rooms and the servants' dining rooms. When they reached the doctor's office, they found Lou waiting to escort her guest back to the Red Room for refreshments.

It was all very cordial. The Hoovers and Roosevelts had been acquainted since the war years, when Franklin D. Roosevelt was Secretary of the Navy in Wilson's cabinet. Both men were liberal in their politics, though from different parties and to a different degree. In the past few years, as Roosevelt rose from governor of New York to president, however, they had seen little of one another. The viciousness of the smear campaign now lay between them, as well as Roosevelt's reluctance to appear to cooperate with Hoover in any way. For the first time in the chief usher's memory, the outgoing president did not invite his successor to dinner on the night before the inauguration. Instead, the Roosevelts were asked in for tea, which was "a rather cool affair all around."[2]

The day before the inauguration, Lou called the White House servants together in the dining room, where she had set out an assortment of items for them to select as mementos. Lillian Parks received a Victrola. Lou told them to be sure to speak to her if they should meet again, even if she didn't at first recognize them out of uniform. With tears in her eyes she assured Lillian's mother, Senior Maid Maggie Rogers, that "my husband will live to do great things for his country."[3]

On March 4, 1933, the Hoovers left the White House. A crowd of some five thousand people saw them off at Washington's Union Station. They were accompanied by their two sons and several friends and former aides. At Philadelphia, the party separated, Lou and Herbert Jr. going west to California, Bert and Allan going on to New York, where Bert had business to attend to.

After a brief stop in Palo Alto, Lou went for a few days to Sierra Madre, where she got her first view of her son Herbert's home and enjoyed playing with her grandchildren. While there, she received word of the sudden death of French Strother, Bert's former administrative assistant and speech writer. Bert attended Strother's funeral in Washington on the 13th and then joined Lou in California.

Being out of office, Bert observes in his *Memoirs*, was "emancipation from a sort of peonage."[4] Soon after his return to California, he and Lou set off on a vacation—"the first for so many years," Lou claimed.[5] They drove up past Lake Tahoe to Reno and back through Death Valley, a pleasant if not leisurely tour. Bert "did keep us going on the Death Valley trip," Lou wrote to her friend Florence Stewart in Arizona.[6] They were up at 6:30 every morning, and drove steadily until 6 P.M. covering an average of 350 to 450 miles per day. Nevertheless, Lou enjoyed their time together. "I try to convince myself that to gad about with him is one of my duties,—and I am never home!"[7] They went to Yosemite in May, staying at the Ahwanee Hotel, whose manager Don Tressider was a Stanford graduate and a trustee of the university.

Although Bert had never used his presidential salary for personal needs, Lou worried that now that he was no longer drawing a federal paycheck, they might need to watch their pennies. "I am going to have to make strenuous economies," she wrote Allan.[8] "We have spent in the past, instead of being thrifty."[9] Her concern, as usual, was not for herself—"we will still have a roof and enough to eat and wear, and even for one or two people to look after us"—but for her husband, who was "so accustomed to directing the activities of many men, and thus achieving much more than he could by his unaided efforts. . . . If he is to be free in the next four years to help get this country back to sanity . . . we all have to do our part to scrape together as much in the way of funds as we can manage."[10] She herself would make do with only one secretary, and she would have to do without her personal maid, Agnes Thompson, since Agnes did not wish to leave Washington. Her charities would also have to be cut back. She informed Aunt Lill that her monthly $75 check would be reduced, although the regular $30 payments from Aunt Jennie's estate would not be affected.

As it turned out, Lou's fears were exaggerated. The family's financial base was still secure. With the necessity for extensive entertaining now ended, their expenses were considerably lower. Gradually, a new regime established itself. Lou discovered that she could live quite comfortably, and still manage to help those of her friends and relatives whom she felt needed assistance, without limiting Bert's activities in the least.

Agnes Thompson did come west with her for a few months, but missed her family too much to stay longer. Mildred Hall remained at her post as "general roustabout," while her fiancé, Allen Campbell, looked for a teaching job in San Francisco. Frank and Marie Franquet, the caretakers at the Palo Alto house for the past four years, continued to run the place. Kosta Boris continued on as Bert's valet, and Bert hired Paul Sexson, who had been one of their student house-sitters during his graduate days at Stanford in 1927–28, to be his secretary, a "temporary position" that lasted for three years. It was a much smaller staff than the Hoovers had been used to, but enough to do the job.

Although the hectic pace of the presidential years had abated, there was still more than enough to do in Palo Alto to keep Lou Henry Hoover active and happy. This was the life she had dreamed of living ever since she left England in 1917. Her only disappointment was that Bert preferred to spend most of his time in New York. "New York is the place where a large part of America's intellectual life is transmitted," Bert declared in his *Memoirs*.[11] He would make it his headquarters for the remainder of his life.

Bert was convinced that the Depression had actually ended by late 1932, and that the bank panic of early 1933 could have been stemmed if Roosevelt had joined him in a public statement that would reassure the nation's bankers. In the next few years, Hoover invested in farmland in the San Joaquin Valley in California and in mining ventures in the United States and South America. He continued to speak and write against the New Deal, but his political influence was limited both by continued Democratic opposition and by his own party's reluctance to support the man whom the American people firmly believed had caused the Depression. The opportunity Lou had hoped he would have to "direct many men" in public service projects would have to wait almost a decade, until another world war created a renewed need for humanitarian relief.

In June 1933 Lou was invited to speak at the commencement ceremonies at Whittier College in Whittier, the little town near Los Angeles where she had lived as a girl. She was interested to see the changes that had been made in the town since the days when she had lived there, and was pleased to become reacquainted with people she had known so many years ago. Whittier College elected her to its board of trustees, and she diligently attended the annual board meetings for the next ten years.

Lou was fifty-nine in 1933. Her energy and zest for life were undiminished. Although she remained bitter about the political mudslinging that had cost her husband his bid for reelection, she liked being able to concentrate on the things she most enjoyed: picnics or hiking trips in the mountains, concerts, visits with her grandchildren, and working as a volunteer on projects that appealed to her. She took an active interest in Stanford campus life. In keeping with her philosophy on physical education for everyone, she worked with Stanford's director of the Women's Student Health Service, Dr. Helen Pryor, to provide better athletic opportunities for women students and improved training for physical education teachers. Her home continued to be open to university groups for special events, as when she provided a buffet supper featuring grilled oysters and miniature enchiladas on the terrace for the university's Cap and Gown Society. She also offered her services to various community charitable organizations, including raising funds for the Stanford Convalescent Home's programs supporting the care of chronically ill children in their own homes.

Allan moved from Los Angeles to Fresno that summer, where he became involved in what Lou called the "ranching side of banking." Bert had purchased several ranches in the Bakersfield area. Within a short time, Allan had abandoned banking to take over the running of these ranches full time. It pleased Lou to have her younger son closer to home.

When her friend Mary Vaux Walcott, the elderly Quaker naturalist, came to California in July, Lou took her on a ten-day camping trip through Yosemite. Mildred Hall accompanied them, taking a welcomed break from her job of sorting through the large piles of letters Lou still received every day. Mildred was quite amazed by the stamina of these two elderly women, who took long hours of riding and sleeping on the ground quite for granted.

Although the volume of requests for assistance had declined, Lou still received a good many of them. She did her best to help those whose requests seemed authentic. As time passed, it seemed to her that the percentage of letters from the truly needy decreased substantially, while those simply hoping for a handout increased. She still had her network of friends around the country, who helped her to evaluate the requests and sometimes provided the needed financial aid themselves.

In October 1933 she and Bert went east to meet the Rickards in Chicago, where they attended the "Century of Progress" exhibition together. Lou was not impressed. "Parts of it are amusing," she wrote to Allan afterwards, "parts amazing; most of it dreary; and all singularly reminiscent of California highway architecture as practiced by filling stations and hot dog stands."[12]

Lou and Abbie then went on to Milwaukee for the Girl Scouts' national convention, while Bert accompanied Edgar back to New York. On her way home, Lou visited Girl Scout offices in Seattle and Portland, discussing national policies and local projects with local leaders. The Girl Scouts were pleased to have her more active on the local council, to which she had belonged for many years.

1934 was a year full of new beginnings for those whom Lou considered family. Kosta Boris and his Essie were married in January; Mildred Hall and Allen Campbell, in August. Both were given receptions at the Hoover home. When Del Large married Jean Parker in May, Lou loaned him money to start up a small printing business. Both of Abbie Rickard's daughters had new babies, who duly received gifts from their "Auntie Lou."

In response to the Smithsonian's request for an appropriate gown for her mannikin in their First Ladies exhibit, Lou sent a dress she said was not particularly significant, but one she had enjoyed wearing. It was a floor-length pale green satin with a draped cowl neckline, cap sleeves and a cord-belted waistline. Mary Vaux Walcott supervised its installation. After spending many frustrating hours attempting to arrange the mannikin's hair, Mary finally had to call in Agnes Thompson to do the job for her.

Lou refused, however, to allow her portrait to be hung with those of other First Ladies in the White House until Congress appropriated funds for a portrait of her husband. It was August 1939 before that happened.

Lou traveled frequently during 1934–35, mostly on Girl Scout business. In February she attended a weekend training course at Asilomar, and in March (after a short trip to Waco and Paso Robles) she took part in a Court of Honor at Redwood City. When problems arose in the Los Angeles council, Lou sent advice and names of contacts to Alice Conway, the field representative whom the national organization sent out to clear things up. In May, Lou drove down to Beverley Hills to attend a reception for Girl Scout dignitaries hosted by the new Los Angeles Commissioner Mildred (Mrs. Harvey) Mudd.

Lou took the train east in October to attend a variety of Girl Scout events preceding the convention in Boston, spending the weekend of the convention at Cedar Hill Camp outside Boston. She took Marie McSpadden, a Girl Scout worker who was working on her M.A. at Stanford, with her. Marie had been Lou's temporary secretary during the Los Angeles episode, and now served both as an official delegate to the convention from Palo Alto and Lou's unofficial aide.

Eleanor Roosevelt also attended the Boston convention. She and Lou met briefly before the meeting began. It was the first time the two women had met since the Hoovers left Washington in 1933. They chatted about the White House furniture, housekeeping, and the Lincoln Study. It was, Marie McSpadden said later, a "charming half hour, and then they went down to the auditorium" where Mrs. Roosevelt was officially installed as honorary president of the Girl Scouts. The newspapers, unaware that the meeting had taken place, wrote in their headlines "First Ladies Do Not Speak." Marie was dismayed. "I should have thought of a public briefing, but none of us did . . . everybody was very distressed."[13]

Abbie Rickard came to California in January 1935 to visit the Girl Scouts' Bay Area Council in her capacity as national treasurer. Lou held a tea in her old friend's honor, inviting a crowd of area Girl Scout dignitaries. In March Lou attended the twentieth anniversary celebration of the Pasadena Girl Scouts, rushing home afterwards to entertain Sheila MacDonald, daughter of Britain's Prime Minister Ramsay MacDonald. Sheila's older sister, Ishbel, had visited the Hoovers at the White House several years earlier, during their father's state visit to Washington. Lou was out of town again in April, when Lady Baden-Powell visited San Francisco, but she sent flowers to the chief guide, wife of the Scouting movement's founder.

Happy as she was about Mildred Hall's marriage, Lou was sorry to lose such a competent secretary. It took over a year to find an acceptable replacement. Marie McSpadden was too busy with her studies to accept a full-time position. Melissa Clark, whom Lou hired to replace Mildred in 1934, had trouble learning stenography and suffered two lengthy illnesses, which limited her effectiveness. Lou wrote to Mary Walcott that she was having difficulty keeping up with only one secretary, but could not afford two.

When Melissa left in September 1935 to become director of the Palo Alto Girl Scout Council, she was replaced by Helen Greene. Lou had known Helen for several years. Helen's parents were Stanford graduates and classmates of the Hoovers. As the first members of those early classes to marry, they often served as chaperones on field trips to the Redwoods. Helen herself met Lou for the first time when, as First Lady, she gave a luncheon at the White House for Helen's brother Carl after his wedding, holding it in the Green Room—a choice that Helen believed had been made for its whimsical appropriateness. Helen had helped Lou with her correspondence during the summer of 1930, when the news of Herbert's illness sparked an avalanche of sympathetic letters to the White House. Now she accepted the post of full-time secretary, much to Lou's satisfaction. Helen was quite fond of her employer, whose whimsies she especially enjoyed. Years later, she recalled Lou as rather a lonely woman, isolated from many of her friends by the many honors she had received over the years. Because of their diffidence, Lou always had to take the initiative in social matters, Helen said. She found it sad that this outgoing, sociable woman no longer enjoyed a normal, casual relationship with her peers.

Lou was a proud member of the audience at Stanford's May 1935 commencement, where her husband addressed the new graduates and their guests, seated in the university's football stadium. There had been considerable friction recently between Bert and the university's more liberal faculty, especially with regard to who should control the Hoover War Library. Bert had donated and developed the extensive collection, but the university librarian considered it to be a part of his domain. Issues such as the location of the collection and funding for acquisitions were major points of conflict. Ray Wilbur, Stanford's president and a close friend of Bert's for many years, found himself torn between friendship and his vision of the university's role. Lou felt that the invitation to speak at the commencement, and the subsequent formal dedication of the Hoover War Library, indicated the university's acceptance of her husband's prominent role in American history.

After visiting the San Diego Exposition with Bert in June, Lou returned to Palo Alto, while her husband went back to New York. She attended the Bay Area Girl Scout Council meeting in August, where plans were made for the national convention to be held in San Francisco in October. At that convention Lou was again elected national president of the Girl Scouts. Abbie Rickard, with New York's representative to the board, Flora Whiting, stayed at the Hoover home. To Lou's dismay, Abbie suffered an accident shortly before the convention opened, and could not be present to see her old friend honored once again.

Although Lou had kept in close touch with the Girl Scouts over the years, she found that her role as president had changed since the early 1920s. Then she had been deeply involved in the organization's day-to-day activities; now, she would serve primarily as a figurehead and good-will emissary. Although there were still many familiar faces on the board of directors—Abbie Rickard as treasurer, Harriet Barnes as secretary, Anne Choate as first vice president, and Genevieve Brady as chairman of the board—a new generation of leadership had taken over. The new national director, Constance Rittenhouse, was a competent woman with the kind of tact and energy that Lou had admired in Jane Deeter Rippin. Lou found her much more congenial than her predecessor, Josephine Schain. The regional organization set up in 1932 was functioning well, and membership had continued to rise despite the Depression.

By 1935 Lou's ambitious private housing venture, begun ten years earlier when she and Jean built five houses to be sold or leased at reasonable prices to young faculty members at Stanford, was becoming a burden. The houses had been very well received, and over the years, many members of the faculty had begun to purchase them. Lou had hoped eventually to sell them all. However, few of the purchasers had managed to pay off their mortgages before deciding to move on. Time after time the houses reverted to Lou, who then had to find someone to rent or buy them again. William Hyde, a banker in Palo Alto, served as her agent in this matter. She decided that the time had come to take steps to disengage herself permanently from the properties.

"Practically everything I have is in houses and lots," she once confided to Allan.[14] The Stanford house was in her name; she had tried during the presidency years to rent it out, but without success. Also, the house at 2300 S Street in Washington was hers. It had been rented from 1929–1931 to Senator Frederick Walcott, and then from 1931–1933 to Senator Kean. Since leaving the White House, the Hoovers had preferred to keep it available for Bert to use whenever he was in Washington, although they did rent it briefly to former Secretary of State Frank Kellogg in November and December of 1935. Lou's friends Gertrude Bowman and Alida Henriques kept an eye on it, and a minimal staff continued to run it. Lou also still owned her parents' former home in Monterey, in a neighborhood that was beginning to deteriorate, as well as some acreage her father had acquired on the Monterey peninsula.

Despite Bert's contention that the Depression was almost over by late 1932, its hold on America continued throughout the decade—a situation that Hoover blamed entirely on the New Deal. The younger generation, those who had entered the workforce between 1928 and 1930, was particularly vulnerable.

Several of the Hoover nieces and nephews were struggling financially. Charles McLean, husband of Lou's niece Hulda Hoover, had been working for the California Department of Weights and Measures for seven years without a raise. In 1938, burdened by the expenses of a new house and a third child, he applied for reclassification. Hulda asked Lou if she knew of anyone who might be able to help. Although she noted sadly that the Hoover name had become something of a political liability, Lou still knew many members of California's Republican establishment. She referred Chuck to Republican leader A. C. Mattei. Whether it was Mattei's influence that did the trick or not, Chuck finally got his reclassification and raise in February 1939.

Hulda's sister Louise had also had her share of troubles. Married the same year as her cousin Herbert, Louise had divorced her first husband, Ernest Dunbar, in 1936 and gone to work as a stenographer to support her two young daughters, Della Lou and Judith. In 1938 she married Harold Fouts, an oil company technician, but that marriage also ended in divorce two years later. Louise then went back to work as a secretary in an insurance office.

Del Large, Jean's son, had married Jean Parker in 1934, and now had two sons. His small-scale printing business, the Town Crier, that his Auntie Lou helped him start up had failed, and he returned to Stanford in 1936. His family lived on one of the Hoover ranches in Bakersfield. In 1937 he left school again when he found a job with a building firm in San Francisco.

His sister Janet, whose teenage years Lou had supervised with such concern, had attended Mills College, where she enjoyed the social atmosphere to the detriment of her grades. Lou worried that Janet might not stay in school, and that her friends were not suitable. By the spring of 1934 Janet was working for a newspaper in Carmel and anticipating an inheritance from her Large grandparents. In January 1939 she married Lewis Maverick, a San Francisco native employed by Union Oil.

The Hoover boys were less affected economically by the Depression than their cousins. Herbert Jr. was still working for TWA and delivering lectures at Cal Tech on a regular basis. He was becoming interested in oil exploration, as well as airplane technology, with special emphasis on the legal aspects of oil production. In 1940 he founded United Geophysical Co., an oil exploration firm that would eventually employ some 1,100 people and do $7 million of business annually. Between 1940 and 1947 he patented a number of oil-locating devices, some of which were quite successful. In May 1940 he and Peggy went on a three-month trip to South America, where he was to advise the Costa Rican government on the framing of laws to cover uranium mining. While he was there, he investigated the possibility of establishing a mining venture of his own (in partnership with his father and brother), but a revolution in El Salvador deflected him to Guatemala, where the mine was finally opened.

Since 1934 Allan had been running several ranches his father owned in the Bakersfield area. These ranches produced raisins and other fruits and vegetables, some of which his mother made a point of sending to friends at Christmas. Allan had developed one of the first farm shipping operations in the country, sending a full trainload of produce out every night to markets around the nation. There were four ranches in various parts of the state, which Allan supervised from his headquarters in the San Joaquin valley. He had built a house there, decorating it in reproduction early American. (His mother wrote a friend that Allan had "especially tabooed" the then-popular Mexican or Chinese styles as too trite).

On March 17, 1937, Allan married Margaret Coberley, known to her friends and family as Coby. Coby's family lived in the San Francisco area. Lou was especially fond of Coby. Although she got along quite well with Herbert Jr.'s wife, Peggy, Lou seems to have bonded particularly closely with Coby, who shared her mother-in-law's adventurous spirit. "I certainly was fortunate in the mothers-in-law my sons selected," she wrote a friend in 1941, "and those dear ladies did know how to bring up daughters,—so I have the two delightful ones now without any of the trouble of raising them!"[15] On November 15, 1938, Allan and Coby had their first child, a son named Allan for his father.

Bert and Lou Hoover were now in their sixties. Over the next few years, death began to claim increasing numbers of their friends and relatives. Lou's Uncle Wallace Weed had died in Shell Rock in 1934. In November 1936 her beloved Uncle Will Henry died in Palo Alto at the age of eighty-nine. He had been traveling with his ward, Mary Paul, in southern California when he became ill. Mary took him to the hospital in San Diego, where Joel Boone, the former White House physician now stationed at the San Diego naval base, was able to inform Lou of his condition. Mary herself was not well—she died four months later of a long-standing heart condition at the age of thirty-three.

Another death that struck close to Lou's heart was that of Abbie Rickard, on February 8, 1937. The funeral was held two days later, and Lou, who was in California, was unable to reach New York in time to attend. Lou and Abbie had shared a thirty-two-year friendship, beginning in London during Bert's mining years. They had worked together in relief projects during the first World War, and in Girl Scouting since 1927. Abbie had helped her find a housekeeper for the White House, and always had a room free in her home when Lou needed to spend a few days in New York. Lou would miss her greatly.

In August 1937 the Hoovers' friend Vernon Kellogg succumbed to Parkinson's disease after four years of increasing disability. John Agnew, who had been Bert's close colleague in London so many years ago, died in August 1939 while on a visit to California. In 1940 Mary Vaux Walcott (her Quaker naturalist friend) and Theodore Hoover's wife Mildred both died within a space of four months.

The effect of these losses shows in a letter Lou wrote in October 1937: "We unfortunately are having two of our very dearest friends apparently now suffering their final illnesses, and I am expecting to be called to either one or the other of them, and in opposite directions, at any time. So I just can't plan even the details that I would like to have settled in my calendar."[16]

Her calendar remained active, however. Between 1935 and 1940, she traveled frequently on Girl Scout business, attending board meetings in New York, regional conferences in Iowa and Colorado (1937), and national conventions in Cincinnati (1936), Savannah (1937), Kansas City (1938), and Philadelphia (1939). "I like to preside," she told a reporter in 1931, "because it's so nice and easy. You don't have to do anything; you just introduce others and they do all the work."[17]

Those who knew Lou best, however, knew that she was not one to shirk "the work." During the 1936 convention she hosted a Pioneer Dinner whose honored guests were women like herself whose connection with the Girl Scouts went back to its earliest days. Most of them had attended the 1925 conference on camping at Irondale, Missouri. Guests were encouraged to dress in nineteenth century pioneer costume. Like most of Lou's dinner parties, it was a great success. In March 1936 she traveled to St. Louis and Cincinnati, talking with Girl Scout officials in both cities. In May she was on the road again, visiting Colorado Springs, Salt Lake City, Chicago, and Duluth. On her way home from a 1937 board meeting in Boston, she toured Montana, Wyoming, Washington, and Colorado, where she met with local Girl Scout leaders, encouraging their comments on a nation-wide study that would result in a complete overhaul of the program in 1938. She also allowed herself to be photographed (in uniform) in a 1936 promotional campaign for a new fund-raising project: the annual Girl Scout cookie sale. Even after her term as president ended in 1937, she continued to serve on the board of directors as a vice president.

Another project that occupied Lou's attention in 1935 was the preservation of her husband's birthplace cottage in West Branch, Iowa. Lou had tried to buy the house in 1928 as a birthday present for her husband, but the owner, Mrs. Jennie

Scellars, said she would have to consult her children first, and as they could not be contacted before the birthday arrived, the opportunity passed.

Shortly after Bert's election to the presidency, Mrs. Scellars began showing visitors "the little room where our President was born" for ten cents a person. By mid-1931, some 34,000 people had passed through the home, and two weddings were performed there in 1929. Mrs. Scellars was now making a steady income from tourism, and when the Hoovers again asked in 1930 if she would sell, she refused. When Mrs. Scellars died in 1934, her heirs offered to sell the house to the Hoovers, but at a price that Bert found too steep. He wrote to a friend, Fred Albin, who lived in West Branch, and suggested that Albin buy the house for them "at the lowest price possible." In July 1935 Albin bought the house for $4,500, and in October he transferred the title to Allan Hoover, who had been handling the matter on his parents' behalf.

The house had been enlarged since the days when Bert had lived in it, and was "probably not in condition to last much longer," according to a memo thought to have been written by Lou. There were, she felt, two options: to restore the house to its 1880 appearance, or to demolish it and create a small park on the land (which included twelve lots of land in addition to the house).

By June 1937 the decision had been made to restore. Consulting with Bert, his brother Theodore, and their Aunt Mattie Pemberton, Lou had the newer portions of the house torn down and the cottage wing turned ninety degrees and moved back to its original location facing Downey Street. The Hoover family funded the entire project, but by late 1938 Lou was investigating the possibility of setting up an association to maintain the site in the future. On March 22, 1939, the Herbert Hoover Birthplace Society was incorporated, with Fred Albin as its president. By 1941 the state of Iowa was contributing funds to the site, and other funds were beginning to trickle in, relieving the Hoover family of the responsibility for the society's day-to-day expenses.

Another of Lou's projects, the founding of the Friends of Music at Stanford, began to take shape in 1937. Among the women whom Lou had met during her years in Washington was Elizabeth Sprague Coolidge, a wealthy philanthropist whose love for music led her to commission works from some of the greatest talents of the twentieth century. In addition to sponsoring countless performances, Mrs. Coolidge (no relation to the president of that name) funded the Coolidge Auditorium in the Library of Congress, a concert hall for chamber music that quickly achieved international acclaim.

Over lunch at the White House one day, Mrs. Coolidge asked Lou if there was someplace on the west coast where she could bring her quartets. Lou put her in contact with officials and music lovers at Mills College in San Francisco and at Stanford, where a steady stream of artists began to perform. In June and July 1934 the Pro Arte Quartet of Brussels presented the entire Beethoven string quartet series in six very well received concerts. In order to encourage continuing local support, especially on the financial level, for further such performances, Lou gathered together those of her friends who shared her love for music and formed the Friends of Music.

Beyond the society's immediate goal of supporting concerts, lectures and musical instruction at Stanford, however, lay a more ambitious dream. "It has always seemed to me a great pity," Lou wrote to a potential member in August 1937, "that we did not have a real department of music here, capable of having our graduates leave for the many and diverse fields of life that the University prepares them for with some adequate appreciation of the music that may come their way in the future. . . . I am one of many who have longed for years to have some music courses here for those who are to be busily engaged . . . in other lines. Alas, the University has not had funds to develop sufficiently a department of even this narrow caliber."[18] This dream would be realized ten years later with the establishment of Stanford's department of music.

After a strenuous three months of traveling on behalf of the Girl Scouts, Lou set off in early July 1937 on a ten-day horseback trip through Yosemite with her granddaughter Peggy Ann, her former secretary Philippi Butler, and Phil's daughter Patsy. Phil, who declared herself to be "shy of horses," was assured by Lou that the rides would be very simple, and that they would be accompanied by a professional guide who would see to setting up the tents and preparing meals at the campsites. The trip turned out just as Lou had promised, and was a great success. The two eleven-year-old girls were entranced by her fund of nature lore and campfire tales.

In late October, Lou returned from the Girl Scouts' twenty-fifth anniversary celebration and convention in Savannah, having completed her two-year term as president and been succeeded by Mrs. Frederick Brooke of Washington, D.C. She spent Thanksgiving with Allan and Coby at the ranch, and the next month was delighted to have her entire family together in Palo Alto for Christmas.

But in Europe, events were taking place that would soon threaten Lou's peaceful world.

Chapter 16

A War-Shadowed Twilight

In February 1938 Bert went on a fact-finding tour of Europe, where Hitler's Germany was beginning to show signs of the kind of aggression that many remembered from the early months of 1914. It was the second trip he had made there in the past year. He spent a month traveling to various nations and discussing the political situation with his contacts in European capitals.

Lou remained behind, attending a Girl Scout reunion in Berkeley and working on her many projects—charity fund drives, the West Branch house renovation, the Friends of Music. She was also becoming interested in the activities of Pro-America, a political organization formed a few years earlier by a group of well-to-do, mostly Republican women opposed to the New Deal. Although she agreed with the organization's beliefs, she had refused at first to become openly affiliated with it, fearing the negative effect association with the Hoover name might have on the group.

Lou had first heard of Pro-America in 1935, when a classmate, Agnes Morley Cleaveland, wrote to recommend it to her. Although Lou had never taken part in politics, she was deeply concerned about the direction in which the Roosevelt government seemed to be moving. In 1933 she wrote a lengthy dissertation to Allan about the Constitution in which she said, among other things, that "the success of any system of government depends on the character of the governed, and of the governors." She was appalled at the notion expressed by some editorial writers that the Constitution was outdated. "I think a balanced system of government, with three wheels interlocking, helping one another in orderly functioning, braking one another when any one gets erratic, is better than any dictatorship."[1]

She was also distressed by the apparently superficial grounding in governmental theory that young people were receiving from schools. "Two exceedingly nice boys came in to see us the other day," she wrote to Agnes Cleaveland, "graduating from Stanford University next Monday. . . . We talked briefly about Communism, Socialism, Fascism and Hitlerism, and they were pretty well-grounded in the general outlines of them all. When my husband asked them what they thought of the American system in comparison, they looked very blank and one said, 'Why, we haven't got a system, have we?' . . . They hadn't the faintest idea of what the first amendments to the Constitution [were] nor how they came to be incorporated. . . . They knew absolutely nothing of the principles which Washington, Adams, Jefferson, Hamilton, and even Franklin discussed at such length, nor how they developed until the present day."[2]

In March 1938 Lou held a luncheon for Ruth Simms, chairman of the California Republican Women's Clubs, with some fourteen guests, all of whom were involved to some extent with the party and the Pro-America movement. Lou agreed to become an honorary vice president of Pro-America. She wrote to several friends, recommending it to them, and encouraging them to become involved. It seemed to her that grass-roots opposition to the New Deal needed to be organized, but not necessarily through the existing Republican organization, with its habitual infighting and politicking. She had not forgiven the Republican Old Guard for its lack of support for her husband during his term in office. Pro-America, she explained to her friends, was not affiliated with the Republican party, though most of its members were Republicans. Its only cause was opposition to the New Deal, which its members felt had "practically extinguished the old principles."[3]

In an address before the California Federation of Women's Clubs in 1935, Lou spoke out against the threats to democracy posed by communism and fascism, whose powers in Europe were then increasing. These efforts were the closest she had ever come to active political involvement.

In August 1938 she accompanied Bert to the Rockies on a camping trip, during which she visited the regional Girl Scout office in Colorado and a Girl Scout camp in Utah. She attended the annual Girl Scout convention in Kansas City in October at which a new three-tier program for girls was introduced, and a biennial schedule adopted for national council meetings, to begin after 1939. For the first time, membership in the Girl Scouts had surpassed 500,000.

It may have been that same summer that Lou, now sixty-four, took yet another horseback camping trip to the top of Mt. Whitney in Sequoia Park with her equally elderly Stanford classmates, Isabell McCracken and Parnie Storey. Her secretary, Helen Greene, accompanied them. Like Mildred Hall before her, Helen was amazed at the hardihood of these women. She noted that Lou slept on the ground, although the other two ladies used air mattresses.

Lou was in New York for Girl Scout board meetings in February 1939 when she received the following telegram from Bert in Palo Alto: "We are having a party to celebrate the fortieth anniversary. Its deficiency is that you are not here. But we have in it all the affection that you could wish and another forty years is indicated. We are sending an appropriate mark of the occasion in a few days." It was signed by Bert, Herbert, Peggy, Allan, and Coby.[4]

This casual attitude toward anniversaries was not unusual. Once, when they were living in the White House, Lou arrived home to find that Bert had asked the cook to prepare a cake with dinner. He told her that he had read in the paper that it was his wife's birthday, and thought perhaps a cake would be appropriate. Such things always seemed to take Lou by surprise. She frequently forgot to do her Christmas shopping until the last minute. To avoid embarrassment, she always kept a supply of trinkets suitable for last-minute gift-giving tucked away in a drawer in her dressing room. These were items she had picked up in her travels, and were generally appreciated by their recipients as much as if they had been selected specifically with them in mind.

As soon as the Girl Scout board meetings ended, Bert and Lou took off together for Florida, where they had been invited by their friends Kitty and Jeremiah Milbank to spend a few days fishing on the *Saunterer*. In addition to being one of Hoover's financial backers during his presidential campaigns, Milbank had also invested in several of his new business ventures, including mines in Guatemala and Nevada. Now he was offering financial assistance to the Hoover War Library, to help it acquire materials from the new war beginning in Europe.

Lou attended the Region XI Girl Scout conference in Utah in April 1939. In May she drove with Allan and Coby to West Branch to check on the progress of the birthplace restoration. The three then went on to Washington, where the young Hoovers stayed at 2300 S Street while Lou proceeded to New York on Girl Scout business. At the Girl Scout convention in Philadelphia, she was pleased by the election of another Californian, Mildred Mudd, as national president. Lou had recruited Mildred, whose husband Harvey was a wealthy mining engineer headquartered in the Los Angeles area, to the movement in 1934.

In September 1939 Franklin Roosevelt asked Hoover to meet with him to discuss the organization of relief for the European continent in the war that had just broken out. It was the first time the Democratic President had attempted to consult with Hoover since the 1932 election, but nothing came of it. Hoover, however, was as committed as ever to the concept of non-partisan humanitarian relief. He spent many months working to find a way to get aid through the fighting to Belgium, France, Finland and Poland. As in 1914, he was opposed by Winston Churchill, who believed that the quickest way to end the war was to starve the Germans into submission; the difference this time was that Churchill was no longer a mere Cabinet Secretary, but prime minister of Great Britain. Lou, who shared her husband's feelings in this matter, helped to establish women's committees in America to aid the helpless non-combatants.

"Do not these days,—no, these months," she wrote to Florence Stewart, who had helped her to organize the American relief efforts in London so long ago, "cause a turmoil of emotions! Can't you see it all over there! . . . Don't you exclaim with amazement and horror at the fact that it can all be repeating itself such a little time after."[5] Like her husband, she hoped that this time the United States would be able to keep out of the war. She served as chairman of the Salvation Army's refugee clothing drive, and was active in the Red Cross efforts to collect clothing for European war refugees in New York. She also helped raise funds for her husband's Finnish Relief Fund.

In June 1940 the Women's Division of the National Amateur Athletic Federation finally ended its eighteen-year struggle for survival, merging with the American Association for Health, Physical Education and Recreation. This relieved some of the responsibility from Lou, who had been the organization's chief fundraiser (and often a major funding source), as well as its honorary vice president, ever since it was founded in 1922. She continued, however, to lend her support to efforts to make sports available to all women.

The year 1940 was a watershed in many ways. The stimulus of industry caused by the European war was finally bringing the long Depression to an end. Franklin D. Roosevelt shattered 144 years of tradition by running for—and winning—a third consecutive term as president. Hoover, who had hoped to return to office in 1936 but had not been able to secure his party's approval, once again cast his hat into the ring—and was once again rejected by his party, who selected Wendell Willkie as its standard bearer.

Writing to a friend in September 1940, Lou said, "Just for your own confidential edification I must quote to you what an acquaintance said to me the other day: 'I am spending every ounce of energy and mind I possess on electing Franklin D. Roosevelt for ex-President.' But you can also hunt for the good qualities of Willkie,— and there are really a lot,—and stress them mightily."[6] She accompanied her husband on a campaign trip for Willkie through the Midwest in October, applauding his speeches with the same unbridled enthusiasm she had always given him.

The most important event of 1940 for Lou, though, was not the presidential campaign nor even the birth of another grandson, Andrew, to Allan and Coby on November 9. It was Bert's decision finally to move their family headquarters to the new apartment he had secured in suite 31A of the Waldorf Towers in New York City. Since 1933 he had spent weeks at a time in New York, writing and lecturing on political issues and keeping abreast of American public opinion. Now he proposed to remain there year-round, and he wanted Lou with him.

"Take a look at the arrangements and camp here," he suggested in a telegram on November 30. Lou, who had loyally followed her husband everywhere he went since the first day of their marriage, agreed to this final uprooting with the same uncomplaining resignation she had shown when he decided to run for president. She settled easily into the elegant hotel whose other permanent residents included the Duke and Duchess of Windsor, Cole Porter, and the future Shah of Iran.

Neither life in the White House nor living in close proximity to such wealthy and aristocratic neighbors could affect Lou's down-to-earth character. One evening, some guests arrived at the Waldorf apartment for dinner. They looked around for their hostess, and not seeing her, asked where she was. "She's there," Bert replied, gesturing toward the table. "A light went out, and she knows all about these things so I let her fix them." At that moment, Lou emerged from under the table-cloth and greeted her guests as graciously as if nothing unusual had happened.[7]

In December the Hoovers rented the yacht *Virago* from a friend and invited the Richard Hannas—at whose Californian ranch at the foot of Mount Lassen Bert and Lou had spent a restful few days in July—to join them on a fishing holiday. Their old Washington neighbor, journalist Mark Sullivan, whose wife had recently passed away, was another guest. The party drifted quietly through the clear Caribbean waters off the Florida coast. It was a peaceful interlude in a world rapidly descending into chaos.

When she returned to New York in January 1941, Lou attended the twenty-first anniversary celebration of the Girls' Commercial High School. Its principal, her old schoolmate Evelyn Allan, was preparing to retire from the school which she had headed for its entire existence. Evelyn's work in the field of vocational training for young women was highly regarded. At her side on this occasion was the thirteen-year-old girl whom she had adopted two years previously, and whose name she had changed from Doris Louella Weston to Lou Weston Allan. She had made a special point of introducing Lou to her new namesake.

In April Lou accompanied Constance Rittenhouse, the Girl Scout national director, on a tour of the northwestern states, and then went on to California to attend the board of trustees meetings at Whittier College. Lou and Bert spent July 4th with the Hannas at their ranch. In August Allan and Coby joined them in a trip through the mountains of southern Colorado and northern New Mexico.

But most of the summer was taken up with the preparations for Stanford's fiftieth anniversary celebration, and the official opening of the Hoover Institute on War, Revolution and Peace, now established in its own building on the campus. Bert gave a speech at the Stanford anniversary ceremony on October 1. Herbert Jr. and Allan and their families came up to Palo Alto for the dedication ceremony. It was the first time the whole family had been together since young Andy's birth almost a year before.

After the Stanford ceremonies, Bert took the train back to New York. He was eager to complete the final draft of his book, *America's First Crusade*, to be published in December. Lou followed by car, taking a leisurely drive with her old friend Susan Dyer through Arizona, New Mexico, Oklahoma, Indiana, and Ohio. The ostensible reason for the trip was to bring the car east for Bert, but for Lou it was an excuse for yet another adventure. She and Sue visited friends along the way and stopped briefly at Lou's parents' childhood home in Wooster, Ohio.

Like many Americans, the Hoovers were enjoying a quiet day in the country on December 7, 1941. As they drove back to New York from their weekend in Bucks County, Pennsylvania, Bert asked Lou to turn off the radio, so as to prolong the peaceful atmosphere of their holiday. Thus, it was not until they reached the Waldorf that they learned the news of Japan's sudden attack on Pearl Harbor.

Lou was particularly upset by the news, because her sister, Jean, was in Honolulu. Janet's husband, Lewis Maverick, was an officer in the army reserve, and had been activated in 1940. Transferred into the regular army with the rank of lieutenant, he was assigned to Honolulu in September. Janet joined him there a few months later. It soon became apparent that their marriage was in trouble. In August 1941 Jean had boarded a steamship for Honolulu. She was, she wrote to Lou, "the world's worst sailor—second only to Bert,"[8] but her daughter needed her, and so she must go. While many Americans, including Lou, believed that war with Japan was imminent, Jean had reported that in Hawaii "there seems to be a feeling of perfect safety."[9] She was staying with Janet in the Mavericks' home just outside the city when the attack came. At first, they thought it was a drill, but they soon learned differently.

Frantic concerning her sister's safety, Lou managed to contact Lewis's commanding officer, who assured her that Jean and Janet were well. Soon a letter arrived from Jean, describing the events of December 7, and repeating the same assurances. Because mail to Hawaii was now restricted, Lou set up a round-robin system to keep the family informed of Jean's affairs.

There appears to have been some scandal connected with Lewis Maverick's service in Hawaii. "Maverick, on advice, resigned when his term was up and returned to the Mainland," Lou wrote to her husband.[10] Janet remained in Honolulu, where she found a job as secretary to a bus and taxi company, replacing a man who had left to join the army. She also divorced Maverick. During the next year, Janet and Jean often gave parties for the young officers who passed through the Honolulu area. Jean claimed that while the army provided plenty of entertainment for enlisted men, the officers were relatively neglected. In October 1942 Janet married one of these officers, Rhodes Brooks of South Carolina. The following spring, Jean and her daughter finally returned to the States.

Lou went back to California in January 1942 to wind up the trusteeship of the little houses on the Stanford campus. She found the west coast in the grip of panic, certain that Japan would follow up its Pearl Harbor success with an attack on the American mainland. Del Large was considering the wisdom of sending his family to stay at one of the Hoover ranches, away from the military bases in the San Francisco area. Theodore Hoover had taken charge of the coastal watch for the section of coast on his ranch, and had actually sighted a submarine one day.

Lou found it all highly entertaining. "We are really very unconcerned over all the really amusing war preparations going on here," she wrote Bert's cousin Harriette Odell back in Kansas. "Palo Alto is hysterically busy. Everyone is doing his or her bit but the amateurish attempts are awfully funny and very often get lost in complications."[11]

The Hoover sons (now aged thirty-nine and thirty-five) did not serve in the army during World War II, but they were involved in war-related work. Allan's agricultural shipping organization was a part of the nation's food supply network. Herbert applied his mechanical aptitude to the testing of various mechanisms designed to improve military aviation.

Lou had intended to return to New York in February 1942, but one thing after another kept her in Palo Alto through the summer. She looked after the children for Allan and Coby while they took a short trip east in February, then in March she drove down to Los Angeles to check on her aunt and uncle, Jessie and Ed Jones, and on Bert's sister May, all of whom were ill. (May and her family had returned to California some years earlier, and now lived in Santa Monica.) Bert and his old friend Hugh Gibson, the former Ambassador to Belgium who was now director of Bert's committee for Polish and Belgian relief, arrived in April and took Lou with them on a fishing trip to Oregon. From there, she went to Butte, Montana, for a Girl Scout conference. Then it was back to southern California for Whittier College's annual board meeting. In July, Lou took Herbert Jr.'s youngest, twelve-year-old Joanie, for a long-promised ten-day horseback trip up Mount Lassen, stopping on the way to visit with the Hannas at their ranch.

A proposal that spring by Stanford's Quaker chaplain, Dr. David Elton Trueblood, to build a meeting house on the campus met with her approval. To Bert she confessed that the Quaker meeting in Palo Alto "bores me so I just don't go to it."[12] She missed the inspirational leadership of Professor Augustus Murray, who had died in 1940.

Lou and Bert had decided to turn the Stanford house over to the university to be used as the president's official residence. Ray Lyman Wilbur had retired as president at the end of 1941, assuming the honorary post of chancellor, and in August 1942 the board of trustees elected its new chairman, Don Tressider, as Wilbur's successor. The Hoovers had known Tressider for many years, although they were not as close to him as they had been to Ray Wilbur. He had been their host on many occasions when he was manager of the Ahwanee Hotel in Yosemite Park, and he had served with Bert for several years on the university's board of trustees.

During her free moments, Lou had begun weeding out her boxes of papers in the Palo Alto house. She had acquired a new secretary to help her with this task, as Helen Greene had left in 1937 to be married. Lou hired Bernice Miller, a friend and classmate of Hulda Hoover McLean, to replace Helen. Bunny, as she was called, went with Lou to New York, where Bert preempted her to work on his book. Soon Bunny was working full time for Bert, and Lou had to find another new secretary. In 1942 she hired Edith Harcourt to help with her correspondence and files. Dare McMullin, who was now living on the east coast, also helped Lou to organize her files and her budgets.

Now in her sixty-ninth year, Lou Henry Hoover was beginning to feel the passage of time. She had never been one to admit to weakness, taking her occasional illnesses with a wry humor. Nevertheless, she seems to have had a sense of an approaching end as the year 1943 passed. Perhaps it was the process of cleaning out her home, and turning it over to someone else, that inspired her, in November 1943, to write a letter to her sons that would serve as a holographic will.

This was not her first will. In early 1924 she had signed a short, simple will dividing her estate among her husband and sons. It was this will she sought to change with her letter to her sons later that same year, when she was worried about her sister Jean's financial status. In 1928 she changed her mind again, and prepared a typed memo prepared with the advice of William Mullendore, the Los Angeles lawyer who had been Bert's assistant counsel in the Food Administration and had provided the Hoovers with legal advice for many years. This will again divided her estate among her husband and sons. But with all the confusion involved in moving her files out of the California house, she had lost track of it, so she decided to write her wishes out again, in case of sudden need.

To Bert, she left her share in their community property and the funds, investments and securities listed in her name. The Stanford house furnishings, any real estate with the exception of her Washington, D.C. property (the house at 2300 S Street), and any cash left in her bank account, she left to her two sons, share and share alike. "I [am] a lucky woman," she wrote, "to have my life's trails alongside the paths of three such men and boys. . . . You have both been good boys, and an immeasurable source of happiness and satisfaction to me."[13]

The Hoovers spent part of the summer in Palo Alto, living in a rented home on campus, as they had done in the years before the house at 623 Mirada was built. In the fall, their oldest grandchild, Peggy Ann, entered Stanford as a freshman, carrying on the family tradition. Kosta Boris, Bert's former valet, proudly displayed his newborn son for the Hoovers' admiration. In October, Lou traveled to Cleveland to attend her last Girl Scout convention. For Lou Hoover, it was a very quiet year.

In the afternoon of Friday, January 7, 1944, Lou and Bunny Miller went to a concert given by an old friend, the harpist Mildred Dilling, in New York. When the concert ended, Lou said to Bunny, "Let's walk home—the air feels so good." But after a few minutes, she changed her mind, and asked Bunny to hail a cab. They reached the Waldorf Astoria and rode up in the elevator to the thirty-first floor, where Lou told Bunny good night.

Edgar Rickard was with Bert that evening, as they were to attend a dinner together. Lou went into the bedroom. When Bert went in a few minutes later to say goodbye before leaving for the dinner engagement, he found her lying on the floor by the bed. She had suffered a fatal stroke. A doctor was immediately called, but all attempts to revive her failed.

Bert was stunned. "She's gone," he said. As he struggled to come to terms with his loss, Edgar Rickard and Bunny Miller took charge. Edgar called the boys, while Bunny dealt with arrangements for the funeral and obituary.

More than 1,500 mourners filled St. Bartholomew's Episcopal Church next door to the Waldorf Astoria on Monday morning, January 10. Behind the family, several rows of pews had been reserved for two hundred uniformed Girl Scouts. Close family friends Edgar Rickard, Hugh Gibson, and Lewis Strauss were all present. Gertrude Bowman came up from Washington. Long-time servants Ellis Sampson and Leon Thompson also came north for the service.

The coffin was covered with a blanket of smilax, sweet peas, lilacs, and red roses. A choir sang some of Lou's favorite hymns: "Nearer, My God, to Thee," "I Heard a Voice," "Hark, Hark My Soul," and the Twenty-Third Psalm. The rector of St. Bartholomew's, the Rev. Dr. George Paull T. Sargent, conducted the service, and the Rev. Dr. Rufus Jones, chairman of the American Friends Service Committee, read passages from First Corinthians, Revelation, and the Gospel of St. John. There was no eulogy. At the end of the service, Dr. Sargent led Bert and his sons out through a side door, to spare them the ordeal of greeting the crowd.

The casket was taken to Grand Central Station, where it was placed aboard the 4:20 train for the West Coast. Bert, his sons, and Bunny Miller accompanied it. Lou was buried at Alta Mesa Cemetery in her beloved Palo Alto.

"I was married one day and sailed for China the next," she once told Mildred Hall. "I found there was pioneering to do in China thirty odd years ago—and in the mountains of Burma, and on the deserts of West Australia, and in New Zealand and Tasmania and the Ural mountains 'before the war.' I wondered sometimes then if my pioneering was only half pretend. For I always kept a home in California to come back to once or twice a year—not because it was the last stand of the special pioneers whom I adored, not because I thought it had become the last full beautiful flower of civilization—which I did. (The more I saw of other civilizations, the firmer I *knew* that.) But because I never saw a more comfortable, more beautiful spot to settle down in—in which I could ultimately sit in a rocker (I never *did* outgrow a rocker) before a fire (even in July) and dream of places I had been—of the things of many sorts I had seen. For long years, in the back of my mind, I carried the idea that one lived vitally in order to store up memories to live quietly when activity was done. Alas, I find that life always has so much action, so many duties, that there is no time to reminisce."[14]

On July 21, 1944, the London String Quartet performed a memorial concert at Stanford University in honor of Lou Henry Hoover. They played Schubert's Quintet Opus 163 and Brahams' Sextet Opus 18. It was a fitting tribute to the woman whose love for good music had brought a high quality of professional performances to the West Coast.

Later that year, Bert officially gave the house at 623 Mirada to the university. He asked that it be called the Lou Henry Hoover House in memory of the woman who had designed, built and loved it for so many years. The old "Seeing Cairo Fund," established thirty-five years earlier by the Hoovers and Rickards to finance joint vacations around the world, was dissolved, its proceeds donated to the Hoover War Library in Lou's memory. In the fall, shortly after the presidential election that gave Franklin Roosevelt his fourth consecutive term in office, the house at 2300 S Street in Washington was sold for $87,250. Bert had now disposed of all their joint property. For the next twenty years, Herbert Hoover lived in New York, in the apartment on the thirty-first floor of the Waldorf Astoria, alone except for his staff.

In one of his last acts before his death in 1964, Bert ordered that his wife's papers—letters, manuscripts, memoranda, souvenirs, some 220,000 items in all—be sealed for a further twenty years. He didn't want her memory to be marred, he said, by the publication of some sharp words she might have written in defense of those she loved. It was a final tribute by a man who thoroughly understood and respected his wife's reticent character.

Epilogue

One Last Move

In late October 1964, the Rev. Thomas Hulme, rector of Grace Episcopal Church in Cedar Rapids, Iowa, received a telephone call from John Turner, director of the prestigious Turner Mortuary and a long-time member of his parish. He had a very special favor to ask, Turner said. He had asked the Bishop of Iowa to do it, but the bishop was not free and had suggested Rev. Hulme take his place. The body of Mrs. Hoover was being brought to West Branch, where her husband had recently been buried with great ceremony, and the family wanted an Episcopal priest to preside over her recommittal. There was to be absolutely no publicity; Hulme was sworn to secrecy on the subject. He would be picked up at the church on Sunday morning, October 29, at 7:30. Arrangements had been made for another priest to take his 8 A.M. service. Not even his wife was to know where he was going.

Intrigued, and aware that the arrangements were already so far along that it would be awkward for him to refuse, the Rev. Hulme agreed. Promptly at 7:30, a black limousine appeared behind the church, whisking him away from his startled congregation and down the interstate to the Hoover birthplace at West Branch. A Secret Service car accompanied them; when they reached the gravesite, he saw still more Secret Service men scattered around the site. "There was one behind every tree," Hulme later recalled, smiling.[1]

In the chill, drizzly October morning, the young priest read the burial service from his prayer book as Lou Henry Hoover's casket was lowered into the ground beside her husband's grave. As he said the final words, John Turner leaned over and whispered, "Now she's in holy ground—do you think you could just extend the consecration a little further.?" He gestured towards the former president's grave.

Hulme nodded, swinging his arm a little wider as he made the sign of the cross over the graves.

When the service ended, Father Hulme returned to his limousine and was taken back to Cedar Rapids, where he arrived in time to conduct the 10 A.M. service. With some difficulty, he managed to keep from explaining to his curious parishioners—and his wife—where he had been. Finally, around noon, a formal announcement came over the radio that Lou Henry Hoover had been reburied beside her husband in West Branch that morning. The quiet, inconspicuous service was completely in keeping with the character of a woman who had always preferred to keep personal matters private.

Appendix A

Families

HENRY FAMILY

William Henry (1818–1856) m. Mary Ann Dwire (1827–1912)

    Charles Delano Henry (1845–1928) m. Florence Ida Weed (1849–1921)

      Lou Henry (1874–1944) m. Herbert Hoover (1874–1964)

        Herbert (1903–1969)

        Allan (1907–1993)

      Jean Henry (1882–1958) m. Guthrie Large

        Janet Large (1912–1982) m. Lewis Maverick
                       m. Rhodes Brooks

        Delano Large (1913–1983) m. Jean Parker

        Walter Sidney Large (1916–1922)

    William Dwire Henry (1847–1936)

    Addison Morgan Henry (1848–1906) m. Ann (Nannie) Mole (1864–?)

      Addison V. Henry

      Mary Henry

      Dorothy Henry (1893–1975) m. John (Jack) Matthews

        William

        John III

        two others

WEED FAMILY

Phineas K. Weed (1821–1895) m. Philomelia Sophia Scobey (1827–1897)

Florence Ida (1849–1921) m. Charles Delano Henry (1845–1928)
see above

Jennie Alice (1852–1927) m. Judson Powers
m. George Mager (died 1921)

Wallace Phineas (1858–1934) m. Lillian Stewart (1861–1945)

Arle Gideon (1886–1967) m. Blanche

Jessie Scobey (1866–?) m. Edward Jones (1864–1942)

HOOVER FAMILY

Jesse Clark Hoover (1846–1880) m. Hulda Minthorn (1848–1884)

Herbert Clark (1874–1964) m. Lou Henry (1874–1944)

Herbert Charles (1903–1969) m. Margaret Watson (1905–1983)

Margaret Ann (1926–) m. Richard Brigham

Herbert III "Pete" (1927–) m. Meredith McGilvray

Joan Ledlie (1930–) m. Leland Vowles (div.)

Allan Henry (1907–1993) m. Margaret Coberly (1911–)

Allan Jr. (1938–) m. Marian Cutler (div.)

Andrew (1940–) m. Victoria Talman (div.)
m. Jean Williams

Lou Henry (1943–)

Theodore Jesse Hoover (1871–1955) m. Mildred Crew Brooke (1872–1940)

Mildred Brooke (1901–1983) m. Cornelius Willis

Theodore (1925–)

David (1926–)

Mildred Anne (1932–)

Hulda Brooke (1906–) m. Charles McLean

Charles Alexander (1931–)

Allan Hoover (1935–)

Robertson Brooke (1939–)

Louise Brooke (1908–1985) m. Ernest Dunbar (div.)
m. Harold J. Fouts (div.)
m. Kenneth Stevenson (div.)
m. William Hauselt (div.)

Della Lou Dunbar (1926–)

Judith Dawn Dunbar (1928–)

Mary Blanche "May" Hoover (1876–1953) m. Cornelieus Van Ness Leavitt (1874–1962)

Van Ness Hoover (1907–1992) m. Dorothy Berry (div.)
m. Patricia Rheinschild

two sons

Appendix B

Secretaries, Aides, Servants, and Friends

SECRETARIES

Laurine Anderson, 1914–20 (HH secy) m. Stanwood Small

Dare Stark, 1918–22 m. John Hays McMullin

Susan Bristol, 1922–23 NAAF/WD

Philippi Harding, 1920–24, 1930–32 m. Frederick Butler

Louisette Aubert Losh, 1922–24 m. William Losh

Virginia Burks, 1924–25

Anna Fitzhugh, 1925–26

Martha Noyes, 1926–27

Ruth Fesler, 1928–31 m. Robert Lipman

Mildred Hall, 1927–34 m. T. Allen Campbell

Mary Randolph, 1928–29

Doris Goss, 1930–33

Marie McSpadden, 1934 m. John Sands

Melissa Clark, 1934–35

Helen Greene, 1930, 1935–37 m. Bolton White

Bernice "Bunnie" Miller, 1938–44

Edith Harcourt, 1942–44

AIDES

Catherine Fletcher, 1914–17

Gertrude Bowman, 1917–44

Alida Henriques, 1917–42

Caroline Goodhue, 1920–27

Susan Dyer, 1918–44

George Harrison, 1919–23

SERVANTS

Washington, D.C.

Alfred Butler, gardener and handyman, 1917–33

Carrie Butler, maid, 1917–22

Ellis Sampson, butler, 1921–33

Leon and Agnes Thompson, houseman and maid, 1926–33

Mary Rattley, cook, 1921–29

Kosta Boris, Hoover's valet, 1919–34

Palo Alto

Henry ?, cook, 1919–22

Alfred Butler, caretaker, 1920–22

Carrie Butler, housekeeper, 1920–22

Clarence and Bessie Doleman, caretakers, 1922–26

Carrie Butler Massenburg and Bland Massenburg, caretakers, 1927–29

Frank and Marie Franquet, caretakers, 1929–33

Frank Lee, cook, 1933–41

Robert Perry, watchman, 1929–41

David Sanquinetti, gardener, 1929–41

Mary Gianelli, caretaker, 1935–41

Monterey

Matias Estella, houseboy, 1921–29

Philip Anastosi, caretaker, 1929–35

White House

Ava Long, housekeeper

Irwin Hoover, chief usher

Ellis Sampson, chief butler

Encarnacion Rodriguez, assistant butler

Leon Thompson, butler

Alonzo Fields, butler

Katherine Bruckner, head cook

Hannah Heffernan, second cook

Maggie Rogers, chief maid

Agnes Thompson, personal maid

Annie Fulton, maid

Nora Mannix, maid

Lillian Carter, maid

FRIENDS

Ephraim D. Adams, Stanford University professor of history

John Agnew, Australian mining engineer, HH's colleague in London

Evelyn Wight Allan, Stanford schoolmate, sorority sister, principal of Girls' Commercial High School, NYC

Sarah L. Arnold, former dean of Simmons College, Girl Scout president, 1925–28

Mary Austin, popular writer

Mary Bainbridge, wife of U.S. secretary in Beijing, 1900

Lindon & Josephine Bates, prominent engineer, colleagues of Hoovers in CRB, son died on *Lusitania*

Julius & Harriet Barnes, grain dealer, CRB/ARA official, wife on Girl Scout executive council

Genevieve Brady, wife of wealthy philanthropist, chairman of Girl Scout executive council

John C. Branner, geology professor, Stanford—president of Stanford

Joel T. Boone, navy doctor, White House doctor under Harding, Coolidge, and Hoover

Ethel Bagg Bullard, colleague of LHH in London and Washington during World War I

A. B. Clark, professor of art, Stanford University

Birge Clark, architect

Agnes Morley Cleaveland, college classmate, active in Pro America movement

Katherine Jewell Everts, founder of camp and school of arts in Vermont

Adeline Fuller, classmate of Jean Henry, colleague in Food Administration Club

Hugh Gibson, diplomat, ambassador, colleague of HH in CRB

Lillian Gilbreth, management engineer, served on Girl Scout board

David Starr Jordan, Stanford's first president, active in peace movement pre–World War I

Edith Starr Jordan, daughter of David S. Jordan, college friend of LHH

Vernon & Charlotte Kellogg, instructor at Stanford when Hoovers were students, colleagues on CRB/ARA, both wrote biographical sketches of Hoovers

Charles & Anne Lindbergh, "Lucky Lindy," aviator

Edith G. Macy, Chairman of Girl Scout executive board, 1918–25

Marie M. Meloney, editor of *Delineator* and *NY Herald Tribune Sunday Magazine*, founder of Better Homes movement

Jeremiah & Kitty Milbank, wealthy philanthropist, raised money for HH's campaign, War Library

Harvey & Mildred Mudd, wealthy California mining engineer, wife was president of Girl Scouts, 1939–41

Augustus T. Murray, Stanford professor of religion, prominent Quaker preacher, preached at Washington Meeting House

Harriette Miles Odell, cousin of HH

Mary Paul, Native American ward and companion to William Henry

Mark & Florence Requa, California mining engineer, HH assistant in Food Administration

Lawrence Richey, HH's secretary, 1917–33

Edgar & Abbie Rickard, former editor of *Mining Magazine*, HH's assistant in CRB/ARA, handled Hoovers' financial affairs, Abbie was Treasurer of Girl Scouts

James Rippin, architect

Jane Deeter Rippin, Executive Director of Girl Scouts, 1918–30, later president of NAAF/WD

Florence Stewart, colleague in London, moved to Arizona for health reasons

Thomas & Parnie Storey, professor of hygiene at Stanford and CCNY, Parnie was classmate of LHH

Lewis Strauss, NY banker, HH's secretary, 1917–19

French Strother, HH's administrative assistant and speech writer

Mark Sullivan, prominent journalist, neighbor on S Street in Washington

Alonzo E. Taylor, MD, served on CRB/ARA and Food Administration

Mrs. Tiru-Navuk-Arasu, Ceylonese friend

Donald Tressider, manager of Ahwanee Hotel in Yosemite Park, Stanford president

Mary Vaux Walcott, geographer, naturalist, artist, prominent Quaker, widow of director of Smithsonian Institution

Ray Lyman Wilbur, classmate of HH, MD, Stanford president 1916–43, secretary of interior, 1929–33

Christine Vest Witcofski, teacher at Rapidan School

Appendix C

Honorary Awards Given to Lou Henry Hoover

1914	Gold Medal from Mining & Metallurgical Society
1916	Letter of thanks from Queen of Belgium
1918	Queen Elizabeth Medal (Great Britain)
1919	Chevalier, Order of Leopold (Belgium)
1921	Certificate from Polish Children of Jaworow
1921	Letter of thanks from women of Stollberg, Saxony
1923	Honorary degree, Mills College
1928	Honorary degree, Whittier College
1929	Certificate from Latvian National Women's League
1929	Honorary degree, Swarthmore College
1930	Honorary degree, Elmira College
1930	Lace from Belgian delegation
1931	Honorary degree (LLD: Social Services), Goucher College
1931	Medal, Yorktown Sesquitennial Commission
1932	Honorary degree, Tufts University
1932	Honorary degree, Wooster College

Notes

PROLOGUE

1. Charlotte Kellogg, "The Young Hoovers," *Saturday Evening Post*, March 2, 1928.

2. Ruth Fesler Lipman, Oral History interview, 1967, Herbert Hoover Presidential Library (Hereafter abbreviated as HHPL).

3. Karen Blair, *The Clubwoman as Feminist (1868–1914)* (New York: Holmes & Meier, 1980).

4. Mary Daughtery, New York *Journal*, June 15, 1928, "Women's Suffrage and Feminism," Lou Henry Hoover (Hereafter abbreviated as LHH). Subject files, HHPL.

5. LHH speech in Toledo, Ohio, 1932.

6. LHH speech at Girl Scout Convention, St. Louis, 1926.

7. LHH letter to Mrs. George T. Gerlinger, February 16, 1942. Mary Austin was a noted writer with whom the Hoovers were acquainted at one time.

8. Blair, *The Clubwoman as Feminist.*

CHAPTER 1

1. Mary Ann Dwire Henry to William Henry, April 7, 1876, LHH Correspondence files, HHPL.

2. Ibid.

3. LHH school essay, June 8, 1888, HHPL.

4. LHH to Mark Sullivan, August 27, 1927, LHH Organization files, HHPL.

5. Ms. written by LHH for her family, undated but after 1932, LHH files, HHPL.

6. LHH letter quoted by Ruth Fesler Lipman in Genealogy file, 1960, LHH files, HHPL.´

7. Ibid.

8. LHH to *St. Nicholas* magazine, December 1887, LHH Correspondence files, HHPL.

9. LHH to Mr. Perry, May 7, 1937, LHH Correspondence files, HHPL.

10. Memo dated 1929, LHH Correspondence files, HHPL.

11. LHH Diary, February 12, 1890, LHH Correspondence files, HHPL.

12. Harley Jordan to LHH, undated, LHH Correspondence files, HHPL.

13. Clipping of interview from *Saturday Evening Post*, June 9, 1928, LHH Correspondence files, HHPL.

14. LHH Diary, May 2, 1891.

15. Philomelia Weed to Florence Henry, May 16, 1893, LHH Correspondence files, HHPL.

CHAPTER 2

1. Quoted in *Stanford Album: A Photographic History*, by Margo Davis and Roxanne Nilan, Stanford University Press, 1989.

2. Will Irwin, *Herbert Hoover: A Reminiscent Biography* (New York: Century, 1928), p. 65.

3. Elizabeth Frazer, "Mrs. Herbert Hoover: Portrait of an American Lady," *Saturday Evening Post*, June 9, 1928.

4. Herbert Hoover (Hereafter abbreviated as HH), *Memoirs of Herbert Hoover*, vol. 1, p. 23 (New York: Macmillan, 1951–52).

5. LHH to Everitt Smith, November 23, 1914, LHH Correspondence Files, HHPL.

6. Richard Norton Smith, *An Uncommon Man* (New York: Simon & Schuster, 1984), p. 70.

7. Jean Henry to Charles Henry, 1901, LHH Correspondence files, HHPL.

8. Irwin, *Herbert Hoover: A Reminiscent Biography*, p. 59.

9. Oral History interview with Susan Dyer, 1966, HHPL.

10. Correspondence with Ida Wehner, 1896–97, LHH Correspondence Files, HHPL.

11. Oral History interview with Adeline (Mrs. Parmer) Fuller, 1967, HHPL.

12. LHH to Joel T. Boone, January 28, 1937, LHH Correspondence files, HHPL.

13. Albert Whittaker to LHH, July 1898, LHH Correspondence files, HHPL.

14. J. C. Branner to LHH, June 26, 1898, July 20, 1898 and February 2, 1899, LHH Correspondence files, HHPL.

15. LHH to L. Evelyn Wight, undated (ca. 1898), LHH Correspondence files, HHPL.

16. Vernon Kellogg, *Herbert Hoover, the Man and His Work* (New York: D. Appleton & Co., 1920), p 68.

17. HH, *Memoirs*, vol. 1, p. 28.

18. Harriette Miles Odell to Theodore Hoover, February 18, 1920; Herbert Hoover to ???, quoted in Helen Pryor, *Lou Henry Hoover: Gallant First Lady* (New York: Dodd Mead, 1969).

19. HH, *Memoirs*, vol. 1, p. 23.

20. As described by Evelyn W. Allan in the February 1944 issue of *The Key* of KKG. The exact wording of this telegram (which was not preserved) is often disputed. The only thing that most of those involved agree upon is that the word "marriage" did not appear in it.

21. LHH to Jean Large and Susan Dyer, fall 1930, LHH Subject Files, HHPL.

22. Florence Henry to Mrs. George Mason, March 12, 1899, LHH Correspondence files, HHPL.

23. Theodore Hoover, memoir:"Being a Statement By an Engineer," undated (ca. 1940), HHPL.

24. Oral History interview with Susan Dyer, 1966, HHPL.

CHAPTER 3

1. LHH Diary, February 11, 1899.

2. LHH, Chinese character studies, LHH papers, HHPL.

3. LHH, notes on Boxer Rebellion, LHH subject files, HHPL.

4. Chu'an Yueh-tung to Helen Downes, 1929, LHH papers, HHPL.

5. HH, *Memoirs*, vol. 1, p. 36.

6. LHH to Jennie Weed Powers, June 14, 1899, LHH Correspondence files, HHPL.

7. LHH Diary, April 27, 1899.

8. LHH Diary, June 9, 1899.

9. LHH Diary, June 7, 1899.

10. LHH, Chinese character studies, LHH Papers, HHPL.

11. Mary Bainbridge to LHH, 1900, LHH Correspondence files, HHPL.

12. LHH Diary, June 13, 1899.

13. Ibid.

14. LHH to Mrs. Cutler, September 15, 1939, LHH Correspondence files, HHPL.

15. HH to Jean Henry, January 12, 1900, LHH Correspondence files, HHPL.

16. LHH to Jean Henry, undated, ca. January 12, 1900, LHH Correspondence files, HHPL.

17. Hulda McLean, *Uncle Bert: A Biographical Portrait of Herbert Hoover,* (West Branch, Iowa: Herbert Hoover Presidential Library Association, 1974), p. 7.

18. LHH Diary, October 27, 1900.

19. LHH to Jennie Weed Powers, undated (1899), LHH Correspondence files, HHPL.

20. LHH to Mary Austin, as quoted in Nash, *The Life of Herbert Hoover*, vol. 1 (New York: W. W. Norten, 1983), p. 104.

21. LHH to Theodore Hoover, undated, LHH Correspondence files, HHPL.

22. LHH Diary, April 10, 1900.

23. LHH to parents, November 1899, LHH Correspondence files, HHPL.

24. LHH to Jean Henry, July 17, 1900, LHH Correspondence files, HHPL.

25. Stanford University *"Alumnus"* Magazine, June 1900. As quoted in Nash, *The Life of Herbert Hoover*, p. 111.

26. LHH to Jean Henry, January 12, 1900, LHH Correspondence files, HHPL.

27. LHH to Jean Henry, undated (January 1900), LHH Correspondence files, HHPL.

28. Harriette Miles Odell to LHH, January 4, 1912, LHH Correspondence files, HHPL.

29. Mansfield Allan to LHH, December 29, 1899, LHH Correspondence files, HHPL.

30. LHH to John C. Branner, November 12, 1899, Branner papers, HHPL.

31. George Nash, *The Life of Herbert Hoover*, vol. 1, pp. 51, 69.

32. Quoted by Allan Hoover, Oral History interview 1986, HHPL.

33. Nash, op. cit., p. 69.

34. HH, Memoirs, vol. 1, p. 46.

35. LHH Diary, April 17, 1900.

36. LHH Diary, April 20, 1900.

37. LHH Diary, June 1, 1900.

38. LHH Diary, June 4, 1900.

39. LHH Diary, June 10, 1900.

40. LHH Narrative on Boxer Rebellion, undated.

41. Ibid.

42. Ibid.

43. Ibid.

44. Mrs. Edward B. Drew, Diary of siege, LHH papers, HHPL.

45. HH account of siege, HH papers, HHPL.

46. HH notes on siege, LHH papers, HHPL.

47. LHH notes on Boxer Rebellion, LHH papers, HHPL.

48. Frederick Palmer, *Ladies Home Journal*, March 1929.

49. Ibid.

50. LHH Subject files, Boxer Rebellion, HHPL.

51. LHH to Evelyn Wight Allan, undated, ca. August 1, 1900, Evelyn Wight Allan papers, HHPL.

52. LHH notes on Boxer Rebellion, LHH papers, HHPL.

53. LHH Diary, August 10, 1900.

54. LHH Diary, October 1, 1900.

55. LHH Diary, October 9 and 11, 1900.

56. LHH Diary, November 1, 1900.

CHAPTER 4

1. Mildred Hall Campbell, Oral History interview, September 1966, HHPL.

2. LHH Diary, March 1901.

3. LHH memo to her children, ca. 1932, LHH papers, HHPL.

4. Ibid.

5. LHH Diary, March 5, 1902.

6. This manuscript is on file in the HHPL, along with the source material Lou used in preparing it.

7. HH, *Memoirs,* vol. 1, p. 85.

8. LHH Diary, July 15–17, 1902.

9. LHH Diary, July 30 and August 9, 1902.

10. LHH memo to her children, ca. 1932.

11. Ibid.

12. Ibid.

13. Ibid.

14. Theodore Hoover, memoir.

15. LHH memo for family, ca. 1918, LHH papers, HHPL.

16. Ibid.

17. HH, *Menoirs*, vol. 1, p. 124.

18. HH, *Memoirs*, vol. 1, p. 76.

19. LHH Diary, December 1903–January 1904.

20. HH to Theodore Hoover, quoted in Nash, *Life of Hoover*, vol. 1, p. 346.

21. Hulda Hoover McLean, *Uncle Bert: A Biographical Portrait of Herbert Hoover* (West Branch, Iowa: Herbert Hoover Presidential Library Association, Inc., 1974), p. 6.

22. Theodore Hoover, memoir (ca. 1940).

23. HH, *Memoirs*, vol. 1, p. 96.

24. Amy Jane Englund, "Mrs. Hoover—Homemaker and World Citizen," *Better Homes & Gardens,* April 1929, p. 64.

CHAPTER 5

1. HH, *Memoirs*, vol. 1, p. 76.

2. Ibid., vol. 1, p. 89.

3. Hulda McLean, *Uncle Bert: A Biographical Portrait of Herbert Hoover,* 1974.

4. HH, *Memoirs*, vol.1, p. 99.

5. LHH notes to family, c1918.

6. LHH to Laurine Anderson Small, undated, 1919, LHH Correspondence files, HHPL.

7. Jean Henry to LHH, March 1909, LHH Correspondence files, HHPL.

8. Jean Henry to LHH, March 8, 1909, LHH Correspondence files, HHPL.

9. Hazel Lyman Noel, "A Chained Book—Now Free to All," *The Canadian Mining and Metallurgical Bulletin* (June 1949), Agricola Collection, HHPL, p. 305.

10. LHH notes for her family, ca. 1932, LHH papers.

11. Irwin, *Herbert Hoover: A Reminiscent Biography* (New York: Century, 1928), p. 212.

12. Ibid., p. 65.

13. LHH to Allan Hoover, February 1929, LHH Correspondence files, HHPL.

14. LHH to Ruth Comfort Mitchell Young, March 20, 1934, LHH Correspondence files, HHPL.

15. Mary Bainbridge to LHH, May 14, 1908, LHH Correspondence files, HHPL.

16. LHH note to family, undated ca. 1932, LHH papers, HHPL.

17. LHH letter (undated; probably to her sons), LHH papers, HHPL.

18. Letterhead of Friends of the Poor, LHH papers, HHPL.

19. LHH to Catherine Fletcher, 1920, LHH Correspondence files, HHPL.

20. Mark C. Carnes in *The Reader's Companion to American History*, ed, by Eric Foner and John A. Garraty (Boston: Houghton Mifflin, 1991), pp. 418–420.

21. Jane C. Croly, *The History of the Woman's Club Movement in America* (New York: Henry G. Allen, 1898).

22. LHH memo to her son Allan, May 1932.

23. Richard N. Smith, *An Uncommon Man* (New York: Simon & Schuster, 1984), p. 77.

24. Quoted in Nash, *Life of Hoover*, vol. 1, p. 504.

25. LHH memo to family, ca. 1918.

26. Ibid.

CHAPTER 6

1. Smith, *An Uncommon Man*, unattributed quote, p. 71.
2. LHH letter to Mrs. Griffiths, January 29, 1915, LHH Correspondence files, HHPL.
3. HH cable to LHH, October 26, 1914, LHH Correspondence files, HHPL.
4. LHH to Jackson Reynolds, November 24, 1914, LHH Correspondence files, HHPL.
5. LHH to her son Herbert, November 25, 1914, LHH Correspondence files, HHPL.
6. HH, *Memoirs*, vol. 1, p. 210.
7. Charlotte Kellogg to LHH, 1916, LHH Correspondence files, HHPL.
8. Adeline Fuller, Oral History interview, 1967, HHPL.
9. HH, *Memoirs*, vol. 1, p. 210.
10. HH memo re LHH, undated, LHH Correspondence files, HHPL.
11. LHH to Laurine Anderson, November 26, 1915, LHH Correspondence files, HHPL.
12. Charlotte Kellogg, "The Young Hoovers," *Saturday Evening Post*, March 2, 1929, p. 166.

CHAPTER 7

1. HH telegram to LHH, May 14, 1917, HH Papers, HHPL.
2. LHH to Laurine Anderson (?), undated ca. March 1919, LHH Subject Files, Food Administration Club, HHPL.
3. Lou used this title for all her assistants, to indicate that their responsibilities were somewhat beyond those of a mere secretary.
4. Irwin, *Herbert Hoover: A Reminiscent Biography*, p. 210.

CHAPTER 8

1. HH cable to LHH, April 22, 1919, Kenneth Colegrove papers, HHPL.
2. Dare Stark to Laurine Anderson Small, February 1919, LHH correspondence files, HHPL.
3. Birge Clark, quoted in Ruth Dennis, *The Homes of the Hoovers*, HHPL, April 1986.
4. Dare Stark to Laurine Small, February 1919, LLH Correspondence files, HHPL.
5. HH, *Memoirs*, vol. 1, p. 481.
6. LHH to Edgar Rickard, November 14, 1919, LLH Correspondence files, HHPL.
7. HH, *Memoirs*, vol. 2, p. 5.
8. LHH to Mrs. Tiru-Navuk-Arasu, February 12, 1921, LLH Correspondence files, HHPL.
9. Oral history interview, Philippi Butler, 1967, HHPL.
10. LHH to Will Henry, undated, ca. January 1929, LHH Correspondence files, HHPL.
11. LHH to her sons, April 20, 1924, LHH Correspondence files, HHPL.
12. LHH to Mrs. Walter Large, undated (1922?), LHH Correspondence files, HHPL.

13. Letters from LHH to Philippi Harding, May–July, 1921, LHH Correspondence files, HHPL.

14. LHH to Alida Henriques, September 4, 1921, LHH Correspondence files, HHPL.

15. LHH to Allan Hoover, undated 1926, LHH Correspondence files, HHPL.

16. LHH to Philippi Harding, July 7, 1921, LHH Correspondence files, HHPL.

CHAPTER 9

1. Letter by supporter to James West, president of Boy Scouts of America, March 21, 1924, in LHH Girl Scout Files, HHPL.

2. "A Homage to Juliette Low," by LHH, read at the 1927 Girl Scout Convention.

3. Ibid.

4. Ibid.

5. Ibid.

6. Letter from Girl Scout leader to LHH, November 9, 1928, LHH Girl Scout Correspondence File, HHPL.

7. Notes from LHH speech to Girl Scout leaders at Boston national council meeting, May 1925.

8. Notes for talk given at Better Homes Program at Little House in Washington, D.C., April 1929.

9. Ibid.

10. LHH to Allan, Herbert and Jean Large, March 17, 1925, LHH Girl Scout Correspondence File, HHPL.

11. LHH to Birdsall Edey, April 30, 1930, LHH Girl Scout Correspondence Files, HHPL.

12. Grace Coolidge to LHH, June 30, 1928, LHH Correspondence files, HHPL.

13. Oral history interview, Marie McSpadden Sands, 1981, HHPL.

14. Confidential reminiscence by LHH to Miss Hodgkins, undated (ca. 1929), in NAAF Subject File, LHH papers, HHPL.

15. *Standards in Athletics for Girls and Women*, American Physical Education Association, 1937.

CHAPTER 10

1. LHH to Mrs. Walter Large, undated 1922, LHH correspondence files, HHPL.

2. Oral history interview with Hulda Hoover McLean, 1985, HHPL.

3. LHH to Evelyn W. Allan, December 12, 1922, LHH Correspondence files, HHPL.

4. See Dale Mayer, "An Uncommon Woman: The Quiet Leadership Style of Lou Henry Hoover," *Presidential Quarterly* 20 (fall 1990): 694.

5. Helen Pryor, *Lou Henry Hoover: Gallant First Lady* (New York: Dodd Mead, 1969).

6. Ibid.

7. LHH to her sons, April 20, 1924, HHPL.

8. Ibid.

9. LHH to Philippi Harding Butler, July 24, 1925, LHH Correspondence files, HHPL.

10. Ibid.

11. Allan Hoover, Oral History interview, 1986, HHPL.

12. Oral history interviews with Hulda Hoover McLean, 1985, and Van Ness Leavitt, 1967, HHPL.

13. LHH to Allan Hoover, October 26, 1927, LHH Correspondence files, HHPL.

CHAPTER 11

1. LHH to her sons, January 1928, LHH Correspondence files, HHPL.

2. LHH to Irene (Mrs. George T.) Gerlinger, October 23, 1941, LHH Correspondence files, HHPL.

3. LHH to Allan Hoover, undated 1928, LHH Correspondence files, HHPL.

4. LHH to her sons, January 1928, LHH Correspondence files, HHPL.

5. LHH to Edna Heald McCoy, September 22, 1928, LHH Correspondence files, HHPL.

6. LHH to Caroline Honnold, October 24, 1928, LHH Correspondence files, HHPL.

7. Dorothy Bowen to Marjorie Bowen, November 7, 1928, courtesy of Marjorie Bowen Gal.

8. Alonzo Fields, "Looking Over the President's Shoulder," *Ladies' Home Journal*, May 1960.

9. Oral History, Lillian Parks, 1971, HHPL.

10. Irwin Hoover, *Forty-Two Years in the White House* (New York: Houghton Mifflin, 1934), p. 181.

11. Irwin "Ike" Hoover to LHH, May 8, 1933, LLH Correspondence files, HHPL.

12. LHH to Grace Coolidge, February 8, 1934, LHH Correspondence files, HHPL.

13. Ruth Fesler Lipman, Oral History interview 1967, HHPL.

14. Hulda Hoover McLean, Oral History interview 1985, HHPL.

15. "Lou Henry Hoover: A Tribute from the Girl Scouts," p. 5, LHH Subject Files, Death and Funeral, HHPL.

16. Oral History, Lillian Parks, 1971, HHPL.

17. Herbert Hoover, Essay on Fishing, HHPL.

18. Charlotte Kellogg, "The Young Hoovers," *Saturday Evening Post*, March 2, 1929.

19. Irwin Hoover, *Forty-Two Years in the White House*, p. 191.

20. LHH to Ruby Logan, April 26, 1930, LHH Correspondence Files, HHPL.

21. Irwin Hoover, *Forty-Two Years in the White House*, pp. 315–316; Ruth Fesler, Oral History interview 1967, HHPL.

CHAPTER 12

1. Irwin Hoover, *Forty-Two Years in the White House*, p. 286.

2. Perle Mesta, "First Ladies I Have Known," *McCall*'s, March 1963.

3. HH, *Memoirs*, vol. 2, p. 324.

4. Ava Long, with Mildred Harrington, "Presidents at Home," *Ladies' Home Journal*, September 1933.

5. Ibid.

6. Mary Randolph, *Presidents and First Ladies* (New York: D. A. Appleton-Century, 1936), p. 143.

7. LHH to Jean Large, June 5, 1930, LHH Correspondence files, HHPL.

8. Oral History, Susan Dyer, interview 1966, HHPL.

9. Oral History, Ruth Fesler, interview 1967, HHPL.

10. Ibid.

11. HH, *Memoirs*, vol. 2, p. 324.

12. Oral history, Agnes Thompson, 1966, HHPL.

13. Glen Plaskin, *Horowitz: A Biography* (New York: William Morrow, 1938), p. 142.

14. LHH to Allan Hoover, June 17, 1929, Allan Hoover papers, HHPL.

15. HH telegram to Allan Hoover, June 17, 1929, Allan Hoover papers, HHPL.

16. LHH to Susan Dyer, September 18, 1929, LHH Correspondence papers, HHPL.

CHAPTER 13

1. Oral History, Admiral Joel T. Boone, interview 1967, HHPL.

2. LHH to Mary Vaux Walcott, April 14, 1937, LHH Correspondence files, HHPL.

3. HH, *Memoirs*, vol. 2, p. 325.

4. Reminiscences of Christine Vest Witcofski, August 1960, LHH papers, HHPL.

5. Ibid.

6. "Lou Henry Hoover: A Tribute from the Girl Scouts," p. 8, LHH subject files, HHPL.

7. LHH to Birdsall Otis Edey, April 30, 1930, LHH subject files, HHPL.

8. LHH to Abigail Rickard, 1930, LHH subject files, HHPL.

9. LHH to Sarah Louise Arnold, July 5, 1930, LHH Correspondence files, HHPL.

10. LHH to Genevieve Brady, April 14, 1930, LHH GS Correspondence files, HHPL.

11. LHH to Hugh Gibson, December 5, 1929, LHH Correspondence files, HHPL.

12. Charlotte Kellogg, "Mrs. Hoover," *Ladies' Home Journal*, September 1930.

13. LHH to Jean Henry Large, October 3, 1930, LHH Correspondence files, HHPL.

14. Ava Long, "Presidents At Home," *Ladies' Home Journal*, September 1933.

CHAPTER 14

1. HH, *Memoirs*, vol. 2, pp. 324–325.

2. Harriette Miles Odell to LHH, undated 1930, LHH Correspondence files, HHPL.

3. LHH to Bertha Heald Goodwin, October 2, 1939, LHH Correspondence files, HHPL.

4. LHH to Allan Hoover, October 3, 1931, LHH Correspondence files, HHPL.

5. R adio broadcast to 4–H clubs, November 7, 1931.

6. Margaret Hoover Brigham, anecdote told at Hoover Library Rededication, October 1997.

7. LHH to her sons, July 1932, Allan Hoover files, HHPL.

8. LHH to Anne Hard, June 20, 1932, LHH Correspondence files, HHPL.

9. LHH to Allan Hoover, undated 1932, Allan Hoover papers, HHPL.

10. Ibid.

11. LHH to Marie M. Meloney, August 11, 1926, LHH Correspondence files, HHPL.

12. LHH to Mary S. Brown, June 10, 1930, LHH Correspondence files, HHPL.

13. LHH to Allan Hoover, undated, Allan Hoover papers, HHPL.

14. Irwin Hoover, *Forty-Two Years in the White House,* Houghton Mifflin, 1934, p. 219.

15. LHH to Allan Hoover, June 1929, Allan Hoover papers, HHPL.

16. LHH to Mary Vaux Walcott, August 16, 1932, LHH Correspondence files, HHPL.

17. Anne Hard to LHH, June 20, 1932; LHH to Anne Hard, June 20, 1932, LHH Correspondence files, HHPL.

18. Irwin Hoover, *Forty-Two Years in the White House,* p. 219.

19. George Nash, *Herbert Hoover and Stanford University* (Palto Alto, Calif.: Hoover Institution Press, Stanford University, 1988), p. 102.

20. Mildred Hall Campbell, Oral History, interview September 1966, HHPL.

21. Oral History, Joel T. Boone, July 22, 1967, HHPL.

22. HH, *Memoirs*, vol. 3, p. 344.

CHAPTER 15

1. LHH to Allan Hoover, December 1932, Allan Hoover papers, HHPL.

2. Irwin Hoover, *Forty-Two Years in the White House,* Houghton Mifflin, 1934, p. 227.

3. Lillian Rogers Parks, *My Thirty Years Backstairs at the White House* (New York: Fleet, 1961), p. 232.

4. HH, *Memoirs*, vol. 3, p. 345.

5. LHH to Sarah Arnold, June 29, 1933, LHH Correspondence files, HHPL.

6. LHH to Florence Stewart, May 10, 1933, LHH Correspondence files, HHPL.

7. LHH to Sarah Arnold, June 29, 1933, LHH Correspondence files, HHPL.

8. LHH to Allan Hoover, January 6, 1933, Allan Hoover papers, HHPL.

9. LHH to Allan Hoover, January 31, 1933, LHH Correspondence files, HHPL.

10. Ibid.

11. HH, *Memoirs*, vol. 3, p. 347.

12. LHH to Allan Hoover, October 22, 1933, Allan Hoover files, HHPL.

13. Marie McSpadden Sands, Oral History interview, 1981, HHPL.

14. LHH to Allan Hoover, November 22, 1932, Allan Hoover files, HHPL.

15. LHH to Helena Hirst, January 16, 1941, LHH Correspondence files, HHPL.

16. LHH to Ruth Hanna Simms, October 29, 1937, LHH Correspondence files, HHPL.

17. "The President's Right Hand," *The Republican Woman*, November 1931.

18. LHH to Mrs. Baldwin, August 14, 1937, LHH Friends of Music Correspondence, HHPL.

CHAPTER 16

1. LHH to Allan Hoover, May 17, 1933, Allan Hoover papers, HHPL.

2. LHH to Agnes Morley Cleaveland, June 13, 1934, LHH Correspondence files, HHPL.

3. LHH to Grace Coolidge, December 23, 1939, LHH Correspondence files, HHPL.

4. HH to LHH, February 9, 1939, LHH Correspondence files, HHPL.

5. LHH to Florence Stewart, February 5, 1940, LHH Correspondence files, HHPL.

6. LLH to Katherine Everts, September 30, 1940, LLH Correspondence files, HHPL.

7. Oral history interview with Edward Anthony, 1969, HHPL.

8. Jean Large to LHH, August 4, 1941, LHH Correspondence files, HHPL.

9. Jean Large to LHH, August 13, 1941, LHH Correspondence files, HHPL.

10. LHH to HH, February 21, 1942, LHH Correspondence files, HHPL.

11. LHH to Harriette Odell, January 27, 1942, LHH Correspondence files, HHPL.

12. LHH to HH, May 4, 1942, LHH Correspondence files, D. E.Trueblood file, HHPL.

13. LHH to Herbert and Allan Hoover (holographic will), November 17, 1943, HHPL.

14. Mildred Hall, memoir, 1971, HHPL.

EPILOGUE

1. Conversation with the Rev. Thomas Hulme, December 1997.

Bibliography

BOOKS

Aikman, Lonnelle. *The Living White House.* 7th ed. Washington, D.C.: White House Historical Association, 1982.

Andreas, A. T., *Illustrated Historical Atlas of the State of Iowa.* Chicago: Andreas Atlas Co., 1875.

Anthony, Carl Sferrazza. *First Ladies: The Saga of the Presidents' Wives and Their Power, 1789–1961,* New York: William Morrow & Company, 1990.

Bailey's Waterloo Directory, 1873–74. Waterloo, Iowa: Bailey & Co., 1873.

Baird's Manual of American College Fraternities. 11th edition, 1927.

Barker, Felix, and Peter Jackson, *The History of London in Maps.* London: Barrie & Jenkins, 1990.

Bassett, Margaret. *Profiles & Portraits of American Presidents and Their Wives.* Freeport, Maine: Bond Wheelwright Co., 1969.

Beckman, George M. *The Modernization of China and Japan.* New York: Harper & Row, 1962.

Blair, Karen J. *The Clubwoman as Feminist (1868–1914).* New York: Holmes & Meier Publishers, 1980.

Boller, Paul F. *Presidential Wives: An Anecdotal History.* New York: Oxford University Press, 1988.

Caroli, Betty Boyd. *First Ladies.* New York: Oxford University Press, 1987.

Carr, William. *History of Germany 1815–1990.* London: Arnold, 1991.

Colbert, Nancy A. *Lou Henry Hoover: The Duty to Serve.* Greensboro, NC: Morgan Reynolds, Inc., 1998.

Congressional Record, 71st Congress, 1st Session, 1929. Vol. 71, part 3, p. 2781.

Corwin, Margaret and Helen Hoy. Waterloo: A Pictorial History. Rock Island, Ill.: Quest Pub., 1983.

Croly, Jane C. *The History of the Woman's Club Movement in America.* New York: Henry G. Allen, 1898.

Daniels, Jonathan. *The Time Between the Wars.* New York: Doubleday, 1966.

Davis, Margo, and Roxanne Nilan. *Stanford Album: A Photographic History 1885–1945,* Palo Alto, Calif.: Stanford University Press, 1989.

Dennis, Ruth. *The Homes of the Hoovers.* West Branch, Iowa: Herbert Hoover Presidential Library Association, Inc., April 1986.

Diller, Daniel C., and Stephen L. Robertson. *The Presidents, First Ladies, and Vice Presidents.* Washington, D.C.: Congressional Quarterly, 1989.

Fairbank, John King. *China: A New History.* Cambridge, Mass.: Belknap Press, 1992.

Foner, Eric, and John A. Garraty, eds. *The Reader's Companion to American History.* Boston: Houghton Mifflin, 1991.

Girl Scouts of the U.S.A. *Highlights of Girl Scouting, 1912–1991.* New York: Girl Scouts of the U.S.A., 1991.

Girl Scouts of the U.S.A. *75 Years of Girl Scouting.* New York: Girl Scouts of the U.S.A., 1986.

Guerrier, Edith. *We Pledged Allegiance: A Librarian's Intimate Story of the United States Food Administration.* Stanford: Stanford University Press, 1941.

Gutin, Myra G. *The President's Partner: The First Lady in the Twentieth Century.* Westport, Conn.: Greenwood Press, 1989.

Hoover, Herbert. *The Memoirs of Herbert Hoover.* 3 vols. New York: Macmillan, 1951–52.

Hoover, Irwin H. *Forty-Two Years in the White House.* Boston: Houghton Mifflin, 1934.

Iowa Census Returns: Schedule 1, vol. 156, 1885. Butler County, pp. 1, 8, 9, 10, 23.

Iowa Census Returns: Schedule 1, vol. 299, 1895. Butler County, pp. 669, 672, 674, 676, 685.

Iowa Executive Council. *Thirteenth State Census. The census of Iowa, as returned in the year 1875.* Des Moines: R. P. Clarksons, 1875.

Irwin, Will. *Herbert Hoover: A Reminiscent Biography.* New York: Century, 1928.

J. G. Shmid's Waterloo City Directory. Waterloo, Iowa: J. G. Shmid, 1886.

Kellogg, Vernon. *Herbert Hoover: The Man and His Work.* New York: D. Appleton & Co., 1920.

Lavender, David. *California: A Bicentennial History.* New York: W. W. Norton, 1976.

Leavitt, Roger. *When Waterloo Was Young.* Waterloo, Iowa: Waterloo Rotary Club, 1929.

Long, Barbara. *Waterloo: Factory City of Iowa.* Waterloo, Iowa: Midwest Research, 1986.

Malone, Dumas. *Dictionary of American Biography.* New York: Scribners, 1935.

Marquis, Albert Nelson, ed. *Who's Who in America.* Chicago: Marquis, 1916–17, 1918–19, 1919–20, 1922–23, 1932–33, 1934–35, 1944, 1950–51.

Martin, Ralph G. *Jennie.* New York: Prentice Hall, 1971.

Mayer, Dale C., ed. *Lou Henry Hoover: Essays on a Busy Life.* Worland, Wyo.: High Plains Publishing Co., 1994.

Mayo, Edith P. *The Smithsonian Book of First Ladies.* New York: Henry Holt & Co., 1996.

McLean, Hulda Hoover. *Uncle Bert: A Biographical Portrait of Herbert Hoover.* West Branch, Iowa: Herbert Hoover Presidential Library Association, Inc., 1974.

Nash, George H. *The Life of Herbert Hoover.* 3 vols. New York: W. W. Norton, 1983.

Nash, George H. *Herbert Hoover and Stanford University.* Palo Alto, Calif.: Hoover Institute Press, Stanford University, 1988.

National Museum of History and Technology. *The First Ladies Hall.* Washington, D.C.: Smithsonian Institution, 3rd printing, 1981.

Notable American Women 1607–1950. Cambridge, Mass.: Belknap Press, 1971.

Paletta, LuAnn. *The World Almanac of First Ladies.* New York: World Almanac, Pharos Books, 1990.

Parks, Lillian Rogers. *My Thirty-Five Years Backstairs at the White House.* New York: Fleet, 1961.

Parrish, Michael. *Anxious Decades: America in Prosperity and Depression 1920–1941.* New York: W. W. Norton, 1992.

Peterson's staff. *Peterson's Guide to Four-Year Colleges.* Princeton, N.J.: Peterson's, 1993.

Plaskin, Glen. *Horowitz: A Biography.* New York: William Morrow, 1938.

Pryor, Helen B. *Lou Henry Hoover: Gallant First Lady.* New York: Dodd Mead, 1969.

Quinn, Sandra L., and Sanford Kanter. *America's Royalty: All the Presidents' Children.* Westport, Conn.: Greenwood Press, 1983.

Randolph, Mary. *Presidents and First Ladies.* New York: D. Appleton-Century, 1936.

Reischauer, Edwin O., and John K. Fairbank. *East Asia: The Great Tradition.* Boston: Houghton Mifflin, 1958.

Sage, Leland. *A History of Iowa.* Ames: Iowa State University Press, 1974.

Schultz, Gladys D., and Daisy G. Lawrence. *Lady from Savannah.* New York: Girl Scouts of the U.S.A., 1958.

Seagrave, Sterling. *Dragon Lady: The Life and Legend of the Last Empress of China.* New York: Alfred A. Knopf, 1992.

Smith, Richard Norton. *An Uncommon Man.* New York: Simon & Schuster, NY, 1984.

Standards in Athletics for Girls and Women. American Physical Education Association, 1937.

Sullivan, Mark. Dan Rather, ed. *Our Times.* New York: Scribners, 1996.

Tannenbaum, Edward R. *1900.* New York: Doubleday Anchor Press, 1976.

Truman, Margaret. *First Ladies.* New York: Random House, 1995.

Tuchman, Barbara. *The Guns of August.* New York: Macmillan, 1962.

U.S. Bureau of the Census. *Fourth Census.* Vol. 9 (Ohio), Bureau of the Census. Washington, D.C., 1820. Stark Co., Perry Township.

U.S. Bureau of the Census. *Fifth Census.* Vol. 15 (Ohio), Bureau of the Census. Washington, D.C., 1830. Stark Co., Tuscarawas Township.

U.S. Bureau of the Census. *Sixth Census.* Vol. 23 (Ohio), Bureau of the Census. Washington, D.C., 1840. Stark Co., Canton Township.

U.S. Bureau of the Census. *Seventh Census.* (Ohio), Bureau of the Census. Washington, D.C., 1850. Wayne Co., Wooster Township.

U.S. Bureau of the Census. *Eighth Census.* Vols. 12, 67 (Iowa and Ohio), Bureau of the Census. Washington, D.C., 1860. Butler Co., IA, Waverly Township; Wayne Co., OH, Wooster Township.

U.S. Bureau of the Census. *Ninth Census.* Vol. 3 (Iowa), Bureau of the Census. Washington, D.C., 1870. Bremer Co., Waverly Township; Butler Co., Shell Rock Township.

U.S. Bureau of the Census. *Tenth Census.* Vols. 2, 4 (Iowa), Bureau of the Census. Washington, D.C., 1880. Butler Co., Shell Rock Township, Black Hawk Co., Waterloo Township.

U.S. Bureau of the Census. *Twelfth Census.* Vol. 9 (Iowa), Bureau of the Census. Washington, D.C., 1900. Butler Co., Shell Rock Township.

Waldrup, Carole Chandler. *Presidents' Wives: The Lives of Forty-Four Women of Strength.* Jefferson, N.C.: McFarland & Co., 1989.

Who Was Who in America. Vol. 1. Chicago: Marquis, 1943.

Wright, Katharine O. *Twenty-Five Years of Girl Scouting.* New York: Girl Scouts of the U.S.A., 1937.

ARTICLES

Boatright, Kevin. "A Simple Little Building." *The Palimpsest* 68 (summer 1987).

Burke, Frank G. "First Ladies as National Leaders." *Prologue* (summer 1987).

Canfield, Dorothy. "A Good Girl Scout." *Good Housekeeping (April 1930).*

Daughtery, Mary. "Women's Suffrage and Feminism." New York *Journal* (February 16, 1942).

Day, David S. "A New Perspective on the 'DePriest Tea' Historiographic Controversy." *Journal of Negro History* 75 (1990).

Englund, Amy Jane. "Mrs. Hoover—Homemaker and World Citizen," *Better Homes & Gardens* (April 1929).

Fields, Alonzo. "Looking Over the President's Shoulder." *Ladies Home Journal* (May 1960).

Frazer, Elizabeth. "Mrs. Herbert Hoover: Portrait of an American Lady." *Saturday Evening Post* (June 9, 1928).

Gould, Lewis. "First Ladies." *American Scholar* (Autumn 1986).

Gould, Lewis. "There's History to Role of First Lady." *The Quill* (March 1996).

Hinshaw, Augusta. "How the Hoovers Brought Up Their Boys." *Parents Magazine* (December 1929).

Hoover, Lou Henry. "Whittier Letter." *St. Nicholas Magazine* (December 1887).

"Hoover's Silent Partner." *Literary Digest* (September 8, 1917).

Howard, Kris. "Legacy of Leadership: Edith Carpenter Macy." *Girl Scout Leader.* (Feb/March 1980).

Kappa Kappa Gamma. *The Key* (February 1944).

Kellogg, Charlotte. "Mrs. Hoover." *Ladies Home Journal* (September 1930).

Kellogg, Charlotte. "The Young Hoovers." *Saturday Evening Post* (March 2, 1929).

Long, Ava. "Presidents at Home." *Ladies Home Journal* (September 1933).

"Lou Henry Hoover, School Girl."*Sioux City Journal* (July 15, 1928).

Mayer, Dale C. "An Uncommon Woman: The Quiet Leadership Style of Lou Henry Hoover." *Presidential Studies Quarterly* vol. 20, no. 4 (fall 1990).

Mayer, Dale C. "Not One to Stay at Home: The Papers of Lou Henry Hoover." *Prologue* 19 (summer 1987).

Melville, Keith. "The First Lady and the Cowgirl." *Pacific Historical Review* (1988).

Mesta, Perle. "First Ladies I Have Known." *McCall's* (March 1963).

"Mrs. Hoover's International Housekeeping." *Literary Digest* (November 24, 1928).

"Mrs. Hoover Honor Guest of Founders." *Whittier News* (May 16, 1938).

Nickel, Hazel Lyman. "A Chained Book—Now Free to All." *The Canadian Mining and Metallurgical Bulletin* (June 1949).

O'Connor, Karen, Bernadette Nye and Laura Van Assendelft. "Wives in the White House: The Political Influence of First Ladies." *Presidential Studies Quarterly* (summer 1996).

"The Other Presidents." *Good Housekeeping* (February 1932).

Palmer, Frederick. "Mrs. Hoover Knows." *Ladies Home Journal* (March 1929).

"The President's Right Hand." *The Republican Woman* (November 1931).

Rothschild, Mary Aikin. "Lou Henry Hoover: Girl Scouting's First Lady." *Girl Scout Leader* (spring 1982).

Rothschild, Mary Aikin. "Women in History: Jane Deeter Rippin." *Girl Scout Leader.* (fall 1981).

Walsh, Thomas. "Herbert Hoover and the Boxer Rebellion." *Prologue* 19 (spring 1987).

Watson, Robert P. "The First Lady Reconsidered: Presidential Partner and Political Institution." *Presidential Studies Quarterly* (Fall 1997).

Watson, Robert P. "Ranking the Presidential Spouses." *The Social Science Journal* vol. 36, no. 1 (1999).

PRIMARY SOURCE MATERIAL (HERBERT HOOVER PRESIDENTIAL LIBRARY, WEST BRANCH, IOWA)

Allan, Mansfield, letter

Anthony, Edward, Oral History

Bainbridge, Mary, letters

Boone, Adm. Joel T., Oral History

Bowen, Dorothy, letter

Branner, John C., letters

Butler, Philippi, Oral History

Campbell, Mildred Hall, Oral History

Chu'an Yueh-tung, letter

Coolidge, Grace, letters

Drew, Mrs. Edward B., diary

Dyer, Susan, Oral History

Fuller, Adeline, Oral History

Hard, Anne, letter

Henry, Mary Ann Dwire, letter

Hoover, Allan, Oral History

Hoover, Herbert, letters

Hoover, Lou Henry, letters, diaries and memos

Hoover, Theodore, memoir

Jordan, Harley, letter

Kellogg, Charlotte, letters

Large, Jean Henry, letters, diary
Lipman, Ruth Fesler, Oral History
McLean, Hulda Hoover, Oral History
McMullin, Dare Stark, letters
Odell, Harriette Miles, letter
Parks, Lillian, Oral History
Sands, Marie McSpadden, Oral History
Thompson, Agnes, Oral History
Weed, Philomelia, letters
Witcofsky, Christine Vest, reminiscence

Index

Harcourt, Edith, 171

Hard, Anne, 147, 151

Harding, Philippi. *See* Butler, Philippi Harding

Harding, Warren G., 82, 105–106

Harrison, George, 80–83, 85, 86, 103, 106, 108, 109

Hauselt, Louise Hoover Dunbar Fouts Stevenson, 111, 160

Henriques, Alida, 71, 74, 78, 119, 145, 160

Henry, Addison Morgan, 5, 6, 29, 57, 112

Henry, Ann (Nannie), 29, 37, 57, 144

Henry, Charles Delano, 5–12, 21, 57, 86, 112, 117, 150; financial gifts to daughters, 55, 84, 108

Henry, Florence Weed, 5–13, 21, 29, 38; health, 9, 81–82, 84, 86

Henry, Jean. *See* Large, Jean Henry

Henry, Mary Ann Dwire, 5, 6, 8, 18, 29, 34, 57, 113

Henry, William Dwire, 5, 6, 84, 117, 141; financial troubles, 108, 144; with mother in North Dakota, 8, 29, 34, 57; with Native American ward, 119, 133, 144, 161

Herbert Hoover Presidential Library, LHH papers in, 2, 4, 174

Hodgkins, Anne, 100

Hoffman, Mira, 97, 139, 140

Honnold, Caroline, 76

Honnold, William L., 64, 68

Hoover, Allan Henry, 82, 113, 116–118, 150, 151, 169, 173; childhood, 45, 54, 72, 77, 80, 81, 83–86, 109–110; correspondence with mother, 2, 113, 116, 147, 155, 167, 172; early education, 68, 75, 77, 82, 85, 87, 106; employment, 149, 150, 156, 161; and father's presidential campaigns, 116–118, 151; higher education, 110–111, 133; and Hoover birthplace project, 163, 167; marriage and family, 161, 168; South American tour,

118; World War I, 65, 69, 75, 81; World War II, 170–171

Hoover, Herbert Clark, 24, 39, 43, 57, 70, 98, 133, 141, 174; and American Committee, 62–63; and Bewick Moreing Company, 20, 30, 34–35, 38, 40–42, 48, 51; birthplace project, 162–163; and Bohemian Club, 107; and Boxer Rebellion, 30–34; character, 16–17, 20–21, 28, 42, 45, 54, 56, 105, 127; and Chinese Mining and Engineering Company, 34–35, 41; Commerce Secretary, 82, 85, 93, 106, 115; and Commission for Relief of Belgium (CRB), 64–65, 68, 70, 71, 75, 81, 82; engineering career, 18, 20, 25–30, 48–49, 51, 58, 69, 72 (*see also* Bewick Moreing Company); Food Administrator, 71–72, 74, 75, 78; lawsuits, 41–42, 44, 51, 146; and Mississippi River flood, 1927, 116; and Panama-Pacific Exposition, 58; post-presidential activities, 154–156, 159, 165, 167–169; presidential campaigns, 115–118, 150–152; private charities, 20, 29, 51, 58, 108, 111, 136, 144; proposed purchase of newspapers, 56, 82; publications, 50, 169; and Rowe defalcation, 41, 42, 44, 58; and Stanford house, 73, 79–80, 171 and Stanford University, 16–18, 49, 56–58, 70, 104, 109, 159, 169, 171; and Waldorf Astoria, 168–169, 172; and World War I peace commission, 77, 81; and World War II, 165, 167, 169

Hoover, Herbert Charles (Herbert Jr.), 86, 150, 153, 154, 167, 172, 173; childhood, 43, 45, 47, 49, 63, 68; early education, 54, 57, 65, 68, 75, 77, 82, 83; employment, 109, 141, 142, 150, 161; and father's presidency, 117, 119, 151; health, 57, 77, 81, 109, 113, 141–142, 158; higher education, 103, 107, 109, 110; homemade car, 81; marriage and family,

About the Author

ANNE BEISER ALLEN is an independent researcher. She writes poetry, fiction, and historical biography, preferring to focus on lesser-known characters whose unique personalities placed them in a position to do exceptional things. Her writings about Iowa people and places have led to her nomination for two different awards.

Recent Titles in
Contributions in American History

ISBN 0-313-31466-7

EAN

9 780313 314667

HARDCOVER BAR CODE